June Antoinette Necchi

Copyright © Published 2024

by June Antoinette Necchi

All rights reserved.

No part of this publication may be reproduced, distributed, or transmitted in any form or by any means, including recording, or other electronic or mechanical methods, without the prior written permission of the publisher, except as permitted by UK copyright law.

For permission requests, contact
junenecchiauthor@gmail.com

Book cover, illustration, and design by June Antoinette Necchi

Year of first publication 2024

June Antoinette Necchi

'The Little Stranger at Your Door'

June Antoinette Necchi

June Antoinette Necchi

b

Dedication

To my beloved family—my four wonderful children Russell, my late daughter Donna, Matthew & Dan, who have been with me through every twist and turn of this journey. Your love and support have been my anchor."

Also, to Leslie Foot and Linda Joyce

Your unwavering support, friendship, and belief in me have made this journey possible. This book is as much yours as it is mine. Thank you for standing by my side and for being the wonderful lights in my life.

With deepest gratitude,
June

June Antoinette Necchi

'Weeping, I thought I saw my

Father

wipe away his tears'

June Antoinette Necchi

Contents

Chapter One 1
   MY BEGINNINGS 1
      EVACUATION 11
      THE FIRST OF MANY HOMES 12
      STONEHOUSE 15
      GHOSTS 18
      ORPHANAGE 23
      MRS PEACH 27
      LAST WARTIME HOME 28
Chapter 3 31
   END OF WAR AND LEAH 31
      SALLY'S NEW BIKE 37
      LEAVING LODGINGS 40
Chapter 4 43
   LEAVING CONVENT 43
Chapter 5 52
   BLACKPOOL HOLIDAY 52
Chapter 6 56
   FIRST COTTAGE 56
Chapter 7 61
   DAD'S CAFE 61

June Antoinette Necchi

Chapter 8 72
   THE HOLLIES 72
Chapter 9 80
   MARRIAGE HAD RUN 80
   ITS COURSE 80
Chapter 10 84
   EGG FARM 84
Chapter 11 87
   CHASING THE DREAM 87
Chapter 12 93
   ARIES 93
Chapter 13 102
   FINNINGS (Bowmaker) 102
   LAURA ASHLEY 105
Chapter 15 112
   DARTMOUTH ROAD 112
   Chapter 16 118
   CLINICAL ONCOLOGIST 118
      PATIENT' LIAISON GROUP' 118
   Chapter 17 121
   BOURNEMOUTH 121
Chapter 18 127
   GRANDCHILDREN 127
Chapter 19 132

THE INTERVENING YEARS..................................132
Chapter 20 135
   PARENTS..135
      DAD'S CLUTTER 137
      THE DANCE LESSONS..................................139
      BUNNY LICHFIELD.......................................140
      CONSCIENTIOUS OBJECTOR 145
      END OF WAR..148
Chapter 21 150
   GWYNETH 150
      THE BUTCHERS SHOP.................................152
   Chapter 22 163
   EXPERIENCES..163
      ERIC 163
      COLONNATO...168
      THE CHINESE MOTHER MAI 170
      PETER 173
Chapter 23 180
   PONTREMOLI ADVENTURE 180
      MY LITTLE ESCAPEE 182
      CEDRIC'S SECRET LIFE 184
      AMNESTY 187
      A DREARY SUNDAY AFTERNOON 193
      MISTER JOE...199

LIFE PAINTING 203
THE LITTLE RED BEETLE 205
DOCTOR HARWOOD 207
EMIL 213
THE RED SKIRT 215
ALLEN THE SCULPTOR 219

Chapters 24 222
HOLIIDAYS 222
FRENCH HOLIDAY 222
DISCOVERING PIETRASANTA 227
SWITZERLAND ITALY 231
PAINTING IN PIETRASANTA 235
THE SWISS OBERLAND 237
PIETRASANTA 241
THE WELSH HOLIDAY 244

Chapter 25 249
KEEPING A ROOF OVER MY HEAD 249
PROBUS 249
FAMILY PLANNING CLINIC 252
INA 270
SUZANNE 271
SARAH AND MIRIAM 276
PRISON LIFE 277
CANNABIS LEAF 281

VULNERABLES UNIT 283
THE WEST INDIAN CULTURE COURSE ...285
FARM CLEANING..292
JOERN 295
CAMBRIDGE 297
MARIA WAGNER' 302
ROYCE AND KAREN....................................305

Chapter 27..313
LOVE STORIES..313
YVETTE AND DON.......................................313
YANTO AND PHYLLIS 319
A WELSH LOVE STORY 320

Chapter 28..325
MY CHILDREN..325
RUSSELL, DONNA, MATTHEW, DAN........325

Chapter 29..331
DAN..331
THE WINDSOR AFFAIR................................333
DAN'S BEDROOM 334
BRATTO...337
DAN DECISION MAKING............................342
WHO IS JOYCE? 348

June Antoinette Necchi

June Antoinette Necchi

June Antoinette Necchi

Chapter One

MY BEGINNINGS

My beginnings, my roots, were bestowed on me by my Italian father and my Welsh mother. Their fathers, my grandfathers, Agostino and Evan, were not to know that their two cultures, that of the Italian and Welsh were to collide in the years to come.

Agostino my grandfather, began his life in Bratto a village in the municipality of Pontremoli, Tuscany, Italy.

An Italian census going back to the 1700's revealed that the Necchi's made a living by working on the land, gathering the porcini mushrooms and chestnuts which grew in abundance, and were sold in the local markets. A handful of the men who had craftsmen skills, carpentry and stonemasonry, were able to increase the family's income by using these skills to maintain the village's houses which were hundreds of years old.

June Antoinette Necchi

Agostino like some of his cousins, was a cabinet maker working for a spell in Florence but living in the village where most were unable to read or write. I learned from the Italian census at that time that my grandfather was the only one in his home who was named as 'Literate'.

The young men eventually decided to join many other Italians at that time by emigrating to England. Agostino walked with two cousins to the Bay of Genoa, a considerable distance from Bratto to board a ship that would take them to an unknown country. I can only imagine their excitement leaving their home in the mountains despite having no knowledge of the English language.

Having arrived in London the young Italians soon spotted an opportunity to open a restaurant in Villier Street located next to Charing Cross station, and according to all accounts was successful, until the National Strike when Agostino allowed hard up customers to put their bills 'on the slate', to be paid later. The 'later date' never materialised, and the restaurant closed.

It was at that restaurant that Agostino met and married Florence the daughter of a gilder, Henry Kell and his wife Emma, and the granddaughter of Marylebone waistcoat makers, George and Elizabeth Kell, and it's this Henry Kell, my great grandfather, who in 1923 sailed to Egypt at the time Tutankhamen's tomb was opened. He had been requested to repair, by gilding,

June Antoinette Necchi

Tutankhamen's chair, which had been discovered in the tomb.

Agostino following the closure of his restaurant, was employed by Waring and Gillow's, a renowned fine furniture company in London. He became supervisor of the parquet floor-laying branch of the company, taking my father, Enrico (known as Bunny), as his apprentice at the age of 13.

I remember the stories of their work, laying the floor of the Tower ballroom, Blackpool, and that of building the Rolls Royce stand in London Earls Court, a stand which was dismantled and erected every year.

Florence and Agostino's family increased until they had 10 children, 6 sons and 4 daughters with my father, Enrico (Bunny) being their second born. The girls, like their ancestors became seamstresses, and the boys, craftsmen, especially in cabinet making.

My Welsh grandfather, Evan, known as Yanto lived in the small village of Pontlottyn in the Rhymney valley in South Wales. He came from a long line of coal miners with a culture of music and dancing, and Chapel twice a day on Sundays.

My grandmother, Amelia left the family when my mother, Gwyneth, was three years old and her brother, Yanto two. Their father brought the children up on his own in their small home which stood at the foot of old stone steps along a track overlooking the river Rhymney.

June Antoinette Necchi

At the top of the steps were three cottages, each with a family. Sarah, a widow whose husband, an army officer who had been killed in action in the First World War, lived in the first cottage with her four children. A kind lady, she had taken pity on her neighbour, Yanto offering help from time to time, then some years later inviting him to move into her home with his children. Despite the crowded conditions Gwyneth enjoyed the company of the two girls, Dolly and Margie, and their brothers, Alfie and Joey.

My mother, Gwyneth, was a lively youngster who together with her brother, Yanto entertained the locals by dancing and singing on stage. In school she excelled at mathematics, and winning a classroom competition, was invited to the home of the head mistress to listen to her new crystal radio.

Yanto and the two boys became firm friends, eventually joining the Royal Navy, while Dolly and Margie left the village to work in London. Gwyneth was already looking into the future, and on leaving school at the age of 14 was also attracted to the 'bright lights' of London where work was readily available for young girls. She went into 'Service' for a Jewish doctor and his wife, and Nanny to his twin babies, as well as general home help, including cooking for the family.

It was at this point that the two worlds of the Welsh village, Pontlottyn, and the mountain village of Bratto Italy, collided. The visiting Italian laundry boy to the

June Antoinette Necchi

doctor's home set his eyes on the new Nanny waiting at

June Antoinette Necchi

the door with the week's laundry, and in his words later, 'took one look at her in her smart Nanny's uniform, fell in love, promising myself to marry her one day'. Bunny, despite his Italian blood, had light blonde hair, while Gwyneth was black haired with olive skin, inherited from her Romany grandmother.

They married when Gwyneth was 18 and Bunny 21, beginning their married life in a London flat with Gwyneth still working for the doctor, and Bunny being given work from time to time by an Italian ice cream company painting signs for cafes and ice cream trikes, as well as shop window dressing for local grocer's shops.

Before long Gwyneth realised that she was expecting a baby. I was due to be born when she was still 18. Apparently she was at work when her labour began prematurely. I was born one month early, leaving them unprepared, So I was put to sleep in a drawer on the floor. Fortunately, her employer, the doctor, allowed her to continue working for him, taking me with her to work each day.

After my birth, my father was keen to boost the family income so taught himself to play the piano accordion, busking each weekend night outside West End theatres.

At that time, they had formed a close friendship with an Irish couple, Bridie and Paddy, who also was able to play the accordion.

June Antoinette Necchi

My mother often talked about the past to me, and one day related a story about this accordion which had been a great source of income in hard times. For me it was a fascinating glimpse into the hardships of that time in history, and of the camaraderie which develops between those sharing the challenges of wartime Britain. This was her story.

"Can Paddy borrow Bunny's piano accordion? Bridie asked me when she turned up at the door one morning. "We've run out of money and Paddy's lost his job. He wants to busk over the weekend to try to earn a few bob to buy some food for the little ones". I knew that Bunny had been guaranteed a few weeks' work for the cafe owner so the accordion would lay unused for a while. Money was hard to find then, and though pregnant again, I felt lucky to still have my job with the doctor, So I was happy to help my friends. It was the mid 1930's with the threat of war hanging over us, but me and Bunny got by with him topping up his wages with odd jobs and busking.

"Gwyneth, when you go to Bridie's can you bring my squeeze box back! There's a big show in the West End at the weekend. I need to do some busking there", Bunny asked me a few weeks later. I told him, "Yes, Bunny, I'll go tomorrow on my day off".

I lifted you from your pram and went down the steps to Bridie's basement flat. "Hell Bridie. Bunny sent me to collect the accordion. Did Paddy manage to make enough money to go to the shops?" "Well, yes, he did, thank you, Gwyneth. He had a good busk".

Bridie was hesitating. "Look Gwyneth, I'm sorry but the accordions not here". "Don't worry, Bridie" I said, "I'll come back later". "That's the problem, Gwyneth. I don't know how to tell you...."

"It's not broken, is it?" "No. I mean I don't know. Oh,, I do wish that Paddy was here to tell you…" "Look, Bridie", I told her. "Whatever the reason, we can sort it out. Then Bunny can go and busk this weekend".

"Bridie spoke quickly now. "Look I may as well……." She was close to tears. "We ran out of money, so Paddy took it to the pawn shop........". Before she could go on I interrupted her, "Don't worry. Just tell me which pawn shop and I'll go and get it".

"As I was trying to tell you Gwyneth. He did pawn it but couldn't afford to get it out and the time ran out".

"What am I going to tell Bunny? "There's me with another baby on the way and will soon have to give up work. That accordion has been our life saver when Bunny's on short time".

Bridie, trying to be helpful, said, "Maybe you should go to the shop and see if it's still there?".

I put you back in your pram and hurried to the shop.

"Sorry, we have a shortage of accordions" "That one sold quickly" I was told by the pawn shop keeper.

June Antoinette Necchi

Back in our little flat I gave Bunny the bad news. He stood thoughtful for a while.

"Well, Gwyneth. Paddy must have been desperate. He's a good man and would never do anyone down. I think I'll go to Gino's in the morning. Maybe he can find me a bit more sign writing".

"June, your dad never failed to reinvent himself when his back was to the wall. The next weekend I watched him standing back from the newly painted trike. He whistled happily as he walked over to collect another.

June Antoinette Necchi

My Welsh grandparents

Amelia my great grandmother

Anne my Romany grandmother

My mother, Yanto, & me

June Antoinette Necchi

My Italian grandparents

Agostino's home in Tuscany

My Italian grandfather

Agostino

My paternal grandmother Florence

My parents on their wedding day

June Antoinette Necchi

EVACUATION

My brother Antonio (Tony) was born 14 months after me. Gwyneth was able to find work when me and Tony were toddlers by putting us in a day nursery. My parents were then able to rent a bigger flat and life settled down.... that was until rumblings of a possible war with Germany were on the horizon.

And then on September the 1st 1939 Germany invaded Poland and on the third of September, England and France declared war on Germany.

I was too young to know what this meant but strange things were happening. My mother put up black blinds to cover the windows. My dad dug a big hole in the garden and put a roof on it. He told me that it was called a shelter. He put a bed down there and said we could sleep there sometimes. Me and my brother thought it was fun.

When we were taken for walks we saw great big balloons as big as houses in fields. They were too big to play with.

Our father told us they were called barrage balloons for 'the war'. Sometimes there were very loud noises in the streets. He told us they were called sirens and if we heard them we had to go and sleep in the shelter.

One day out shopping with my mother the sirens warned of German bombers approaching, and she ran with us to an underground station to shelter with other people. I remember the music down there.

Soon after, our parents told us that they were taking us on a train. We had never been on a train before and were very excited. It was a long way away and they told us that we would see our grandfather. We were shy when we saw him waiting at the station. We didn't know him. Back in his cottage, Sarah, the lady he lived with, put plates of dinner on the table and we played a little while before being put to bed together.

About 2 days later my parents began packing their bags but left our clothes in the bedroom. They told us, "You will live now with your grandfather and Sarah because of 'the war'". We were too young to understand about 'the war'.

Weeping, we stood at the cottage door as we waved goodbye to our parents who hugged and kissed us saying, "We'll come back to see you at Christmas". I thought I saw my father wipe away his tears.

THE FIRST OF MANY HOMES

I was 4 years old, and my brother 3, too young to understand what 'the war' was, and that we had to adapt to a new life in a Welsh cottage far away from the security of life with our parents in London. It felt as though we had been given away but were too young to understand why. Neither did we know that my mother, Gwyneth, thought that we would be safer in this small village, Pontlottyn, set in a Welsh valley, safe from the Germans' bombs.

June Antoinette Necchi

Back inside the cottage, Sarah, sat us down for tea. We were just getting used to her and my grandfather, who until then had been strangers to us. How different life was with these 'strangers. I remember playing on the hearth in front of a coal fire, with Tony, and our breakfasts of lumps of bread in a dish of warm milk with sugar. It was Sarah who taught me to say my prayers at night kneeling at the side of our bed.

There was a pigsty in the garden outside. "Where are the pigs? "I asked Sarah. "Oh, they've all been killed now. We'll have some for dinner tonight".

We made friends with the children in the other cottages and played in the empty pigsty when it was raining, and when the sun came out, ran up and down the nearby mountains. We didn't know until we were older that these were slag heaps, the waste from the village coal mines now covered in grass.

Across the road from Sarah's home, we paddled in a shallow river, the Rhymney, and as children lived in the moment despite the turmoil in our lives created by the war.

Three months is a long time for young children to be separated from their parents. My parents' arrival just before Christmas apparently left Tony and me unmoved.

Telling me years later, my mother said, "We walked into the cottage, and you were both playing on the hearth. You looked up at us as though we were

June Antoinette Necchi

strangers then went on playing". I can only imagine how distraught they were at this, knowing too that they would have to leave us again after Christmas.

It was Easter 1940 when there was a national realisation that the earlier threat by Hitler that his air force would destroy London, hadn't happened. In fact, there was little evidence that a war had begun despite the Germans' conviction that it would all be over in a year. My parents decided, like many, that it was turning out to be a non-war and that they would take us back to our London home.

I had started at the Pontlottyn Infants' school and would now go to a school back in London. I was happy that at last I could be with my parents once more …..though not knowing that this would just prove to be a respite from the war.

September 7th, 1940, was the beginning of the Blitz, 57 nights of the German planes' non-stop bombing of London which would continue until May 1941.

One night with no warning the heavy drone of overhead planes and explosions burst into the night. My parents wrapped us in blankets and ran down the garden to the shelter my father had built when preparing for the war. We lay on the beds he had put underground, putting our fingers in our ears as we listened to the deafening explosions all around us. I was terrified as the bombs raining down from the German bombers lit up the sky. The noises of that night are imprinted on my mind.

June Antoinette Necchi

As day was breaking my father said, "I'm going out to see if our house has been damaged". I cried, saying, "Don't go Daddy. You'll be killed". "I will be alright he told me, "I'm wearing my tin hat".

Years later he told me that while the windows in our house were broken and the door blown out, the house itself was safe to live in, but that the street at the bottom of our garden, and all its houses had been blown up.

When it became clear that the Blitz was going to continue night after night, my parents took us on the train, once again, to live in Wales. They returned to London, my father to work in a bomb damage team and my mother to work in a factory. I went back to the local school in Wales and waited and waited until we would become a family again.

STONEHOUSE

And that day came about towards the end of 1941 when we were taken on the train, not to London, but to a village, Stonehouse, in Gloucestershire, where our next home was a cottage built on a track leading to the Cotswold Hills. A mother and her young daughter, Maureen, lived there, and let out a room to earn a little extra money while the husband was serving abroad.

Looking back, it was an idyllic period in my life. I was reunited with my mother, and while living there a baby sister was born. My father lived in Worcestershire,

June Antoinette Necchi

coming home every six weeks on leave while working as a foreman on a site building a new hospital for the returning wounded troops. I looked forward to him coming to see us. I'd sit on his lap when he was teaching me how to draw and go onto the hills to play with him and Tony.

Life was bliss then. I was back with my family, and had started the local infants' school, my third school. My playground was the Cotswold Hills where with the village children, I spent my time gambolling down the hills, making daisy chains, taking sandwiches for picnics, and playing with none of the fears of bombings and separations that I'd grown used to. I was happy and content.

I didn't know that the clouds of change were beginning to gather and that my life was about to be thrown into turmoil again after just a few contented months in Stonehouse.

My father heard that he was going to be posted to the West Midlands where cooling towers were being constructed. Wanting to be within travelling distance of his family he found lodgings for us in a small mining town, Cannock, which had its own railway station enabling him to travel to see us every six weeks.

The landlady lived alone while her husband was fighting abroad, and like many wives managing on limited incomes, she offered her home to evacuees in return for a weekly payment from the Government.

June Antoinette Necchi

I looked forward to starting the nearby school, St Gregory's Catholic school as the other children like me, were all evacuees. Their school in Margate had transferred its headmaster, Mr Ivory, his two teachers, and all the pupils who had been taken into a variety of homes around the area. The small midland town offered refuge from the war activities which were focussed on cities and ports. The school was in the town centre overlooking an ancient bowling green and only a few hundred yards from where I lived with my baby sister, my brother and my mother.

Unfortunately, after a month the landlady decided that she didn't want children living in her house and my mother had to find other accommodation. Some kindly neighbours were prepared to help. My brother moved into a family along the road. They were warm hearted people who welcomed him into their home, but he cried to be with my mother. He was still only 5 years old and very attached to her. Having found a landlady who was prepared to take her and my baby sister, my mother begged her to take in Tony as well.

I was placed with a family who had two girls a little older than myself.....I would be seven in one month's time, and I was frightened of ghosts......

Leaving the security of the lodgings I had shared briefly with my family, the home that was found for me was a few minutes' walk away.

There were 2 bedrooms in the house, and I was to share a double bed with two sisters who told me. "You must sleep on the side of the bed next to the attic door. Do

June Antoinette Necchi

you know there's a ghost up there? "When they told me

about the ghost. I believed them. I was frightened and cried. I was nearly 7 years old

GHOSTS

The two sisters couldn't understand my London accent which they often laughed at, nor could I understand the dialect of the mining town. I didn't feel as though I belonged there and felt lost with my only comfort going to school each day to spend time with the other evacuees. At school, I was sad at the end of lessons when my mother came to take Tony home because I wanted to go with them. I couldn't understand why 'the war' meant I had to live in a different house, but I was happy when my mother decided to take me away from the house with a ghost and find another home for me.

A little girl, two years older than me, lived in the next home I was sent to. Her name was Sheila. Her father was a local butcher. There were two beds next to each other in the bedroom I shared with her. During the war I had no story books so I couldn't believe it when I saw that Sheila had a big box of Enid Blyton's Sunny Stories at the side of her bed. It was lovely to lie in bed at night and read one of the stories.

Her mother, Kitty, and her father were very kind to me which probably made Sheila a little jealous because she told me. "You can't read my story books anymore". She told her parents that she wanted them to 'send her away'.

June Antoinette Necchi

It had only been a few weeks since I'd had my seventh birthday. It would have been nice to stay there because

June Antoinette Necchi

I played in the fields with children from the street and went fishing for tadpoles in the brook across the road.

My school was quite a long way away, but I didn't mind walking across the fields to the main road that led to the school. It was wintertime and I wore a siren suit my father had made for me to wear when walking to school. It was very furry material and covered me right down to my feet and over my head.

(Many years later my friend Irene, a niece of the butcher, told me, "When I visited they said come and have a peep in the other room at the evacuee in a Teddy Bear suit").

I packed my Teddy Bear suit into my small case as I got ready to leave Sheila's house. I waited for the lady who told me she was from the government. I didn't know where I was going to live next, but I hoped it would be nice.

Waiting, with my small case in my hand, I stood at the front door with the lady from the government. In my case, which I took to every new home, were 2 dresses, a cardigan, knickers, pyjamas and socks and my teddy bear siren suit. I wore my only pair of shoes.

When the door opened a tall lady stood there and the government lady said to her, "Mrs Robinson, this is your new evacuee, June Necchi. She is 7 years old, and you must send her to the evacuee school in the town centre.

June Antoinette Necchi

As she left Mrs Robinson took me upstairs. "This is your bedroom. Put your case down on the floor at the side of the bed and keep your clothes in there". Pointing to the ceiling she said, "Don't ever switch that light on or the police will come. The German planes may see the light through the window and drop bombs on us".

I thought about the ghosts that might be in the dark room with no lights. I'll hide under the blankets then, I told myself. That night I washed myself in the bathroom next door to the bedroom, put on my pyjamas then ran and jumped into bed and hid under the covers.

I didn't want to be disobedient but couldn't help switching the light on one night when I went into my bedroom. I was sure I could see a ghost. Mrs Robinson ran up the stairs. "I heard you switch that light on. I told you not to because of the police. I'm taking the bulb out now so; you can't switch it on again".

The next morning, I ran all the way to school. It was the only certainty I had in my life with so many changes. I felt safe there with the teachers and children who were my only constant in life. I didn't want to go back to Mrs Robinsons but had no one to tell.

I liked it in my school, playing skipping and hopscotch in the playground with my friends there. The school was in part of a building which printed the local newspaper, the Advertiser, owned by the Withington family next door. They had welcomed the school, St Gregory's, from Margate when they were escaping from bombings on the south coast.

June Antoinette Necchi

The building, the original John Wood School built in the 1600's by John Wood, Paternoster Rd. London was in a poor state of repair after the pupils and staff had moved to another location years before. The Advertiser's printing press had been set up there, and at the beginning of the Second World War had offered part of it for evacuees' schooling.

We had two classes on the right of the building divided from each other by long curtains. In one half were pupils aged from 5 to 9, and on the other side of the curtain sat the 10 to 14 years old. (14 was the school leaving age then).

There was one coal burner in front of which, each morning, crates of small bottles of milk were placed too warm through in wintertime. The back yard had a lavatory and a tap in the wall to provide drinking water and hand washing. At the front of the building, overlooking the bowling green, we had the space to play.

With lovely open countryside, nearby, we were taken on Nature walks over the Common, and down lanes to pick wildflowers and gather autumn leaves.

My father visited every 6 weeks to take us to the 'pictures' and to cut my fringe! Every so often with my fringe growing over my eyes, and waiting for my father's visit, my teacher would say, "June Necchi, get your fringe cut!".

The nearly 4 years I was at St Gregory's gave me the stability necessary for me to cope with separation, its teachers and pupils, becoming my 'family'.

June Antoinette Necchi

I remember I loved learning about sums and writing, and in my mind's eye I can still see the small black slates on which we wrote the alphabet and did our arithmetic in white chalk.

It was while I lived with Mrs Robinson that my uncle Eddie was killed in the Arnhem action in Holland. Eddie was 27 and my favourite uncle, so my father sent me a letter telling me of his death. As a solitary child I spoke to no one about it.

(In the 1960's pushing my baby out in town I saw Mrs Robinson for the first time since I was a child. She and her husband stopped to speak to me. "June, I've never forgotten what you said to me when your uncle Eddie had died. I asked you why I hadn't seen you crying. You said, "I only think about nice things like fairies". I hadn't realised until hearing that, that I had found my own way of coping with all the experiences of the war years).

I made friends with the children in the street and each day when I came from school I played with them. Sometimes we went to the nearby park to play on the swings and the slides. It was while I was there I could forget about my family, but only when my friends went home afterwards did I feel lonely again.

Mrs Robinson had a special day each week when she visited a friend who lived a distance away. She told me, "June, I visit this friend every Tuesday. When you come from school you must play in the street until I come back because I take the key with me".

June Antoinette Necchi

One day, big clouds came over while we were playing outside. Then lightning sparked across the sky and thunder rumbled. Quite suddenly the heavens opened, and my friends ran indoors. I stood in the middle of the road, frightened, not knowing where to run to. Mrs Robinson was still visiting her friend. I knew the house was locked so ran to the end of the avenue where a corner shop had a small doorway. Standing there the heavy rain bounced on the step soaking my shoes and dress. I was terrified of the thunder and the lightning and put my fingers in my ears. Frightened, I looked around hoping to see a person, but the roads were deserted. I felt so alone. I felt abandoned and wishing that I could just run to my family, wishing that 'the war' had never happened.

Mrs Robinson came back when the rain had stopped and told me, "Go upstairs. Take your wet clothes off and put them in the airing cupboard". I wanted to have my mother there to help me.

One day the government lady came and asked a lot of questions. After then I had to leave because I wasn't being given good food and had contracted a contagious skin disease.

ORPHANAGE

"June, there isn't another house for you now so I am taking you somewhere and you will have children to play with. You must call the lady who looks after you, matron", the government lady told me.

June Antoinette Necchi

I had never seen such a big house. It had two lots of stairs and very big rooms. The matron took me to a room with lots of beds. She pointed to a bed at the end of the room and said, "Put your pyjamas on the bed and your case at the side". "The lights go off at 8 o'clock. There must be no talking"

I heard children's voices outside and asked if I could go out there. "Yes, you can play in the garden with the other children".

Outside, I asked a child, "Is this your house?". She told me, "No it's an orphanage. We all live here because we don't have any mothers or fathers". "Are you an orphan, too?" "No, I have a Mummy and Daddy. I'm here because of 'the war" I told her. That night I curled up in bed, shivering, and wished that I could see a face I knew, but I was glad that I wasn't an orphan.

I followed the other children downstairs the next morning and sat at a long table where breakfast was set in front of me. I stared fascinated at the solid ball of porridge floating in a sea of cold milk in my breakfast bowl. Everything in the orphanage felt strange and not a bit like a home. The orphans knew each other and were laughing and talking together and went to a different school to mine. I couldn't wait to finish my breakfast and run to school.

It was my safe haven, the one certainty I now had in life and friends there were also separated from their families and spoke in an accent I understood.

June Antoinette Necchi

Back in the classroom our desks had small slates ready for our sums and writing lessons. I looked forward to the end of the afternoon when our teacher would read stories about Brer Rabbit and his friends.

On the way back to the orphanage there was a big house with a broken fence. I crawled through the undergrowth and made a small space where I could hide away. I called it my secret garden. I never told the other children about it and would go and sit in it every day on the way back from school.

I did like to play in the woodland next to the big house. It was called 'Cannock Chase', and I'd climb trees and build camps with the orphans.

Every Saturday night we had to line up on the landing wrapped in towels when one by one we stood up in the bath, were washed down, dried and given a spoon of some mixture.

Then, one morning with no warning the matron called me in her room telling me, "June, pack your bag. You are leaving and going to a new home". I wasn't sorry to leave and was well used to my itinerant life but wondered where I'd be living in what would be my fourth home in this town, and where I would be spending my ninth birthday, more than four and a half years after I officially became an evacuee.

June Antoinette Necchi

An impression of the orphanage

June Antoinette Necchi

MRS PEACH

I was told that at my next house there was a lady called Mrs Peach. I thought that was a very funny name. Mrs Peach was a nice smiley lady who when I arrived at her house, gave me a lovely little black doll that she'd knitted for me. She had two teenage children who were very friendly and played games with me. Her son played the piano accordion, and at night he played music and sang songs. I liked it there. It was strange to sleep in the same bedroom as Mr and Mrs Peach, but they put a small curtain up and I slept in a camp bed on the other side.

Wartime food was rationed so Mrs Peach made a special breakfast for us all on Sunday mornings. A small amount of bacon, egg made from dried egg mixture, fried bread and something I'd never seen before…round black slices. I wasn't sure about it, but Mrs Peach told me, "Eat it up because it's good for you. It's called black pudding, and it's made from pig's blood". I took one bite and held it in the side of my mouth until I went to the toilet and flushed it away.

I made friends with the girl next door, Joy, and played with her every day after school in the gardens. It was nice to have a special friend, but one day the lady from the government came again and told me, "We have a new home for you, June". I didn't know why I had to move again but found out later. Apparently my mother had seen me at school with holes in my socks and the hem of my dress hanging down and thought I was being neglected.

I was used to moving from one home to another but would like to have stayed with Mrs Peach.

LAST WARTIME HOME

I didn't know then that I would feel quite happy in my next home, a home where another evacuee also lived. Dolores came from Ireland, but her father had brought her to live in Birmingham where he joined the police force. He made the decision to find a safe location for his daughter as Birmingham was at risk of bombing when the war broke out. Cannock was only about 20 miles away but considered to be a safe area.

Audrey, the daughter of the house, Dolores and myself, were the same age and we became good friends. The bed we shared was quite small. In those days it was called a three-quarter bed. We found we could fit in this small bed if the three of us slept sideways across it, our feet sticking out the sides. Audrey, Dolores, and I, giggled each night as our pillows kept falling off the sides of the bed and our feet grew cold as they poked out of the other side.

During the war we all adapted to our circumstances no matter how strange and in time they became 'normal'.

Audrey's father was serving his country while his wife 'kept the home fires burning', but money was short and taking in a couple of evacuees was, for many, a way of increasing the family income.

June Antoinette Necchi

At nine years of age at last I felt quite settled by comparison to the last few years when I felt a bit like a parcel being deposited in one home after another.

I had grown used to retreating into my own little world which I was able to take with me wherever I went. Fairies were still my little companions in that world and here in this family I had the chance to do something I'd always wanted to do.....learn to fly and become a fairy!

The garden to the side of the house had no fence and blended with the adjoining field to become one big garden with a brook running through. One day, tired of paddling and catching tadpoles, I asked Audrey's mother if she had something like an old curtain I could use to learn to fly. Along with a couple of safety pins and some string I fastened each end of the curtain to my wrists and the middle of the curtain to the back collar of my dress. I climbed a nearby old tree to the highest branch I dared t and positioning myself opened my arms wide and jumped. I've never forgotten that thrill when I was about to jump, and the expectation that I would fly. When I fell to the ground I couldn't understand what had gone wrong, but this wouldn't stop me trying again....

And then the day came when my host told me, "June, you will be leaving because there has been an announcement on the wireless that the war has ended". This meant nothing to me as I could only ever remember living in 'the war' for 6 years. Still separated

June Antoinette Necchi

from my parents, my brother and my sister it was unimaginable

June Antoinette Necchi

that I could live in a family again like the local children did. I wondered what it would feel like and would it last?

Chapter 3

END OF WAR AND LEAH

When the headmaster of my evacuee school at the end of the war, with his students and staff, had returned to Margate, I had lost my St Gregory's school friends but was beginning to make friends in a Catholic school, St Mary's, close to our lodgings. My life seemed to have been a never-ending series of different homes since the start of the war, and this felt no different. In those six years I had been to four different schools, lived in London, Wales, Gloucestershire and now Staffordshire. I'd lost count of the homes I'd lived in, but dared to hope that life would finally settle down, become normal.

With the ending of the war, it had brought enormous changes for our family. At the same time my father was able to leave London to join my mother who looked for accommodation. Nearby was a terraced house where Jack, a coal miner, and his wife, Leah lived. They had a spare bedroom and front room which they offered my parents.

At the same time my mother's brother, Yanto, had been demobbed from the Royal Navy where he served

June Antoinette Necchi

as a Petty Officer. On returning home to Wales he found that his marriage had broken down. He decided to come to Cannock to be near my mother, his sister. He was able to rent a bedroom in a nearby house, a ground floor front room which opened onto the pavement. As we had only one bedroom in Leah's house, a room which my sister and myself shared with our parents, my brother would leave the house each evening and sleep in Yanto's bedroom. I was beginning to make friends with the local children in my next school close to our lodgings. My life had been a never-ending series of changes since the start of the war, and this felt no different.

My mother's talent for domestic organisation enabled us to settle in and enjoy our new home. The facilities in our living room included a two-bar electric fire, and a tabletop electric stove, both possible when my father converted the house gas lights to electricity, by wiring the whole house.

The kitchen, its green painted brick walls hung with a bath to be filled with kettles of hot water for the weekly bath, and a brown stone sink fed only by cold water, had to be shared with Leah for washing dishes. The 'refrigerator', a wooden box with a mesh door for ventilation, stood in the shade of the yard outside. Also in the yard was a big wooden Dolly tub used for laundering the clothes and linen.

Upstairs, we had one of the two bedrooms sharing it with my sister, my mother and my father. After the many years of separation and the many 'homes 'we'd

June Antoinette Necchi

lived in we were unfazed by the living restrictions of having to share the bedroom, and just happy to be all together at last.

Jack, Leah's husband, worked shifts down a local coal mine years before showers had been installed, and would return home covered in coal dust. Each afternoon when he came from work he'd stand, bare chested, in front of the fire while Leah washed the coal dust from his back and front from a bowl of soapy water on the table. I'd sit watching fascinated from a hearth footstool as little rivers of dust ran down his back. I felt strangely content in this domestic scene, each day sitting at this fireside with the black grate glistening from the glow of the coal.

My mother and Leah formed a strong friendship which sometimes faltered as the result of a minor domestic dispute. It was then that Leah forbade us from walking through their living room to the kitchen giving us no option but to leave by our front door, to make our way up the entry to the kitchen. Climbing down from the high step with her arms filled with dishes and saucepans from the meal she'd cooked in our small front room, proved a bit perilous for my mother, but I suppose that after the ravages of war her determination had been strengthened.

Once they were back on friendly terms, they, together with my father and Jack, went to the local pub, the 'Crystal Fountain', a few doors away. Jack was always tipsy when they got back home and each time I felt

June Antoinette Necchi

nervous not knowing if he would be in a happy mood or

suddenly turn angry. I have never forgotten one particular night.....

I remember Leah as a very pretty woman with a friendly personality, and from my adult perspective now can imagine that her husband would be jealous of her popularity in their local pub. Maybe an incident in the pub that night fuelled his jealousy and anger, but on arriving home he became very aggressive, swearing and shouting at Leah. My father intervened physically to prevent Leah from being hurt. I had never witnessed anger between my parents and was terrified at what may happen. If I am a witness to unexpected angry outbursts I feel the same emotional reaction now.

It was during our 3 years lodging with Leah and Jack that she gave birth to a baby daughter, Anita. I couldn't understand, one day, when I heard Leah crying out upstairs. She kept repeating 'never again' and in my innocence I wondered what was happening to her. Childbirth was a subject never discussed by parents with their children then, and my mother was no exception. I escaped all the noise and activity by going out to play with my friends. Later, seeing Leah smiling and happy, I was filled with wonder as I looked down at this perfect baby girl in her mother's arms, a baby girl I grew to love as I pushed her out in her pram, and played with her.

Time seemed to be standing still which made me happy after the tumultuous war years. I enjoyed playing out

June Antoinette Necchi

with my friends in the empty street which had only one
car, that of my father. Leah's washing line stretched

across the road gave us hours of fun with skipping games. Pavement hopscotch, top and whip, ball games, marbles, all filled our days. We had no toys. We didn't need them. We made our own fun.

The father of my friend, Marlene, had a timber lorry with an extended open back perfect for performing plays and concerts for the local children. At a penny a time they gathered at the end of the lorry to be entertained by Marlene, Dawn and me.

At the beginning of the long summer school holidays and having seen a film about a mermaid we set to work to put a play on which we called Miranda the Mermaid. Sticking paper together to form a mermaid's tail I painted scales in green and blue. Poor Dawn had trouble trying to prevent it splitting on 'stage' but our audience, our playmates, loved it and thought it was a good penny worth of entertainment.

Within four months of being in my new Primary school I sat for a scholarship which gave me a place in a convent school, 'Our Lady of Mercy', in Wolverhampton. This was to be my fifth and final school. I was embarrassed to wear the uniform, especially what I thought was an unsightly navy velour hat which was too big for my head. Not only that but none of my street friends wore school uniforms.

The convent, an austere building with cloisters, housed both nuns and boarding pupils, and was on the other side of town. While enjoying maths and languages, for me

June Antoinette Necchi

there were few creative opportunities, the emphasis being on academic subjects.

I did, though, enjoy the company of friends, particularly Jeanette, a Huntington girl who shared with me walks around the town's galleries and library after school, as well as fun on the bus on the way home.

It was then that my interest in using my sewing machine, running up garments made from my mother's discarded clothes, became a developing hobby which was to see me well over the coming years.

Me, my mother, brother Tony

& sister Sandra

June Antoinette Necchi

June Antoinette Necchi

SALLY'S NEW BIKE

Now, I felt as though I belonged for the first time. We had our own street 'gang' spending all our spare time playing in the street or the fields behind our row of houses. Every day we found different games to play and places to explore. Then one day we were set to have a new experience, one we could never have dreamt about….

"Line up!", commanded Sally standing proudly at the side of her sparkling new bicycle. We were in awe at the sight of this bike. Sally was the first of the street gang to have one, and a new one at that! Her parents, the only businesspeople down our street, ran the Post Office and Newsagents. Sally, their only child stood out like a beacon with her pretty clothes and toys we could only dream about. And now she had the prize possession of a bike!

Us, a motley queue of youngsters prepared to be compliant, anything to achieve a ride on Sally's bike. Obediently, we waited for our names to be called...

"Your turn, June!"

A never to be forgotten moment. I was eleven years old and had never even sat on a bike, let alone had a ride on one. Oh,, that bike and the pleasure and fun it gave me as I wobbled to the end of the road and back.

"Can I have another go!".

"My turn next!"

June Antoinette Necchi

"Sally, I'll give you a sweet if you let me have another go".

Please for more rides echoed around the street.

"I'll decide who has turns". said Sally, with an air of authority.

"I'll be your best friend if you let me have another go Sally".

And so, the afternoon wore on, a mixture of excitement and sulks as we rode up and down from the shop to the end of the road.

Joy of joy, a year later my parents bought me my own bike from the local Co-op on the 'never, never'. That bike became my best friend. I went everywhere on it. Exploring the nearby lanes, and the wonderful woodland in my homemade dirndl skirt, or my 'pedal pushers', fetching the weekly shop from the Co-op each Saturday, and later, peddling to work.

Yes, those first heady days of my wobbling attempts to ride Sally's bike have never left me nor have the memories of belonging to our street gang

June Antoinette Necchi

Me and my street gang 1

June Antoinette Necchi

LEAVING LODGINGS

Apparently, while we were spending 3 years in lodgings, following the end of the war, my parents' names were down for housing both in London and Cannock until the post, one day, brought a letter from the local Council offering them a council house. It was meant to be, because two weeks later a letter came offering us a home in London. Those two weeks could have changed our lives and my story.

It may sound odd to modern ears, but I remember standing at the foot of the stairs of our new home seeing a window casting light on a landing leading to 3 bedrooms and a bathroom. A bathroom! My goodness, we must be posh now! Not only that but we had a garden to the front and back and even a driveway. Oh,, yes and an outside toilet in a building attached to the house.

My mother worked long hours but kept an immaculate home. I remember Mondays were for cleaning the brasses, the windows and the steps. Much of the washing went out and was returned to be dried and ironed. I was promoted as chief ironer, and my brother became adept at cooking breakfasts for both me and my sister.

My mother worked Sundays, so I cut my teeth on how to cook Sunday roasts while she was in work, and my poor Dad was the recipient of my early efforts at making gravy.

June Antoinette Necchi

My sister, six years younger, was at the carefree roller-skating age, though played a part in household chores, too. For me they were halcyon days cycling with friends, exploring the countryside and attempts at tennis in the local park. I was still friends with my old sewing machine

June Antoinette Necchi

Me and my mother

Me my mother and Anne

Chapter 4
LEAVING CONVENT

I couldn't wait to leave school and the confines of a convent education. While I had a love of maths and French they couldn't compensate for the lack of creative subjects, art in particular. 15 was the school leaving age at that time though it was expected that students at the convent would go on to higher education. Maybe my earlier life hadn't prepared me for stability, I don't know.

At this time, I had lived with my parents for only 4 and a half years and in our own family home for a year and a half. Was I always going to be a rolling stone that gathers no moss, I wondered? Was constant change now embedded in my psyche? Or was I making choices for myself for the first time in my life?

I had no idea what I was going to do when I finished school, nor did my parents question me when I asked their permission to leave. Having had no reliance on my parents throughout the war years they may have decided to let me continue this independence. Whatever the reason, they agreed that I finish school if that's what I wanted.

June Antoinette Necchi

Leaving school behind me was quite a heady experience and now, with the stability of a family home I felt free to express ideas.

Each Saturday morning, I used to go with my mother to an Italian cafe for a morning coffee, and a chat with the owner's wife, Mrs Rosa, who my mother had worked for a few years earlier. Coincidentally, two daughters of Mrs Rosa had been my teachers at the convent, teaching religion and cookery, hence Mrs Rosa knew that I had finished school quite suddenly.

Bringing coffees over to our table she directed all her questions to my mother. "Has June decided what she wants to do? "Not yet", my mother replied. "We need another waitress here in the cafe. June can start on Monday". "Of course,", my mother replied, "I will make sure she is here".

This was one of the most memorable conversations of my life. At no point was I involved, nor my opinion asked.

My independent decision to leave school had brought me to this point only one day later when decisions were already being taken out of my hands!

Nevertheless, not to let my mother down, I did turn up promptly at the cafe. My first day proved to be a baptism of fire as the regular bus drivers and conductors came in for their break time cuppas. Their light-hearted banter, "Put the whiskey at the bottom",

June Antoinette Necchi

"Nice to see a new girl here", "Got a boyfriend? "Left me blushing and not knowing how to respond. Making ice cream sodas when my back was turned to the customers, and helping in the ice cream-making shed in the yard on certain days helped me to acclimatise to cafe life and I began to enjoy it.

I was interested when I heard a year later that a local accounts office was looking for a clerk. I was 16 and it had the appeal of other teenagers working there. It was a credit company selling ladies' clothes by door-to-door representatives, and the clerk's job was to record all sales and weekly payments. I enjoyed the challenge of the maths involved…. Unbelievably then, all calculations were made in the head!

The 'offices' themselves were part of a dilapidated Victorian house, the kitchen a vast place with a walk-in pantry. The large brown stone sink had only a cold-water tap. In nightmarish winter conditions we took it in turns to make the mid-morning, and afternoon drinks.

My own 'office' consisted of a large table and cardboard boxes for files. The gas fire gave out insufficient heat which we combatted by wearing coats and hats in cold weather. Mice frequently ran under the table and chairs, when one of the clerks, Sally, would try chasing them with a shovel.

The company's secretary, Miss German, was a lady quite lacking in confidence, seeming to belong to the Victorian era. I had no problem one very hot summer's

June Antoinette Necchi

day in persuading her that we all take our tables and files

out onto the yard which overlooked an overgrown south facing garden. And she agreed!

We were five girls keeping the accounts for the Bristol company using our town as a base for its representatives. There were 3 of us, teenagers, (though that word had not yet been invented,) and two twenty-five-year-olds. Their 'maturity' demanded a respect reserved for older people. They kept us in line. We filled our morning and lunch breaks with a variety of activities, maybe knitting, crocheting, filling in crosswords. My desk was littered with sketches of dresses I hoped to make up for myself.

I had an idea after seeing boxes of lady's dresses in the stockroom, dresses which to a girl's eyes were old fashioned and boring, and I still can't believe the confidence of the young when I approached the boss visiting from Bristol one day, asking him would he like me to send him a few designs for his clothing factory team. He was interested and asked me to send my designs to his company in Bristol.

I set to work enjoying putting the details of pin tucking, pockets, pleats and piping. At last, I had found a career, I thought! The completed designs were given the thumbs down. They would be too labour intensive, I was told, hence too expensive to produce. Oh, well, at least I could design for myself and friends.

And then 'Rock n Roll' arrived! It bought the Teddy Boys, the draped jackets, the heavy soled 'creeper

June Antoinette Necchi

'shoes, and the juke boxes filling the night in town with

June Antoinette Necchi

the music of Bill Hayley, Everly Brothers, Elvis Presley, Buddy Holly and many more.

The town became alive with music and dance in this new era!

Not sure what the fathers and grandfathers spending their days down the local mines thought about this 'new world'! But there was no stopping it.

The weekend influx of blue suited airmen filled out the dance halls, romances began, and so many girls eventually married their uniformed lovers.

The cinemas were always full with the back seats chosen by courting couples who had an eye kept on them by the usherettes whose torches picked them out from time to time.

Incredibly smoking was allowed in cinemas then with ashtrays fixed to the top of the back of seats.

As youngsters, we felt with changing attitudes that we had the world in the palm of our hands and that the future was ours. They were exciting times…

My brother, a popular teenager who always had a string of friends wandering through our open house was a young fashion follower and wasted no time in asking me to 'drainpipe' his trousers.

Each Friday his friends spent their wages at the local men's shop, Fosters, mainly buying trousers, not quite as wide as sailors' trousers but far too wide for these would-be Teddy Boys. They'd make a beeline for our house clutching their newly bought trousers and stand in line. "June, can you drainpipe these for tomorrow night's dance.? "Will five shillings be alright? I'll make a Slim Jim tie for free, too". I'd tell them

That was a better deal than the local Fosters who charged double that, ensuring that I was able to supplement my office wages. I was young but already learning the lesson that it was possible to earn money myself.

Parents then weren't too happy about this latest craze with their sons' 'creeper' shoes, drape jackets, drainpipe trousers, and the DA haircut, a big quiff at the front, and long hair at the back combed with a line running down the middle.

Some parents, including my mother, were worried about what the neighbours would say about their son's outrageous new fashions. "June, we're going to a wedding, and I don't want you to narrow Tony's new trousers less than 18 inches".

"June", asked my brother a few days later, "Mum, bought me a pair of trousers for the wedding. Can you drainpipe them to 12 inches, please?" I will, but you know I'll be in trouble, don't you? "And I was.

My ideas for business were coming thick and fast, and with the confidence of the young I had ideas which I wanted to put in practice, finding my independence exciting. I was happy with my life, my family, and my friends, Irene, Joy, Sally and Anne, bringing a new permanence to my life.

"June, d'you like my bubble cut? "My friend, Irene, asked me one day. "Went to Hopkins hairdressers and they permed it for me. They said it was a new fashion. What d'you think?" Ooh,! it looks lovely. Not sure about a perm, but I might go and get an urchin cut there."

"Hey, Irene, I bought myself one of those new hair shaders from Woolworths. Going to try it out for the dance tonight"....

These were our first tentative steps in growing up, and my mother was well meaning but determined to help me in my journey to 'grow up'. "June, I think you should give up your Bobby Sox and start wearing stockings. Put this suspender belt on and I'll show you what to do". I thought that it was a bit of a weird contraption but still respectful of my mother's wishes I fastened it around my waist. I didn't even want to wear stockings but complied anyway.

I was only a year or two out of my Convent school gym dress and navy baggy knickers and felt too young to be wearing women's things. There was another problem. It was Mum's old suspender belt, and the elastic suspenders had no stretch as the elastic was old. Now this seemed ok when standing up and walking to the park with my friends to watch a game of tennis, but there was a problem when I tried to sit on the park

June Antoinette Necchi

bench.......the suspenders refused to stretch to allow me to bend and sit down. My friends found this funny.

June Antoinette Necchi

There was only one thing I could do. "Watch", I said to them as I stood a distance from the bench, and with my legs rigid, flopped back onto it. That was the end of Mum's suspender belt and back to my Bobby Sox.

The highlights of our week! Making our way to the town centre, hearing our favourite bands playing in the three local dance halls. The rock 'n roll era had caught on in a big way flooding the dance halls with young RAF, as well as with local youngsters. We danced and changed partners on crowded floors, the 'drain-piped' boys, and the girls with their sugar starched petticoats filling out their wide skirted dresses. Life was for living! These days would go on and on! Repeating the line from Mary Hopkins' song,

"Those were the days, my friend

We thought they'd never end

We'd sing and dance forever and a day

We'd live the life we choose

We'd fight and never lose

For we were young and sure to have our way....

Those were the days, oh, yes, they were the days" ...

June Antoinette Necchi

Not quite the style baggy jacket missing

But close, you get the idea

June Antoinette Necchi

Chapter 5
BLACKPOOL HOLIDAY

It was the '50's. I was 17, and a few months before, my friends and I had planned a seaside holiday together…. and we couldn't wait to spend time on Blackpool's sands.

For a year we had saved up from our jobs, Irene, Anne and Joy working in dress shops, and me with Sally in an accounts' office. The plans were laid. We booked a guest house sharing one bedroom, and on our sewing machines run up yards of material bought from the local market into dirndl skirts, sun tops and boleros, ready for the Blackpool sun.

Giggling and chattering we climbed aboard the coach which was to take us to the 'glittering lights' of Blackpool. This was heady stuff! Our first grown up holiday. And so, we set off with our parents' words of warning ringing in our ears, "Don't speak to strangers! Don't stay out late! Wrap up warm!"

The first impression of the guest house tarnished our expectations of our dream holiday as we all stared at the shabby shared room, with shabby covered beds,

June Antoinette Necchi

and shabby curtains. Still, we had no intention of spending

time indoors.... our holiday was to be sunbathing on the 'golden' sands of Blackpool' by day, and out in Blackpool's illuminations by night, or dancing in the Tower ballroom. Nor did we care the next morning about the scantiness of the breakfast, or the urging by the landlady to leave the house immediately after we'd eaten.

We stepped out that first day wearing our homemade sundresses, ballerina style pumps and the newly fashionable shoulder bags. Jumper or coat? Never! Blue skies promised a good day so off so we went to the beach.

"Where's the sea?" Asked Sally. "There, there, in the distance", we cried, "Can you see it?" Soon we peeled off our dresses to our swimsuits underneath and stretched out in the warmth of the sun, but our feeling of 'grown-up-ness' bubbled over attracting the attention of a group of boys nearby. Lacking sophistication, we began chasing each other around darting looks at the boys as we ran. Plucking up courage, I called over, "Will you take a photo of us, please"?

We didn't fall in love that week, but we enjoyed meeting up to dance with the boys at the Tower ballroom each night and sharing bags of chips as we wandered along the streets after the dance.

Stepping off the coach a week later, we arrived home sporting 'Kiss Me Quick' sun hats. We didn't know then that we had passed a big milestone in our lives.

June Antoinette Necchi

We had chosen our 'adventure', financed it ourselves, came

June Antoinette Necchi

home with a few 'bob' and proved we could look after ourselves.....and were confidently planning the next year's holiday.

It was the 1950's and the world was surely our oyster!

How then did I find myself a few months later the target of a jealous teenage boy?

My childhood, largely spent as an evacuee living with a series of strangers, had left me compliant and subservient. Despite my attempts to finish my relationship with him I became a reluctant bride at the age of 20.

My mother found a cottage for sale next to my uncle's house. She thought it would make a nice first home. I had never confided in my parents about my boyfriend, so they had no idea of the pressures I was under. I was young and went along with the decisions that were being made for me. This compliancy, a leftover from my childhood experiences, I accepted.

And so, a new beginning in another home.

June Antoinette Necchi

Homemade dresses

Anne, Joy, Irene & me

Joy, me, Iren & Sally

Anne, Sally, Me and Joy

Chapter 6
FIRST COTTAGE

Imagine it, a two up two down tiny cottage for five hundred pounds! It had been modernised with a red Formica work surface and a single white sink. And there was a shiny new gas stove! A 9 feet by 10 feet living room stepped down from the kitchen and was heated by an open fire, the only source of heating in the house. A second room only slightly larger led off the living room to the front door. Enclosed stairs led up to two bedrooms, the smaller resembling the size of a roomy cupboard. There was no bath or shower, and the only toilet was located midway up the long narrow, overgrown garden.

Nevertheless, the sale went ahead and in no time out came 'a girl's best friend' my old treadle Singer sewing machine, which quickly ran up red and white gingham curtains and red tie backs to be hung at the tiny kitchen window. Now it really did look like a doll's house!

A cloth I'd embroidered covered a bottles' crate on which stood proudly an ex-RAF radio given to me by my father. I was fascinated to be able to listen to news from around the world. Though televisions were becoming available, few people had them and certainly it never crossed my mind that we should ever have one.

June Antoinette Necchi

Having a bath a few nights a week involved me taking a bus to my parents' home a few miles away followed by a 10-minute walk.

June Antoinette Necchi

I was 20 and had been married only 4 months when I developed a taste for Kraft cream cheese triangles. I couldn't get enough of them! Still working in the accounts' office, on my trip up to the tuck shop along the road to buy sweet snacks for the girls at coffee break, I'd come back with cream cheeses for myself

"Why do you keep eating all those cheeses?" The girls in the office asked me. "Oh, I just fancy them, they're lovely", I replied. "You should try them". This was until a mature clerk asked. "You're not pregnant are you"? Oh,, no I haven't decided to have a baby yet".

So much for a convent education where the only reproduction education involved rabbits and their babies. Not only that, my mother, having been raised in the valleys of Wales where such 'things' weren't talked about, neglected to talk to me about such 'things'. Nevertheless, I revelled in the thought that I was to have my own baby creating my own family life.

The news I was pregnant had the effect of a starting gun, sewing maternity clothes, baby's nighties, knitted matinee jackets, baby vests and pram suits as well as buying a book entitled, how a Baby is Born. Unimaginable now in this enlightened age.

"Where's your dustbin and has it a lid"? demanded the visiting midwife after my pregnancy had been confirmed. Those were the metal dustbin days. No plastic or recycling bags, everything, food etc, put straight into the dustbin. My positive response

June Antoinette Necchi

appeared to meet the midwife's criteria to give birth in the cottage.

June Antoinette Necchi

The fact that there was no hot water supply, and that the antiquated toilet was a trip up the back garden was apparently irrelevant, posing no problems for a home birth. Only a last-minute medical emergency prompting a premature delivery of my under 4 pounds baby boy, saved me from giving birth in uncivilised conditions, and allowed me the luxury of a clinical hospital environment.

It was at this point I realised that with the birth of my son, Russell, my life had changed forever. I had created my own family and stability and fallen in love with my adorable baby with his olive skin and dark hair.

At just 21 I was catapulted into a 'mother's' life with all its routines and was learning fast. Nappies, the sort you boil and wash after use filled the enamel bucket, and stood boiling on the gas stove every day while they bubbled away. I was busy at the sink washing my baby's hand knitted woollens, knitted during my pregnancy.

Mondays were challenging days. There was bed linen, towels, tablecloths and shirts all waiting for the weekly boil. I struggled with buckets filled with cold water taken from the kitchen to the boiler house, a little brick building attached to the garden toilet, and a big, galvanised bowl set into the wall topped with a wooden lid.

Once the weekly whitewash filled the boiler all that remained was to light the fire beneath to heat the water.

June Antoinette Necchi

Often it took many false starts before the fire lit, but it eventually brought the water to boiling point. When I decided, with continual poking and prodding of the washing, that it had boiled sufficiently, I planned the next stage of this laundry operation which was to carefully transfer it to a waiting bucket with the use of washing tongs, carry it back down the garden to the kitchen sink, where I rinsed again and again to remove soap traces.

Finally pegging it out, the resulting gleaming linen and baby whites satisfyingly danced on the garden's washing line when they were pegged out in sunshine. On rainy days the cottage took on the appearance of a Chinese laundry.

A mother's pride and joy.... the high coach-built pram! Daily, I proudly pushed my baby in his Silver Cross pram with its pretty covers to the shops, a two mile walk into town. Leaving this big pram outside shops, there were none of the modern-day fears of abduction, and one would see lines of prams in the town centre while mothers shopped inside.

And at home every self-respecting mother no matter how young, had her 'routines. Each morning, I bathed, dressed and fed my baby, tucked him up in his pram then put him into the garden while I got on with my routine, boil the nappies, hand wash baby clothes, and do the 'housework' until his feeding time.

After that, dressed in outdoor clothes I set off for the daily constitutional walk. Buying the groceries for the evening meal was another daily routine and though

June Antoinette Necchi

milk and bread were delivered to the door, all other food had

June Antoinette Necchi

to be bought from the individual shops, butcher, greengrocer and grocery provision shops. That was until the advent of supermarkets.

It was a simple ordered life with no expectations of 'luxuries' or 'me time' but it worked. A glance into the future would have held me spellbound, a future with automatic washing machines, dishwashers, in house bathrooms and en-suites, constant hot water, central heating, technology in all its forms and a car or two sitting outside for shopping trips, school runs and leisure.

Surely not!

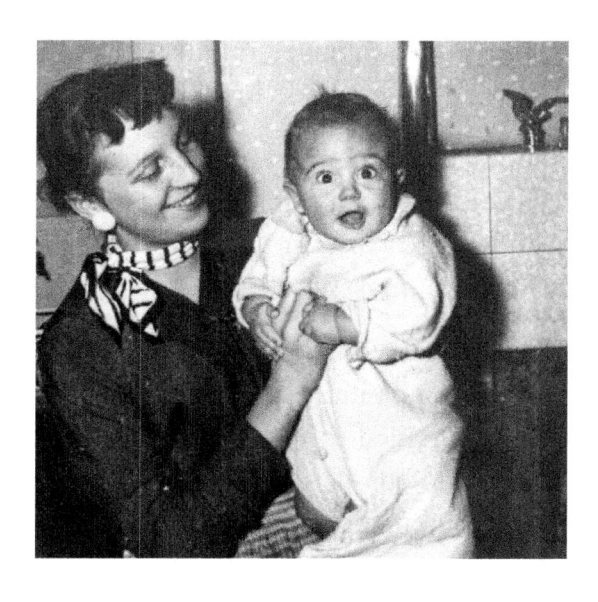

Me and my first-born Russell 1

June Antoinette Necchi

Chapter 7
DAD'S CAFE

When my baby, Russell, was a few months old my father bought a cafe, quite a big 2 room place which seated about 40 customers. I was happy to work as a waitress for a couple of hours a day. A big attraction for local office and factory workers was the huge juke box which stood in the corner. The popular music of the day, Bill Haley's Rock and Roll, Lonnie Donegal's skiffle, Elvis Presley, Pat Boone, rang out in the busy cafe creating a great ambience for customers. It was the age of the jukebox and people loved it.

At the time an Irish company in the area was putting new infrastructure in place for North Sea gas supplies and its workers, and early in the morning, sent in their orders for lunches...massive steaks, chips and eggs.

The cafe was alive with not only the music but the noisy friendly Irish banter, while my sister-in-law and I ran around with loaded trays of food and drinks trying to balance on ridiculously high heeled shoes. Each early morning Dad made an enormous amount of bread pudding, loading it into trays in the oven, such was the demand for it.

June Antoinette Necchi

We all enjoyed this new challenge, but restless after a few months I gave up my job, preferring to enjoy my baby and settle into our next home, an Edwardian semi this time with a bathroom and hot water.... albeit heated by a coal fire in the kitchen Triplex grate. Access to the shops and the local park improved our quality of life after having lived for nearly 2 years in the isolated cottage. I also had a new responsibility, that of being day Carer for my brother's baby daughter, Maria, the same age as Russell. Both babies easily fitted into my big high pram as I walked them out each day. I loved caring for them. If I could have looked into the future I would have been surprised to see a succession of family's children being part of my household....

My treadle sewing machine found a nice corner in the sitting room, and in another corner stood a 12" consol, television. Both the teatime news of the day, and the post lunch Bill and Ben programmes for little ones, could just about be seen through a hazy screen. Nevertheless, we felt that we were going up in the world!

A little dreamt about car was to become a reality a few years later.... As for modern appliances I'd graduated from the outhouse copper in which I boiled my 'whites' to a plug in electric galvanised huge bowl on the red tiled kitchen floor. Sometimes, distracted by the now crawling babies in the next room, I'd return to find bubbling soapy water across the kitchen floor from

June Antoinette Necchi

the overflowing boiler. Generally seeing the 'glass half full', I couldn't help but tell myself how lucky I was to no longer bucket water up the garden to prepare for the weekly wash.

My attempt at serious dressmaking got underway in the evenings with my determination to boost the family income. I was surprised to find ladies who were willing to pay generously to have dresses made to patterns they supplied. I had to take it more seriously for these customers than for my Teddy Boy teenagers, as they were more demanding and were paying more for my work. I was still having a struggle of these boys, bringing in their new trousers to be 'drain piped', after work on Fridays, but I was now running quite a profitable little sewing home business by evening, and mothering the babies by day.

When Russell was about two I began to think about another baby. I was used t and enjoyed motherhood, so the time seemed about right. It felt as though my life was complete with the birth of my daughter, Donna, the following year

The early morning summer sun shone through the windows as my darling child came quietly into the world. It felt like a surreal experience as she was born only minutes after I had been taken into the delivery room. I was in disbelief as I held her in my arms and studied her little face, her fingers and toes, as I stroked her head and wound her dark hair around my fingers. The name I'd already chosen, should I have a daughter, linked to my Italian blood...Donna, Italian meaning 'woman'.

June Antoinette Necchi

There began a period of contentment amid my little family, a time in my life which I really appreciated after my fractured early life.

Sitting on my dad's knee. a pencil in my hand, and him teaching me how to draw, is one of my earliest memories. Now, looking back, I can see that he was the instigator of many things in my life after that. I had always trusted him implicitly, so when he came up with the idea of me using my spare room to boost our income, I was immediately interested. "How about we deal in second hand furniture? I'll buy pieces in from Wolverhampton's auction rooms, bring them back in my van, and use your front room as a 'shop'. We can split the profits". "Deal done, Dad!"

Even better, when he suggested that I might like to go along with him, I jumped at the chance.....we were always good buddies, enjoying sharing time and ideas. Each Thursday we'd set off with my 4- and 1-year olds on board, beginning our tour of the sales rooms with mugs of tea and bacon sandwiches from the snacks room. These first two children, unlike my later two hyperactive sons, were never a problem while we checked out the motley collection of goods up for auction. It's funny about these sale rooms, you spot something unusual and think it's the one thing you've always wanted.

I had no intention of buying anything that day until the auctioneer held up a World War 1 flying helmet. I've

June Antoinette Necchi

no idea why, but this ancient, crumpled leather helmet held

instant appeal for me, and I wanted it. Was it because it represented a young pilot and his flying experiences early in the century? Was it that it should be in the hands of someone who cared about his experiences and maybe even his death? With limited finances, I joined in the bidding determined to keep going until it reached the limit I could afford. You can see that all these years on I have remembered this flying helmet, and still regret that I was outbid.

I rather enjoyed running my little business on the side as it served two purposes, one, it brought in money, and two it gave me an opportunity to meet people. My in - housework wasn't exactly getting out of hand, but I was kept busy with the children, the dressmaking and furniture sales.

The 4 happy years that we spent in that Victorian house were not without 'incidents' I feel a little embarrassed to tell you about this. I think I may have been a bit neurotic as a young mother because when my young son lay poorly with measles and was sick, I assumed he had been bleeding, yes, he had drunk a red fruit drink earlier. I was taking no chances. With no telephone, I ran up to my doctor's house, knocked on his door, disturbing his Sunday lunch, and asked him to visit urgently. What a wonderful doctor he was. A doctor of the old school.

Thoughtfully, leaving his lunch, he drove to my house to examine Russell who was lying prostrate in a

June Antoinette Necchi

darkened room. Much to my embarrassment he confirmed that it was the fruit drink that I'd given

June Antoinette Necchi

Russell. But then said, "You were right to call me out because bleeding can be a serious side effect of measles" adding, "Would you please open those curtains. It's an old wife's tale that the room should be darkened".

I awoke two nights later to acrid smoke filling the upstairs. Rushing downstairs, I found the embers in the fireplace bright red. Looking up the chimney, I panicked, seeing the chimney aglow with fire.

Running outside I was horrified to see flames pouring from the chimney. I knew it was imperative that I called the Fire Service. If only we had a telephone.... The Fire Station was across the other side of the marketplace so grabbing our dog, I left my husband in charge, while I ran across the town to the fire station, while my poor dog must have wondered, why this middle of the night run?

It took two engines only minutes to arrive at my home. I was concerned for my sleeping neighbours at the clatter of ladders going up to the roof and the sound of firemen's boots up the entry. Tarpaulin was stretched across the living room floor as hoses flooded the chimney with water. My baby woke, crying, while my 3-year-old was still running a temperature from the measles he had contracted 3 days before.

Bringing baby Donna, downstairs and into the light of the room I saw that she too was covered in red measles spots. Seven firefighters in protective clothing and

June Antoinette Necchi

huge head gear, water flooding the tarpaulin, and this sick baby in the middle of it all felt surreal.

June Antoinette Necchi

The following morning Dr McGeough had to pay yet another urgent visit. This time to me. The middle of the night dash appeared to have triggered a bout of pleurisy.

They say things come in threes.

I was enjoying life, but some months later, with sales dropping, a good friend, Maureen, came up with the suggestion that we apply for an advertised position with the Express and Star, a leading Wolverhampton evening newspaper. It was a position we could share if we were lucky enough to both have successful interviews. It entailed interviewing prospective customers on their doorsteps and was evening work which fitted in well with our families. With no experience of representative work, we were surprised to be accepted as interviewers. Wow! working for a successful newspaper!

We were thrilled to attend the meetings in Wolverhampton and be part of the newspaper.

The interviewing had to be done on Thursday and Friday evenings of each week, which we understood, naively, that we were to interview to gather householders' views on the newspaper. I say, naively, because in fact we were 'saleswomen'!

The newspaper had been delivered free of charge to a set number of houses, 5 nights a week. Mine and Maureen's job was to do a hard sell, convincing householders that they sign up for a regular delivery. I

June Antoinette Necchi

must add that neither me, or Maureen, were saleswomen material! Still, we looked forward to a brief escape from domestic duties for a few hours an evening and were too courteous to back out when we discovered the reality of the job.

"Have you enjoyed the Express and Star this week", I would begin with. The responses varied. "I never asked for the delivery! Never read newspapers, duck".

Then another, "Oh,, please come inside". That was hopeful, I'd think, and happily went into the house and accepted the invitation to sit down, but politely refused a cup of tea. This was an' interview' I grew quite used to over time as I sat and listened to the life story of a lonely widow, sympathising with her, understanding that this was another lonely person willing to invite another person into her life, however briefly. Eventually, I would mumble, "Would you like to order the newspaper, do you think?" "Oh, no dear. I never read newspapers". An hour later leaving the house, I'd catch up with Maureen who because she was equally empathetic, was experiencing the same problems.

"How many orders, have you?" we'd ask each other. "Let's put it this way, we'll never make a fortune, will we?"

One night, I experienced what felt like a piece of theatre. The man of the house answered the door. My immediate impression was that he was going to give me a resounding, "No".

June Antoinette Necchi

"Good evening, Sir", I said, smiling. "Oh, hello", he said. "I wonder if you have enjoyed reading our newspaper this week" "Yes, it wasn't bad. The sports reports were ok". "I'm glad about that. Do you think you would like to place a regular order with your local newsagent? "I was surprised when he agreed instantly, but at that point he was interrupted by the appearance of his wife at the door. "We agreed that we weren't having that paper!" She was loud and angry. "Well, I've changed my mind!" he told her. "Just because a young woman has come to the door. That's the reason!"

Not wanting to be caught up in a domestic dispute I left them arguing at the door, making up my mind that a saleswoman job was not meant for me

It was during this time that needing an extra bedroom, we moved house. This was my third home since marriage, moving on as my family grew, and convenient for my interviewing work as the rail station was only a few hundred yards away. It was a dormer bungalow situated in Mill Street close to the town centre, and had coal fired central heating, a south facing garden and was adjacent to fields.

After 3 years of canvassing, I decided to resign from the newspaper, staying just long enough to earn enough to buy my children's winter shoes.

You know those times when you look back and think, yes, life was pretty perfect then? Well, those years, after our move to Mill Street were certainly like that, seeming to be idyllic. It was only a few years since I had lived in the primitive cottage, and here we had central heating and constant hot water. The price may

June Antoinette Necchi

have been that it was labour intensive, the solid fuel boiler requiring a regular top of coal to keep the whole system going, as well as the ash to clear out, but what a small price to pay for these up to date living conditions.

I showed my new freestanding washing machine, an Electrolux, to my friends who were quite impressed. Why wouldn't they be? It may have held only a small workload but for the first time I had a machine which washed the clothes for me! No more lifting clothes out with washing tongs to transfer to the sink, but a wringer, with hand operated rollers. It may have been a struggle putting sheets through there but only required concentration and determination, and of course a whole morning!

(Then, it would have been unbelievable that, one day, I would feed my washing into a machine and switch it on, knowing that while socialising with friends over a coffee, my new kitchen 'friend' would be doing the washing for me. Or, that electric dryers would end the days of running in and out of the house to the washing line in between showers. While the 'white goods' kitchen was still an undreamt-of future, with even a domestic fridge still not on the horizon).

Russell was about 8 when I asked him to tell his teacher that he no longer wanted his morning milk allowance at school. He was too young for me to explain that the daily news had prompted this change. When my milk man called for my weekly milk bill, I asked him to stop all my deliveries, embarrassed,

June Antoinette Necchi

because I felt an explanation was due, I said, "I'm sorry to have to cancel

June Antoinette Necchi

my daily deliveries but there has been a nuclear leak in the north". This poor man looked at me as though I was 'losing' it. I continued, "You see it has contaminated the waters and land around that area and I know that your milk originates from that part of the country". He looked blankly at me as I over egged the situation by saying, "You see, I don't want my young children being subjected to that radioactive Strontium 90. Do you know that it has a half-life of 90 years!" I added, "Will you please give my apologies to your boss as this is not a reflection on the quality of his milk (oh,, dear, me over egging again). I imagined him, back at base telling his boss, "You won't believe what I'm going to tell you" …..

Despite my neurosis about my children's health, they were well balanced by the fun we all had, my house being the house where local kids came to play. The boys sliding down the bannisters, the girls playing 'houses', the dog and his puppies charging around under everybody's feet. Theme parks hadn't yet been invented but we had 'Cannock Park' and the Chase for picnics, and for the kids to run about. Simple days which have given us treasured memories……

Chapter 8

THE HOLLIES

Some years before my marriage ended I was always on the lookout to make money as a young mother at home. I have from time to time thought it made good sense to list one's abilities and assets, and one obvious asset was that we had a house which was attractive and welcoming. We also had a spare room, if pushed, and I could cook a good meal and cope with most unexpected situations.

Unaware of the commercial possibilities of these assets, the day came when, immersed in domesticity, they gave me the chance to make money without setting foot outside of my door. No investment of cash was needed, no overheads, no boss and no forms to be filled in. All of this in exchange for a regular sum of money which amounted to nearly half of my husband's earnings.. It sounds like everyone's idea of freedom.

This time it was my mother who had a hand in it. She was a cook at a nearby hotel. It was a popular hotel, the Hollies, its main disadvantage being that it had only 7 bedrooms. Apparently, while the owner was away on holiday the relief manager double booked a bedroom. Now the thought of two lots of guests fighting over one bedroom threw him into a panic. Not only that but what about the prospect of being reported to the owner by the guest without a bed.

He gathered the staff together and pleaded that one of them give one night's shelter to the stranded visitor. People living in the provinces tend to be much more cautious and private than city folk, so their excuses came thick and fast......until it came to my mother. She's always been good at volunteering me in my absence so when it came to her turn she responded with, "Oh, my daughter who lives nearby would be only too happy to help out".

"June", my mother said when she appeared at my house, at her lunch break. "Can you sort a bedroom out for tonight for one guest. He'll be here at about 9 I knew you would help as the manager had double booked the room, all you need to do is give him a breakfast cuppa, clean towels and a nice room for the night".

"But Mum, what room have I got?". "Just put the kids in one room for the night. June don't make things difficult. You want to earn more money don't you?" "Well, that's true". I could feel that I was losing this argument as my mind made a quick flip mentally listing what needed to be done to switch the kids, toys, clothes, not to mention a hasty touching up of the room's chipped skirting board. Happy or not, by teatime, exhausted after the spring cleaning and

June Antoinette Necchi

reorganising the house, I had prepared the bedroom for my first guest.

June Antoinette Necchi

As though it was a holiday or National emergency my children were falling about with excitement. With the afternoon's swift house-about they had been restored to sharing a bedroom once more. My family had been weaned on my flurries of activity whenever I 'changed gear' into yet another money-making scheme and they certainly seemed to thrive on it.... I'd go so far as to say it made them feel secure.

My first duties as a landlady began with the arrival of my guest in the evening.... not at 9 o'clock as advised by my mother but at 6 o'clock. I was pleased that my day's frantic activity had resulted in the 'guest' room being ready to receive the visitor. A small bowl of freshly cut flowers stood on a bedside table and a pretty lamp gave the room a soft glow.

We exchanged self-conscious introductions while I desperately hoped that I resembled a businesswoman who knew what she was about. To look efficient, I asked, "What arrangements would you like to make for the morning?" (that seemed to go down well, anyway). "Can I have a 7 am call, please?" His next question took me by surprise, "Where is the lounge, please. I've had a long day, eaten early at the hotel, and just need to relax for the evening".

The lounge? Did he mean the only 'lounge' we had, the family room, the room where the kids watched TV, the room where I sat at my sewing machine in the evenings? Not to mention the intermittent invasion of

June Antoinette Necchi

some of the puppies born under the stairs to our Border Collie.

June Antoinette Necchi

"I must apologise. We don't have a separate lounge, and this one can get quite busy". "That's fine, Madam", my guest told me, so the die was cast. I was in the hosting business.

Imagine how surprised I was when the Hotel owner phoned me to say that my first guest had requested to stay at my house each time he came to the area.

What a marvellous way to earn money, and even better when the hotel owner returned from holiday he asked if I would become the 'annexe' for his hotel a few hundred yards away. Just one thing remained that I plan each evening like a general planning a campaign. Children's story time over they'd be tucked into bed. An action packed half hour would follow; dishes would be washed, vacuuming done, and the general devastation left by the children cleared in record time. It's funny because I've always been good at theory but there's usually a gap between that and the practice of it. And I'd done it again!

Still, perseverance prevailed and the financial reward from a succession of professional guests proved to be a reliable source of income and allowed me to be a home-based mother....my prime object.

It was some months later that a young man, Cavan, who had just qualified as an art teacher had come from Bernard Castle to take a post at the local College and had been sent to me as a guest. After a couple of weeks, he asked if he could stay on a semi-permanent basis. He was quiet and respectful and stayed for some time until he met his future wife.

The local grapevine (people actually talked to each other then) proved useful when 2 graduates from a local company phoned to ask me for accommodation, telling me that they were prepared to share a bedroom. My little hand wringer electric washing machine worked hard to keep up with 5 bed changes each week, the graduates' shirts, and undies, as well as my family wash! Clothesline drying was sometimes a problem, but I wasn't to be deterred. By now my earnings matched my husband's allowing us to buy our first car, a Morris Minor estate. Now we would be able to take camping holidays both here and abroad, for the first time!

It was then that an advert caught my eye.

'Optician's receptionist wanted, 2 or 3 hours weekly'.

As it was only minutes from my house I immediately applied thinking that I would enjoy an outside interest.

I thought it better to state at the outset when I was interviewed, as the hours were few, would I be able to take my daughter with me. "She's a quiet little 4-year-old who will be able to amuse herself while I work at the desk". As a father of two the optician was understanding and agreed.... if I would be offered the job.

June Antoinette Necchi

"There is just one other thing I need to tell you", I told him, "I intend to have another baby in maybe 3 years' time". I was surprised and pleased to be offered the job and a year later when Donna started school, I began working school hours.

We had a good working relationship, and I enjoyed the challenge of the complex NHS paperwork and the exchanges with the patients. My boss seemed surprised when I reminded him two years later that he would need to employ and train a new assistant as I was planning my third child. "Oh, you're not still talking about babies, are you, June"?

I did tell you that when I started, didn't I?"

I left one month before my son was born but agreed to do the paperwork for the next year from home.....flexible working which saw me pushing my baby's pram 3 times a week to collect or deliver the paperwork.

With a reduced work load I was now able to enjoy my lively little toddler, Matthew, a handsome child with a shock of black hair and blue eyes. As my other children were in school Matthew was like an only child enjoying my full attention. And when they were home he was the centre of their attention. They were happy days with no thought of what was to come.

'Go ahead people go gas'.

Saturday evenings were family evenings. Board games, usually Cluedo or Monopoly or a game of cards, filled the evening. One Saturday was a little different. I had read in our evening newspaper that the Gas Board were promoting gas as the energy of the future replacing electricity and coal and were publicising a competition with a first prize of an installation of automatic gas central heating. The question asked was "choose 8 of the following 12 reasons why you would like gas central heating installed "A slogan then had to be added. This was fun as I decided on a slogan with alliteration giving my kids the opportunity to come up with as many G words as they could. We spent hours but I finally came up with the simple slogan '*GO AHEAD PEOPLE GO GAS*'. (in that era 'go ahead' was a popular expression').

Ok, it had given us a fun evening, I posted it off and forgot about it.

That year, now with 3 children, and just one paying guest, we decided that it was time to move house, and with the local council putting land up for sale for private house building I applied for a plot with a southwest aspect on the edge of the green belt. It was only a fifteen minutes' walk from town, and the children's school. A deposit of £1000 pounds was payable within a month and with our attractive chalet bungalow on the market I was confident that we could meet the deadline. What I hadn't taken into consideration was that interest rates were high, and the housing market sluggish.

With no viewings, when the deadline came to an end I took the risk to ask the bank for a bridging loan to secure the plot of land. With the added anxiety about meeting the interest payments on the loan, and with no

June Antoinette Necchi

viewings, a letter came through the door marked Gas Board. I opened it, reluctantly, expecting a high winter gas bill but couldn't believe my eyes. The Saturday evening spent filling in the competition for a full house of central heating had won the first prize! The installation could be made when the house building stage was ready for it.

Sometimes dreams do come true. 2 days later a lady knocked on my front door asking to view the house and telling me that she and her husband had always admired it as they walked by each day, and they were prepared to make a cash purchase. There is a God in Heaven I told myself!

Soon after that we were invited to a Birmingham theatre where Jim Davidson handed over the paperwork for that first prize.

June Antoinette Necchi

Chapter 9

MARRIAGE HAD RUN ITS COURSE

With the completion of our house sale, we moved in with my parents while we awaited the building of the new house. Surprisingly, it was quite an easy transition with my parents loving having family around them again, and me happy to spend time with them. Not having the responsibilities of my own home was a very enjoyable period giving me time to reflect on both the past and future years. I'd been very home based but now had time to consider outside activities.

I had probably always 'known' that my marriage would eventually end. Engrossed in family routines, too busy for a social life, and enjoying my creative interests had not enabled me to question mine, and my husband's incompatibilities. After all, creating a family life had been my focus and I had hoped that I would be able to bring my children up in relative security, despite a nagging question, 'what happens when the children leave home'?

I was excited to begin two evening courses, English Language and Art at the local college, along with other young mothers all keen to begin professional careers. It was pretty heady stuff after my domestic routines. I felt it was a new start in life not knowing where it would take me....

I made a mistake the first evening and found myself in an English Literature class, for which I had not registered. I was embarrassed but did find it absorbing, encouraged by friends who told me, "You can choose 3 subjects for the price of two. Come and join us". I decided then to go along weekly to the literature group, too.

As with most groups, we bonded quickly and were enthusiastic about our studies and began to socialise regularly when our lecturers were often present.

This socialising developed into easy occasions when our families were involved, too. We all had things in common. Inevitably, this led to conversations and a growing intimacy with likeminded individual something I had not experienced in my marriage. My relationship with one of the lecturers became quite close, sharing many conversations. I was naive not to imagine that it might damage my marriage, despite highlighting the personal differences between me and my husband. Our incompatibilities had been brought to the surface by my growing independence, and an understanding of my hitherto compliance.

'There was no turning back'.

June Antoinette Necchi

After about two years or so I was upset and shocked to find that I would no longer be able to stay with my husband. Yes, we had children but very little else in common and I was faced with an impossible decision.

The breakup was very painful for us all, disrupting the family in a way I had never imagined, made so much more traumatic by my husband's reactions. I moved into my parent's home with my two youngest children. My eldest son was 17 and in a settled relationship. I rented a flat and began a relationship with the college lecturer. Neither of us found this new start easy because of our concerns about our family. About 2 years later, we had a child, a son, Dan, sealing our relationship.

After the security of an 18-year marriage I had taken a step into the unknown. Yes, I realised that I would be financially independent since I had decided to give up any claim on the marriage home.

(At a much later date, a Court hearing, brought by my husband, awarded me 50% of all possessions which I turned down. As it had been my decision to end my marriage I felt that I should not undermine his financial security. Eventually I accepted a nominal payment of £3000).

I began a job requiring me to work through the night as a telephonist for deputising doctors, who covered a large area responding to emergency medical calls.

June Antoinette Necchi

However inconvenient for family life, it boosted my income along with another menial job on a farm. I was fazed by none of this as for the first time in my life I had complete freedom of choice to organise my life in the way I wanted to.......but always the wellbeing of my children was foremost in my mind. My boss sent me to a town 10 miles away to work, a shift starting at one in the morning and finishing at 7am but quite soon this proved to be incompatible with family life.

The 'office' was on the first floor of a dilapidated shop located in a dark street with a reputation for prostitution and drug dealing. Parking on a large, nearby, unlit piece of rough ground, I ran to the shop and waited anxiously for the telephonist upstairs to let me in. The 'office' itself was a dark, dusty room with other rooms leading off, and all very run down. As I arrived, the previous telephonist went off duty and I worked alone throughout the night. I felt very uneasy with the whole experience and felt at risk, so after a few weekends I resigned.

Chapter 10
EGG FARM

Clearing the ashes from the previous night and lighting a fire for an elderly disabled lady who lived in a tiny bungalow on the edge of town, was an early start 7 days a week for me. After a couple of hours of preparing her meal so for the day and lighting her fire I was free to organise the rest of my day.

When I first started the job I was pregnant with my fourth child, Dan, and though I found the work quite easy, the old car I was using presented problems each morning......it wouldn't start unless I used the starting handle several times. This became more difficult as the months passed, but on arriving at the old lady's I was able to make a cup of tea for us both, and rest while we chatted.

My baby was born 2 weeks early and home 24 hours later. He was lovely child and clearly a sensitive one as he slept very little, only happy to share my bed.

It gave me time to reflect on my previous part time job, egg collecting, a job I couldn't leave soon enough once I realised what it involved....

June Antoinette Necchi

It was a job which immediately appealed to me for a few reasons. One, that it was on a farm in the middle of the countryside. Two that it was a morning only job, and three, that it would satisfy the romantic in me. Or so I thought.

My vivid imagination had seen me wearing a large pinafore, and a wide straw hat with a basket over my arm, as I strolled amongst the many chickens collecting their recently laid eggs......In retrospect I realise that I had created my own interpretation of egg collecting taken from the paintings in my old Victorian books.

Where were the wandering chickens in a farm to begin with? There was no farmyard or indeed, farm buildings. What greeted me was what looked like large warehouses sitting in the middle of fields. My first impressions of walking into one of these was of a very unpleasant smell, and of the ear-piercing sounds of trapped birds fighting to escape from their cages. I could see that there were six birds in a cage, I was horrified at what I saw. Birds, their heads poking out and their necks being hurt in their constant attempts to escape. I'd signed up for the job and had to do it until I found alternative employment.

Christmas was around the corner and the turkeys had been fattened up ready for the Festive table. I was upset at having been given the job of chasing the turkeys around, grabbing them and delivering them into a fenced off area. The inside story of these bird factories and the loss of quality of life for these birds

June Antoinette Necchi

instigated my leaving and left me with a conscience
that I was unable

June Antoinette Necchi

to do anything about the pathetic lives of these battery hens.

June Antoinette Necchi

Chapter 11
CHASING THE DREAM

Eager to be more independent and leave the home I had rented from my parents following my divorce, I was aware that my small financial settlement would be too small a settlement to buy a property other than one in a near-derelict condition. I drove around a three-mile radius after dropping my 10-year-old son at school each morning, with his young brother, Dan, eighteen months old, sitting impatiently in the back seat of my old banger while I searched for a wreck of a property which I could afford.

To my delight an old cottage, the end one of three, and backing onto a magnificent area of outstanding natural beauty, stood, apparently unloved and uncared for over many years. There appeared to be no one living there so I dared to take a peek inside.

Clearly it was uninhabited and had been for a long time. I was intrigued. The large garden was completely overgrown. An antique hand wringer stood on the backyard, and peeping through the window I could see low beamed ceilings and an old brown sink in the primitive kitchen. An arched roof over the heavy old front door was shrouded in ivy, while the long south facing garden was a sea of poppies amongst the long grasses.

This was my dream home……'I'll leave a note in the door' I said to myself suggesting that I am interested in buying it. But then, maybe no one would find it Nevertheless, I dropped a message through the letter box and was surprised to hear later from a local estate agent that, in fact, the cottage was in the process of being sold. The selling price was £5000! I'd just missed the boat and was devastated at my timing.

It must have been a week or so later while pushing my toddler into town I had a sudden urge to hurry into the estate agent who was selling the cottage. What drove me to do this? I have no idea, but I kept walking faster and faster until I almost ran, rushed into the office, breathless. I felt foolish when the receptionist asked, "Can I help you?".

Why was I there? I wasn't sure. "Um, the cottage in Stafford Rd, I suppose the sale has gone through?"

"Well, actually, we have just had a call to say that the buyer is no longer interested". I couldn't believe it and thought I must be dreaming the whole scenario. I had to act quickly if I was to secure the cottage……

Now in those days, it was 1976, a down payment as a deposit showed an act of good faith that the prospective buyer seriously intended to go ahead with

June Antoinette Necchi

the purchase, and though I knew that my bank account was empty I had to be quick.....and I had got my cheque book in my bag.

"Will a cheque for one hundred pounds secure the cottage for me?" "Certainly", she responded as I reached for my cheque book.

Time was of the essence now if I had to prevent my cheque bouncing, so hot footed it with my toddler down to my mother's.

"Can I borrow a hundred pounds. Give you it back later. I'm buying a lovely little cottage. Perfect for me and my sons. You'll love the garden".

Now you might wonder how I could buy even a £5000 property with no money especially as it had to be a cash sale due to its condition, but having secured the cottage nothing was going to stand in my way now.

Sitting in his office the solicitor listened patiently to my story, and to the fact that I was awaiting a divorce settlement from my marital home, though I was unsure exactly when I would receive it. "I know what I'll do. I will go with you to the bank, explain your circumstances and request a loan to purchase the house with an extra £2000 for improvements".

What a nice solicitor! He took me along to my bank manager advising him to give me a loan of £7000 which was agreed in minutes! I walked out in disbelief. I was to be the owner of my dream cottage, though minutes before I had no money and an overdraft!

June Antoinette Necchi

It was with great excitement that we moved in, and my father immediately began installing a second-hand kitchen, nothing flashy but with character.

The daub and wattle ceilings with their timber beams gave the kitchen the homeliest feel, especially when I hung my baby's nappies from them on wet days. The view from the south facing kitchen window of the working coal mine was to the right, and the magnificent landscape to the left, prompting me to name the view the 'beauty and the beast' giving me a strong sense of the past when the village was inhabited by coal miners. I would imagine them, the noise from their heavy boots resounding along the road. Imagine too that there would have been boys as young as nine working down the mine in the 1700's when the cottage was built, and quite possibly a mother looking through the same kitchen window waving to her husband and son as they walked to work.

'Steep stone steps wound round upstairs to 3 bedrooms which led off a narrow landing running across the back of the cottage, with windows at floor level and with a panoramic view across pine tree forests. There was no bathroom, but the additional loan enabled me to have a tiled walk-in shower room built from space stolen from the adjoining bedroom. Having improved the kitchen, and installed a hot water and heating system, my father thought it might be a good idea to remove the green tiled Triplex grate from the sitting room. He asked, "June, would you like me to take out the Triplex grate?

June Antoinette Necchi

After all," he commented, "It was a relatively recent addition, probably in the 1930's, so behind it must stand the fireplace allowing us to take it back to its original state".

I was as enthusiastic as my father, "Please, I can't wait to see behind there". The huge inglenook with a massive oak beam straddling the wall was a revelation, and though the beam was wood wormed there was no sign of recent activity. We stood back and stared, unable to believe what we had discovered. "So, this is how they cooked and kept warm 230 years ago," said my father.

After cleaning up the old brickwork he placed a coal basket in position and built bookshelves into one side of the inglenook. What a dramatic centrepiece it was!

That winter we experienced heavy snowfalls with blizzards and bitterly cold weather. The road outside, impassable, due to drifting. I joined the kids playing across the road and rolling in the snow storing up memories for their futures.

When spring arrived, we crossed the road and climbed the manmade 'mountain', a slag heap from the nearby coal mine, now overgrown with grass, shrubs, and picnicked at the top. Each season in the cottage was giving us a wealth of simple experiences.

My old banger which kept breaking down resulting in my 10-year-old son pushing it down the hill to get started most mornings was not the reason that I put the cottage on the market a year later, but the village

June Antoinette Necchi

rumour divulged to me that the cottage was haunted. That was a

June Antoinette Necchi

challenge too far bringing back memories of my childhood fear of ghosts.

My sketch of my dream cottage 1

June Antoinette Necchi

Chapter 12

ARIES

The New Year's camaraderie of the merry groups celebrating in the lively pub only served to pick out the isolated figures with their expressionless faces. It shocked me that on this night of all nights there would be some alone, and uninvited. Always an idealist with a keen desire to put the world to rights, I made up my mind that night to work on a solution to the problem of loneliness! (This of course was before the advent of internet dating which was to replace the personal columns in newspapers which were the original 'meeting places' for those looking for friendship or love).

Early January always acts like a starter gun hurtling me into intense activity prompted by a rush of ideas and this year was to be no different...... and so the Aries Friendship Agency was born.

It gradually dawned on me that in my first flush of compassion for individuals I had neglected to consider the details involved in such a venture expecting as always that the details would take care of themselves. Never much interested in the minutiae of planning, I experienced a sense of frustration chasing up character references for myself before the local newspapers would accept my adverts in their Personal column.

I set about preparing the advert, deciding that short and simple to alleviate the thrice weekly advertising costs was the best advert to arrive at.

Ages 18 to 80! That would attract a wide range of people to start with. Loneliness is no respecter of age, so I thought it important to open it up for everyone regardless of age.In order to attract genuine people, it seemed necessary to include the word 'sincere' as well as 'genuine friendship'

After hours of lost sleep my mind awash with subtle variations and nuances of descriptions I was surprised that the advert I came up with was so mundane.

'WOULD YOU LIKE TO MEET SINCERE PEOPLE FOR GENUINE FRIENDSHIPS?'

It was at this point I realised that I should not use my private address, so my brother intervened offering the use of an 'office 'address at a flat above his business premises. Two more problems remained, one, the design and printing of an application form, and two a meeting with my bank manager to create a 'business' account, an account which necessitated the invention of a pseudonym for myself. A pseudonym, as I wished to protect my privacy by not using my own name, but nevertheless a name as a 'personal' contact for the members.

That proved quite easy as certain Christian names conjured up a sense of solidarity, of reliability I thought. So, *ELIZABETH* it was. A bit more thought was needed for the surname but a call from a friend who knew my search was on, came from the local council office she was working in, "June, I have an idea for the name. There's an Irish Roads and Highways firm working outside. Their name is *SHAND*".

And so 'Elizabeth Shand' was 'born'. My interest in astrology persuaded me to name the group *'THE ARIES FRIENDSHIP AGENCY'*. Next task was to create an application form which I did by sending to a personal column dating company for one of their forms. This way I could be sure that I would be able to give it a professional touch by including the details a reputable company had been using. There was one difference with mine. It had an astrological slant which I was keen to point out to potential members. Now with everything in place I was ready to launch my dream to connect isolated individuals.....

In retrospect I realise that I might have found that I had bitten off more than I could chew but my Aries astrological sign rarely accepts defeat once a dream is in place. The first requests for membership came within a few days of the first advert. They came from a mix of ages, and situations, as well as a couple of men insisting on certain criteria...... no red heads, no glasses, no overweight ladies!

June Antoinette Necchi

I soon realised that I quickly needed to build a healthy membership to match friends. A wide readership area was covered by the newspaper in which I'd placed the adverts and so the membership grew quite quickly confirming my original views that loneliness was a problem for many.

There were some unusual requests, one from a man who in his words, "wanted to meet a lady to live with as I work night shifts, and it would be nice to come home to someone who would cook my breakfast".

Another was from a lady who worked as a hospital Sister, a mother of 3 teenage sons. She complained that previous relationships with men had ended because all they wanted to do was take her out for dinner whereas she had hoped that they would share her sons' great interest in bikes and motorbikes. To me this seemed a bit of a tall order in a budding relationship, and though loathe to make personal contact with members I decided to write to her suggesting that if a relationship developed then there was the possibility that he would become involved with her sons and their hobby. I thought it was certainly a bit premature to expect such involvement at an early stage.

To meet her requirements, I found that there was only one member who was a possible match, but I was uncertain of his nationality, therefore thought it was necessary to contact him. I was reassured by the information. He was Polish, and a lecturer in

June Antoinette Necchi

mechanics at a local college. I tried not to get excited by what I thought was his suitability.... her sons' interest in all things mechanical could be a winner.

I was disappointed to hear nothing more from either of these members.... that was until about 6 months later I received through the post a sweetly scented thank you card.

"Dear Elizabeth, thank you so much for bringing us together. We are to be married next month"

This one card had made it all worthwhile.

A disappointing outcome was that of a communication between a late middle-aged woman and a man of the same age. He lived about 15 miles from her. She lived in a hamlet where time seems to have stood still. She wrote telling me that she had never left her parents' home, looking after them until they passed away. She was lonely and felt that she would like to meet a man for companionship. This would be her first venture into a relationship as she had never had a boyfriend.

The man whose name I offered her was also single and looking for companionship. One problem leapt from his application form.... he didn't drive, had only a bike, and there was no public transport to the cottage where the lady lived. He was not fazed about cycling to see her and wrote telling her when he would arrive. Given my original idea for the Friendship Agency, to bring lonely people together, I was quite hopeful that their loneliness may be eased by meeting each other.

June Antoinette Necchi

Only a few days later I received a letter from the lady telling me that as she heard the latch on the front garden gate she peered from behind the curtains and took fright seeing a man pushing his cycle up the garden path. Too scared to answer the door, she bent down hiding under the window. A lifetime of never leaving her rural home and of being a dutiful daughter, caring for her parents, had not prepared her for modern society or for relationships with the opposite sex. A very Victorian story, and sad, too.

Only four local people became members of the Aries Friendship Agency. One, a retired man who I knew by sight, had been recently widowed and asked if I could find a female friend for him. Fortunately, a lady of similar age lived only about 2 miles away, so I was happy to exchange their details.

I admit I was a little perturbed to receive a note from the lady saying that the gentleman had met her off the bus and taken her to his home nearby. She was taken aback when, after having a cup of tea with him, he invited her to go upstairs.... and she did. There in his bedroom he opened a wardrobe door revealing a rail of ladies' clothes. "If you become my lady friend you can have all of my late wife's things". Now, I happened to know that his wife was a well-built lady. His new friend told me that she herself scarcely weighed 8 stone! She didn't make a return trip to his home but obviously wanted to give the relationship a try under different circumstances, so invited him to her home.

June Antoinette Necchi

Since they had decided that I was their mediator he contacted me with his complaint. "I caught a bus to her house, but she had warned me that I must go after dark in case her neighbours saw me, and not to go to the front door. I nearly fell over trying to find my way up the dark entry to the back door". A further complaint from her was that he showed more attention to his dog than her. I was probably as disappointed as this lonely couple was.

Unfortunately, I was unable to find a suitable friend either for him, or for her. Nevertheless, I still wonder if they continue to contact each other from time to time to ease their loneliness…

At this time in my life, I used to do a morning walk into town taking my toddler, Dan, in his pushchair, always hopeful that he would fall asleep, though sleep wasn't a word he was familiar with. I was on a mission to have a coffee at the local coffee shop while my little one entertained the customers. A particular fan of his was the manager, a friendly Northern lady who I shared daily chats with, and who had confided in me that her husband of 35 years had left her. She was very independent, and I had no doubt that she would easily cope with being single and financially independent.

Opening my agency's mail one morning I found an application from her to become a member. Clearly, this was a bit close to home but due to my privacy arrangements, I could accept her request and she would

June Antoinette Necchi

never know that Elizabeth Shand was in fact baby Dan's mother, the regular morning coffee customer.

June Antoinette Necchi

I read with interest the details on her application form. Born under the sign of Virgo the earth sign. Loves opera. (well, that was unusual). The first person who had joined the agency was a man who lived a few miles from my base. I had not been able to match him up with a friend because of his domestic situation. He was divorced and was raising single handed teenage children. He had no job, no car, and lived in rented property.... but his great interest was opera! Not only that his birth sign was Capricorn, another earth sign! Despite their social differences there was at least a shared interest, so I took a chance and exchanged their names..... but heard nothing.

That was until I went into the cafe one morning and asked after her. Oh, she's gone out of town to buy her wedding outfit," the waitress told me.

"I didn't realise that she was getting married," I said. "Yes, she's met a man from the personal column in the newspaper". I guessed that she had joined another agency but was happy that she had found happiness.

In the cafe the next day, she told me excitedly, "I met him through Elizabeth Shand, and can you believe it, we both love opera! We are having a wonderful time together". "I'm so happy for you both", I told her.

A year later while out in town I bumped into her and her husband. "We have just had our first Anniversary," she told me, "And we and our family are having a lovely life". Should I have told her the part I played in their lives? I didn't think so.

June Antoinette Necchi

By now I had run down my agency preparing the ground for the online dating companies. My original dream of bringing together lonely individuals seemed to have been at least partially successful having brought happiness to the four individual so who may never have met had it not been for Elizabeth Shand.

June Antoinette Necchi

Chapter 13
FINNINGS (Bowmaker)

I hoisted my 3-year-old onto the back of my bike. "Where are we going, Mummy?" "To nursery darling, to play with other little boys and girls". "Don't want to!" "There are some lovely toys to play with". "Don't want to go. Can I come with you?" It's only for grown-ups. I won't be long"

And so began the first day of handing my last child over into the safe keeping of someone else. While I was beginning my first day's work in the accounts' department of Bowmaker's Dan would be in the care of St Mary's nursery.

With the closing down of my Friendship Agency I had approached an employment company and being asked what work experience I'd had in the past I had to think carefully as to what work would be regarded as my suitability to the jobs the agency had on offer. My four years in an accounts office, as a teenager, was picked up by my interviewer who didn't question my ability to move on from handwritten accounting to more modern methods. This worried me a little. I was still focussing on the fact that I could choose my hours of work,

June Antoinette Necchi

starting and finishing to fit in with my children. Yes, the wages were pathetic, but at least I could retain control over my time. I was offered the job and accepted.

I hadn't thought to consult my three-year-old who clearly wasn't in agreement and was now rebelling. That was a difficult parting for him, and for me, and I was already regretting my acceptance of the job. But I had made the commitment to the job agency so I must give it a try. My previous accounts office, as a teenager, consisted of a huge old table with seating for six, and customers' records 'filed' into shoe box type cardboard boxes with fountain pens for recording payments. Contacting the customers relied on writing letters to them. I was anxious that I would not be able to adapt to modern technology.

Concerned with sorting out the practical arrangements that needed to be in place to go out to work, I hadn't considered how different working conditions would be in a modern business centre compared to the decrepit Victorian house I had first worked in as accounts clerk. I was in awe as I took my place at a desk in the huge open plan space. I was equally in awe at the powder room, a base, apparently for touching up hair and makeup before starting work. I couldn't help but compare it with the old brick walls and lack of hot water in my first office kitchen. Yes, I had found myself in a different age.

At that time Bowmaker, a major UK /American company employed 27 agency workers who could be directed to work in any number of departments.

June Antoinette Necchi

I nearly landed a permanent post there when the Company Secretary, after 3 weeks, offered me a full-time position, but I turned it down for two reasons. Having children, I didn't want to work full time, but nor did I want to be tied into a proper career for years. That had no appeal for me despite the financial security. That's the trouble with those of us who have creative leanings. ...and are born under the sign of Aries...we like new challenges.

It was there that I met Anne, who was to become a lifelong friend, and who I was to hijack into running a home business with me after a recession put us Agency staff out of work. For me, the timing was right, as after 3 years there I was increasingly frustrated by the

repetition of the work. And it was time to move on

my early mode of transport

June Antoinette Necchi

Chapter 14

LAURA ASHLEY

With no warning of my job loss, I knew I had no time to lose in finding another way of earning an income. I came up with an idea to start a small home-grown business, that of putting on parties in people's homes. As Laura Ashley designs were very popular it seemed a good idea to make household items with their fabrics. Surely a good seller!

I let the idea brew over the weekend before calling my friend and colleague, Anne, on Monday morning. I had to be careful how I approached her, because while we were close friends there was a distinct difference in as much as I leapt, often too quickly, onto my latest ideas, whereas Anne would be far more moderate in her responses. Our differing characteristics had always served us well when working on joint projects in the accounts' department. In other words, I could rely on Anne to pick out any weaknesses in my ideas, while I could be the pacemaker.

On Monday morning I phoned, saying "Anne, can you sew?" "Yes, June, I can. Why?" "Have you a sewing machine?" "I have. Why?" "That's it then. We're in business. Home parties. Laura Ashley fabrics. How about we take the train to Birmingham tomorrow to choose some. fabrics Today I'll get cracking on a few designs for home items, cushion covers, serviettes, tray cloths, even baby stuff like cot bedding. What do you think?"

I think this was a bit hasty for Anne but then she knew me well and often found it fun to jump on my bandwagon. Aware that we had dramatically lost our incomes, our first 'business' decision was to not incur unnecessary expenses. "Anne, I'll make sandwiches for lunch. We'll push the boat out and buy a coffee in Birmingham. That's all".

We stood on the platform of the local station feeling like schoolgirls playing truant, already enjoying the freedom from the working environment in which we'd been 'trapped' for 3 years. It was beginning to feel like quite heady stuff.

We'd made the decision to buy 5 metres each of different fabrics. Already it was becoming clear what our roles would be in our new business, Anne with her attention to detail was the ideal candidate to keep a watchful eye on the income and outgoings, and that same attention to detail was essential for the finishing of certain items we were planning to make. I fell naturally into the role of ideas person, of pattern making and hand sewing. Since Anne lived a couple of miles from me, and I had no car, I would have to use the only form of transport I had, my bicycle. A rucksack solved the problem of transporting material, and a raincoat to combat the weather, when necessary.

We were both excited when I revealed the prototype patterns for our first items and soon we were cutting out pieces ready for sewing. I had thrown in a 'wild card', that of a pyjama holder in the shape of a large stuffed doll with a back opening for the night wear. I had paid no heed to the time required for the hand sewing involved in this and was yet to learn the lesson of time management in business.

We spent all week building up the stock ready for our first Laura Ashley Home Parties, Unfortunately, by midweek we had run out of filling for the cushions but were saved by the offer from Anne's mother of several old feather eiderdowns. Arriving on my bicycle at Anne's house in heavy rain I set about cutting up the eiderdowns which were stored in the garage. I hadn't planned for the cascading feathers as I released them, or for how I would be able to 'harvest' them to stuff into the cushions but having set them free I had no option but to gather those I could and fill the cushions. Anne's garage, set back from her house, was overlooked by the window of a neighbour, whose expression as I came out my arms loaded with cushions and feathers clinging to my wet clothes, was one of disbelief.

Once happy with the stock and with our first home party booked, there was just one problem to resolve… that of transporting the goods. As usual, my father who

June Antoinette Necchi

had always encouraged my entrepreneurial efforts stepped

up offering us the use of his car. We were excited and couldn't wait. We were pleased with the colourful collection of goods we laid out in the host's home as we waited for the guests to arrive. When the time came the group who'd been invited happily sorted through the items on display with some wanting to buy, others wanting to order in different colours and the evening ended with drinks and biscuits being served by the host.

This first evening had, we thought, been a success both in terms of sales as well as socially. We were pleased with a successful launch.

Over the following weeks and months our business grew, incurring more and more hours of sewing, and shopping for more fabrics. By Christmas, based on Anne's calculations, we decided that we were due for a Christmas bonus, so we planned a day out in Birmingham, minus sandwiches this time, instead treating ourselves to lunch in an Italian restaurant.

While choosing a few Christmas gifts Anne spotted a man's overcoat, a stylish one with a fur collar. "June, I've got to buy that for my hubby's Christmas present. He's been so patient with our home being turned into a workshop and his evening meal being served late. It's the least I can do."

Soon, with healthy accounts and a full order book I felt this was the time to invest in our own transport, become independent.

June Antoinette Necchi

Sitting in the bank manager's office I felt confident that once he'd heard me out he would consider a loan for a small van to transport our goods.

I began by asking him, "Have you heard of Laura Ashley? "He seemed pleased to point to my fabric bag, "Yes, that's a Laura Ashley bag, isn't it?" (actually, it wasn't, but it felt prudent not to start with a negative). "Well, yes, it is", I replied. This felt like a positive start. It was then that he began closely examining my banking history on his desk.

"Mrs Necchi, what about your other business". (What's he talking about? Oh,, he must have been given the wrong bank details.) "These are your bank statements, Mrs Necchi. Can you tell me about your other business, please?" I felt I was on the losing end as I asked, "What business, is that?" Your Aries Friendship business, Mrs Necchi". (Why's he dragging that up? I closed that some time ago after running it for 3 years…..I must have forgotten to let him know.)

"Oh,, that," I replied, breezily, "With internet dating taking off it was no longer a viable business. I'm here today to request a loan to purchase a van for our business. We have full order books and up to date accounts and feel that now is the time to expand". (Maybe this is the time for me to add a little more to convince him) "Yes, we've done so well that my partner was able to purchase an expensive fur collared coat for her husband as a Christmas present".

June Antoinette Necchi

He looked over his glasses, and with a serious look on his face said, "Mrs Necchi, do you think that expensive purchases like that should be made when the money would be better spent towards the van you need? I'm sorry I am not able to advance you a loan".

Fate intervened a week later when Anne told me, "June, the number of orders we have would keep me busy at my sewing machine 6 days a week. I wouldn't have time to keep my house up to the standard I like. You know I'm a bit OCD when it comes to cleaning. Please take someone else on to help you run the business".

"I won't do that, Anne, we have worked well together, but don't worry, I will decide what to do next".

June Antoinette Necchi

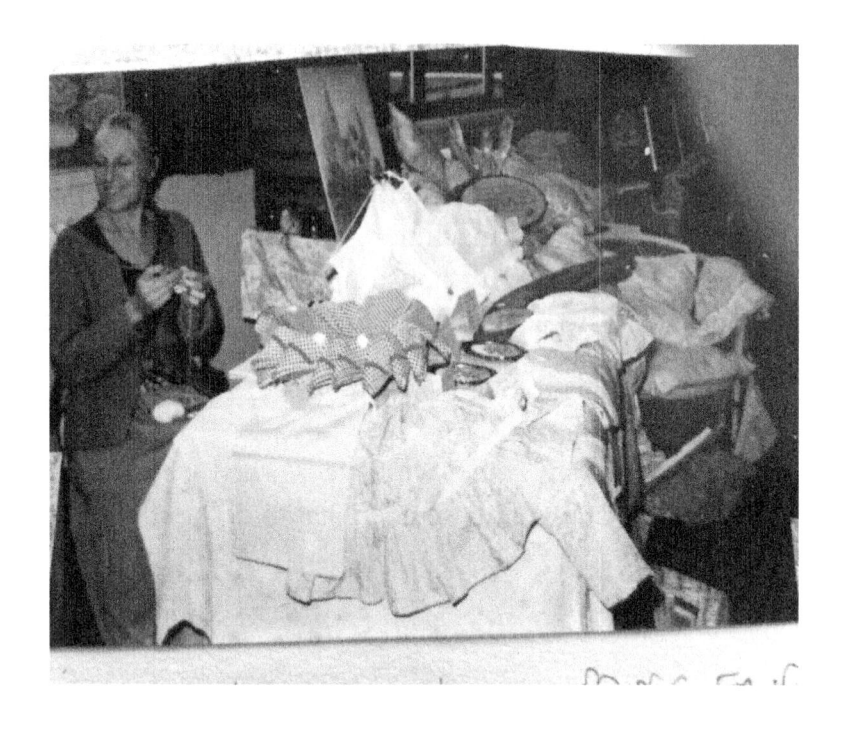

The start of my sewing career

Chapter 15

DARTMOUTH ROAD

Life was moving on. My first 2 children, Russell and Donna were married. Matthew was in senior school and Dan, just 6 years old. It was time for another move, maybe this time to a house with central heating, and an easy walk to the schools. With Dan in nursery at 3 years old, and then in school, I had been able to increase my earnings, and my careful housekeeping costs, together with some home sewing, enabled me to consider another house move.

It was a period,1980, when there was a shortage of houses for sale resulting in an offer often having been made before the advert reached the House Agents' windows. There was nothing for it, but to visit each agent first thing in the morning after I'd taken Dan to school.

My luck was in one morning when the agent told me that a house had just gone on the market. It was close to the town centre and schools, and was a bit run down, hence its low price. I couldn't get there quick enough as I knew that time was of the essence. Cycling, I arrived there a few minutes later to find that no one

June Antoinette Necchi

was home. Peeping through the windows and a quick look at the south

June Antoinette Necchi

facing back garden made up my mind. I was determined to buy it and was prepared to do what was necessary to update it.

Back at the agents I offered them the asking price and in the same breath asked them to put my house on the market. That apparently clinched the sale for them. I spent the next 2 days touching up my paintwork and tidying the garden. At this point the agents hadn't yet put a Sale board up.

It was 48 hours later that I came home to find a note in my door. It was a request to buy my house at the asking price, and within weeks we had moved into our new home in time to prepare for Christmas.

This marked the beginning of a new life for us as a family. Feeling much more settled, I took up painting and joined a local art group. My interest in flower painting moved on to portrait painting.

I had been an admirer of Anwar Sadat, recognised as a man of peace, and was dreadfully upset one morning to wake up to the news that he had been assassinated. The front cover of a newspaper displayed a photograph of him, smiling, and looking up to a flyover in the sky. He was shot seconds after the photograph was taken.

That weekend I painted his portrait and hung it in an exhibition in my local library. I will never know why but it was stolen a week later prompting the local newspaper to make a 'story' of it and arrive at my door

June Antoinette Necchi

wanting photographs. I found the publicity a bit embarrassing, but it triggered an interest in my work by some readers who phoned asking for painting lessons. Reluctant to give lessons, but for financial reasons, I decided that I could at least offer basic starter sessions.

Amazingly, my small group of 3 passed the word around until I had 6 students. I was enjoying this teaching and found that I was able to keep a few steps ahead of them by studying painting techniques in my spare time. The social aspect of the lessons proved to be a popular part of the sessions.... something I enjoyed immensely.

Requests began to come in for portrait commissions, usually single portraits but occasionally groups of children. I would probably have settled for painting portraits as a hobby, but I needed to boost my income which was the big driver.

Overtime I had several interesting requests. One day I had a phone call asking if I could copy a portrait of a deceased family member, a sketch by a street artist. It had been found in the attic of the caller's grandmother's house following her death. I was intrigued to be part of this story and looked forward to seeing the picture.

It was a charcoal head and shoulders drawing of a handsome young man, his shirt collar and tie suggesting the turn of the Victorian era. I very much enjoyed painting this subject, and believe I came to 'know' my subject? Indeed, I think I fell a little in love with him! His family were thrilled to see their long-lost

June Antoinette Necchi

relative come to life on the canvas, and I was happy to have been able to achieve this for them.

June Antoinette Necchi

Life in this new home brought a much-needed stability to our family life with my youngest son eventually moving to Senior school and his brother starting an apprenticeship. Meanwhile I had gained a Teaching certificate in Art and was teaching art in a variety of places, prison, college evening classes, weekly youth centre evenings across the county as well as private lessons at home and in the local library. In some strange way I felt that I had 'arrived' finally with everything in place.

My relationship remained strong with Dan's father, but unconventional, with me choosing to live separately while sharing our interests, family and time together. We were each other's soul mate.

And then clouds began forming when my daughter Donna; a mother of two young children, was admitted one evening to an Accident and Emergency department having suffered a major seizure. Having worked on weekend medical emergency services for three years I had a limited understanding of symptoms and causes. My big fear was that the seizure had heralded a brain tumour. I tried to convince myself that as Donna's two children had serious responses a couple of weeks before to minor surgery, I hoped and prayed that the seizure was a belated response to her anxiety. I was wrong. Donna was quickly diagnosed with a glioblastoma brain tumour. We were warned immediately after surgery that her condition was incurable with a prognosis of "Donna may have 6 or 9 months, 12 if you are lucky."

June Antoinette Necchi

My daughter's family life fell apart at that, and my life would never be the same.

I've published a book on Amazon "Kissing Donna Better" which tells of her brain tumour journey

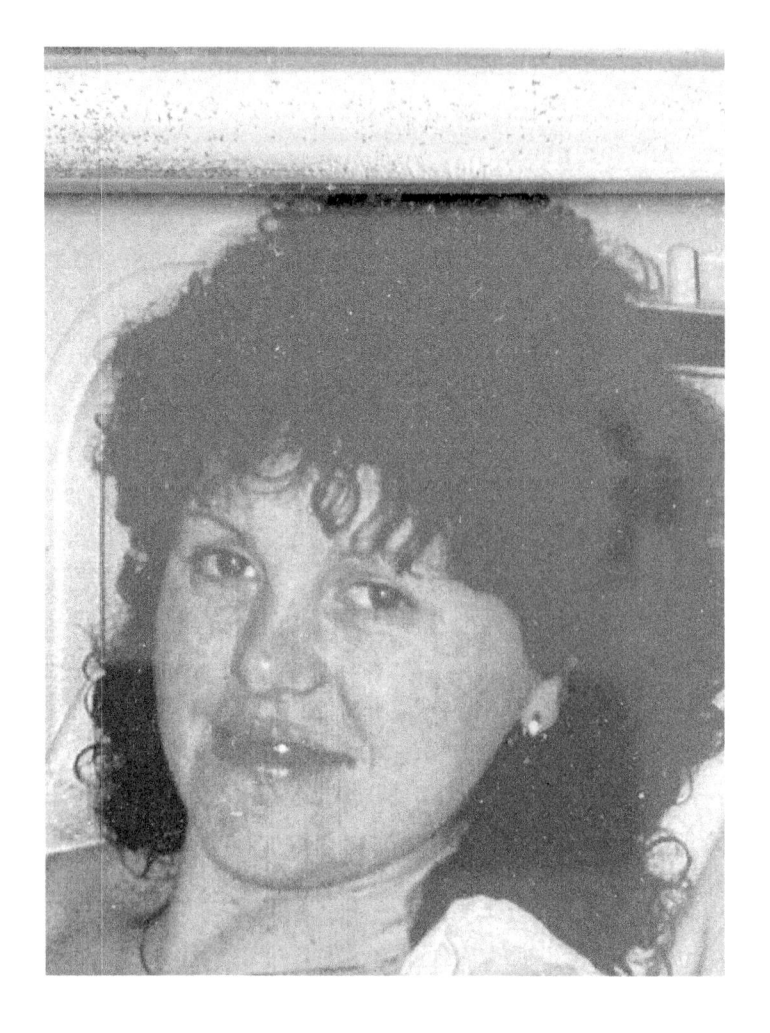

Beautiful Donna

June Antoinette Necchi

My Dartmouth Rd home

My commission for a family portrait

This photo appeared in the newspaper

June Antoinette Necchi

Chapter 16
CLINICAL ONCOLOGIST PATIENT' LIAISON GROUP'

A notice in the national press caught my eye one day. It was by the College of Radiology in London requesting participants to join a new panel whose aim was improvement in cancer care. There were to be six oncologists and six cancer patients whose experiences would be addressed, and changes recommended, where possible.

I decided to apply despite not having had cancer myself but felt that as I had accompanied my daughter through her glioblastoma brain tumour journey, until her death, that I had witnessed her experiences as a cancer patient, and therefore would be able to speak on her behalf. Following an interview at the college a few weeks later I was offered a place on the newly established group, the Clinical Oncologists Patient Liaison Group, a group which was to run for 3 years.

The college itself was a very impressive building in Portland Place London, with beautiful staircases and grand rooms. On the first day we all took our seats around the table in the conference room. There were six oncologists, five members of the public who had experienced cancer, a secretary, and me. It was interesting to see that the professionals there displayed their names minus their titles which made for a less formal meeting. The oncologists represented various parts of the British Isles, while the patients came from more accessible parts of the country.

The first session consisted of the reasons why the group had been formed…..to improve cancer care by listening to the experiences of the cancer patients in the group and addressing any negative situations they had been subjected to. They ranged from anxieties about lack of privacy or information etc all of which had a bearing on how cancer patients coped with their condition.

I was able to recount my daughter's experiences, namely a lack of privacy on two occasions, which distressed her. For her first radiotherapy session, which causes most patients to be anxious, and often distressed, Donna left the Radiotherapy room carrying her wig in her hands as there was no mirror to fit and adjust it. The nearest mirror was in the ladies' toilets at the far end of the large reception area. This entailed her walking through rows of seated patients. Her surgery stitches, 48 on either side of her head, caused her considerable embarrassment while walking through the public area. My suggestion at the Clinical Oncologists Patient Liaison Group was to raise this privacy point where it was concluded that the obvious solution was to provide a mirror in the treatment room, a thoughtful

June Antoinette Necchi

and practical solution at only minimal cost to the NHS, but for maximum benefit to patients.

June Antoinette Necchi

When a cancer patient is hospitalised while still having ongoing radiation treatment daily, as my daughter was, it necessitates a hospital porter taking the patient on a stretcher to the treatment room. Unfortunately, my daughter's stretcher was positioned in the same area as the outpatients' seating, and in full view of them. I felt that not only was this a serious lack of privacy but also for those out-patients who may have been upset by my daughter's condition, while themselves on a cancer journey.

Over 3 years the members of C.O.P.L.G. produced two publications, one, 'Is your Radiotherapy unit Cancer Friendly?' And two 'Is Your Chemotherapy Unit Cancer Friendly?' They were sent to 64 hospitals and included the groups' suggestions. Acting on mine, mirrors were advised to be placed in treatment rooms, and screens erected in public waiting areas for inpatients awaiting treatment. I was pleased on my daughter's behalf to have these privacy experiences addressed, and to have been part of the Clinical Oncologists' Patient Liaison Group.

June Antoinette Necchi

Chapter 17

BOURNEMOUTH

Two of my sons had made their home in Bournemouth, one, Matthew, in business, the other, Dan, as a student at the art university. I had remained in the Midlands caring for my two grandsons after the death of their mother, my daughter, Donna. Now they were more independent, the time felt right to move south. Not only that, but one of my two sons who was living in Bournemouth was planning to start a family, and as he said, "We want their grandmother to be part of their lives. A new chapter was about to open in my life....

I liked the idea of that, and put my house on the market, and began looking for a new home in the south. My 87-year-old mother had no intention of being left behind and lost no time in finding a home in Bournemouth, moving down a few months before me! Having found a home near the sea, as well as a buyer for mine, things moved quickly. That was until I had a call from the estate agents to say that I had been out bid.

I was in Bournemouth for the weekend, and so drove around looking for another property. My house was under offer, so I had to find somewhere post haste. I toured the area spotting a For Sale sign on the gate of a

June Antoinette Necchi

large house which was divided into apartments. Was the

June Antoinette Necchi

flat for sale on the ground floor, south or north facing, or was it on the first floor? A lovely cottage garden was on the south side, but surely it was too much to hope for. Was the advertised apartment under offer, anyway?

Later, I was due to meet my sons and mother for lunch before I returned home, so time was of the essence. Thank heavens for mobile phones! A quick call to the agent whose office was a few hundred yards away, gave me the information I needed. "No, there is no offer on the property. It has just come on the market. And yes, it's the ground floor". With the sea at one end of the road, and the high street at the other, this all seems too good to be true. Mulling over what this change of location would mean; I was still having reservations about leaving my grandsons in the midlands….. I had been their daycare substitute mother for the last 9 years, and while they were now both teenagers, this was to be another 'loss' for them, as well as for me.

I would also be leaving behind my first son and his family, and as a mother hen, I liked all my chicks around me. I had to remind myself, and him, that my home in Bournemouth would always be their home, and only a three-hour drive away.

A call from the agent came. "You can do a viewing in five minutes. I will meet you there". Gosh this dream was becoming a reality!

June Antoinette Necchi

Stepping through the front door into the hall I knew that this was to be my 'happy ever after' home. I loved the original features, and didn't mind that the kitchen needed an overhaul or that the sunroom was tatty. This was meant to be, and I would enjoy putting my stamp on it. A roomy apartment, it would easily accommodate my visiting family. Who could resist a holiday by the sea? My youngest son's philosophical reply to me when I said "I'm not sure how I will feel about leaving my home. It holds so many memories", "Mum, it is only four walls, so you just pack up the memories and take them with you".

The sale went through quite seamlessly, and I moved down a few weeks later. Now I could wait for my new grandchild. Had my sons been keeping something from me? In the first six years they made me a Nonna five times over! Happy days.

Three months after coming to Bournemouth we celebrated the first Christmas of what was to be many in my new home. Life was looking good. My mother was happy for the family to be reunited, and like me, was looking forward to my son's new baby in the spring.

In the New Year, with time on my hands, I made enquiries about voluntary work in the area and made an appointment with a Macmillan Hospice. Wondering what I might have to offer, I thought that I might be able to read a book to patients, or chat with them

June Antoinette Necchi

In life sometimes the 'planets' meet, it's said, and that day was one of those. It came as a complete surprise when the head of the Day Unit at the hospice, noting my previous experience, said "We have a patient in the Day Unit who would like to paint in water colours. We have

June Antoinette Necchi

lots of activities, but no painting. Would you like to try a few sessions for him?" Would I? I was thrilled, though nervous at the prospect. I immediately agreed, and accepted working as a volunteer one day a week.

I had no idea what to expect as I drove to the Christchurch Hospice about two miles from my home. I had decided to do a demonstration about colour for my first visit hoping that there would be a few interested patients. The unit itself consisted of a big activities area, an adjoining lounge encircled by comfortable chairs, a dining area, a kitchen and massage therapy room. Background music, and laughter was my first impression as I went in the first day. Some patients, with morning drinks, sat chatting in the lounge area, and at the activities table, others sat painting pieces of pottery. I immediately knew that I would love working there.

After sharing a coffee with the staff, I now had to take the bull by the horns, introduce myself to the patients, and hopefully encourage a few to watch my first demonstration. John, the patient who had made the inquiry about painting, was the first 'student' to join me at the table. We had a chat, and I found out that he was a retired commercial pilot, who being confined to a wheelchair, now had his activities limited. He told me that he was keen to do watercolour painting. What a good idea for someone whose movements were restricted! I had decided against demonstrating water colour painting at this first session but use pastels instead to quickly produce a range of colour effects.

June Antoinette Necchi

Three more patients decided, with him, that they would join my next lesson.

I came home relieved and enthusiastic about this new position. Now, I need to gather painting material and textbooks ready for next time. I had a phone call from the Head of the unit telling me to buy any material so and she would reimburse me. This was a great start. I increased my days to three, enabling patients across the board to join in.

I increased my days to three, enabling patients across the board to join in. I discovered that as a volunteer in a hospice you become one of that 'family', developing relationships with each other, and updating shared personal news. And the most surprising feature of that 'family' was the happy atmosphere, the laughter, and the joking between us all.

John went on to paint many pictures in a few subjects, his favourite being that of horses though he attempted other subjects, one, a copy of Vettriano's painting of a couple dancing on the beach, given to his wife on their anniversary.

His family built a 'painting room' onto his house though sadly after a few years he and his wife had to leave their rural home for an apartment where he could have daily personal care. At his funeral celebration his family were proud to have an exhibition of his paintings in a public space. A well-remembered friend.

June Antoinette Necchi

My 15 years' experience in the hospice has left me with many memories of forged relationships, and with each visit there, the humbling feelings as I walked out each day of being thankful for good health.

Bournemouth family day out

Matteo

Chapter 18

GRANDCHILDREN

My grandchildren arrived in quick succession. The first, Camilla in 2005, Matteo in 2007, Amelie, 2008, Isotta, 2009 and Gabriel in 2011.

While Matteo's birth was a normal delivery, he was diagnosed with a 'small heart murmur' and given an appointment for a check-up two weeks later.

Visiting him at home when he was five days old I was alarmed at his fast heart rate. The GP who saw him the following day had him urgently admitted to a local hospital.

On examination it was realised he needed to be taken to the paediatric department of Southampton Hospital where it was discovered that he had severe stenosis of his aortic valve, as well as an abnormal aortic artery. Surgery was needed as soon as possible to save his life…. but first his body stress had to be reduced. A general anaesthetic was given, and surgery to stretch the aortic valve began in the early hours of the next day.

Awaiting news that heart surgery had begun on Matteo was the longest night until we were given the news that it was completed and successful. This darling baby had survived and now we must play the waiting game. It was several weeks before we could bring him home, and now with a Naso tube as he had become swallow phobic, a condition that was to last for the next five years.

We had begun a long journey of emergency admissions, of infections, and two more open heart surgeries. Matteo 'graduated' to a portable floor standing milk machine, and then to a Peg inserted in his stomach.

On the rare occasions that his parents went out for a meal I was fearful, baby sitting, that I would make a mistake when removing his Peg to connect him to the milk machine. His timed feed was given as he lay asleep in his cot.

Armed with reading glasses to ensure that I had reconnected the Peg correctly, and my phone, in case an emergency arose, it was worthwhile to give his exhausted parents a couple of hours out of the house.

The Southampton Paediatric Unit was always available to advise his parents and gave my son a direct emergency line.

The time had come when Matteo's valve transplant could wait no longer. Twice, his aortic valve had been' stretched', but now it had to be replaced. It had been hoped that it could be done when he was in his teens, but at four and a half, it could wait no longer.

June Antoinette Necchi

The plan was to remove the aortic valve and replace it with his own healthy pulmonary one. A salvaged valve would then replace the pulmonary valve. My son had been warned by the retired heart surgeon, Magdi

June Antoinette Necchi

Yacoub, that he was to use only a surgeon who was familiar with this procedure.

We placed our faith in the chief surgeon, and his two assisting heart surgeons, and were told exactly what was proposed in the complex surgery.

They were tense and difficult hours as we sat together, waiting. Seven and a half hours later my son and his wife were called into an adjacent room and the planned procedure was described in detail.

"It had been a success and a crisis which occurred early in the surgery, which was life threatening, had been overcome. The transplant had gone well. Before taking Matteo off the life support machine, I decided to do a little plastic surgery. Matteo won't want his three operation 'tramlines' down the middle of his chest. He now has only one." This thoughtful surgeon told them.

How would we ever be able to thank him and his colleagues for giving Matteo a normal life? Now we could go forward and get down to the business of family life, which now included a sister, Isotta, for Matteo and Camilla.

My younger son Dan and his partner surprised us, and themselves, by bringing Amelie and Gabriel into the fold over the next 4 years.

My 'retirement' now included noisy Sunday dinner times and regular requests for sleepovers organised by the kids. 'Putty in their hands 'might describe the last few years, but I wouldn't change a thing......

June Antoinette Necchi

It was the end of an era when my mother passed away in 2015 following a fracture and requiring a stay in a care home. We knew that it would never be easy for her but hoped that she would become a little more mobile and be able to return home.

As it became clear that her condition would not improve, she methodically began withdrawing, no longer prepared to be taken into the lounge, or join in with activities, and eventually asking to have her meals in her room. Finally, she asked not to be taken out of bed, or sit in an armchair. As in life, my feisty, independent mother remained in charge until the end. She was a Christian and told us, "I have no fear of death, but I don't want to leave my family".

Our family regard her as a legend remembering her sense of fun, her singing voice, her protection of the family, and the ever-open house where food was always on the table.

June Antoinette Necchi

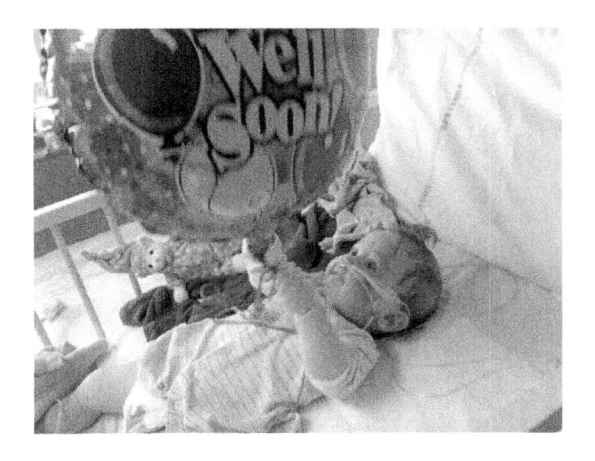

grandson Matteo

Amelie, Camilla, Isotta, Gabriel, Matteo,

Grandchildren

Chapter 19

THE INTERVENING YEARS

I didn't realise that leaving the area I had lived in, and been happy in for most of my life, would be enriched by my move south to Bournemouth. My family life, my 'art as therapy' work, and the opportunity to be involved with a creative community, has gifted me a contented and fulfilling life by the sea.

The years have been filled with teaching art in my own home, joining writing groups, taking in foreign students, and until last year, for four years, opening my home for Airbnb guests…an experience I enjoyed.

I have still not put to rest my quest for proving a theory I have chased for years…that of the trigger for multiple sclerosis. It has, and continues to be, a fascinating study. (One of the subjects of my next book)

I've dabbled in sculpture, in Argentine tango lessons, tap dancing, but have remained true to art and writing publishing my first book, Kissing Donna Better, in 2021.

It describes the brain tumour journey of my darling daughter, and how she met all the challenges that cancer can bring.

June Antoinette Necchi

I will be forever proud of Donna who remains a light in my life.

June Antoinette Necchi

One of my Portraits

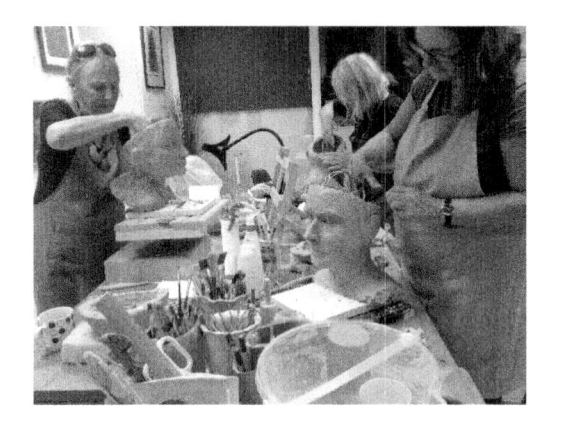

Deep in concentration

hollowing out a portrait of my father

My sculpture tutor Linda Joyce

June Antoinette Necchi

Chapter 20
PARENTS

Bunny, my father, a natural entrepreneur, doting father, grandfather, and devoted to my mother, Gwyneth. Born in London, the second of ten children to Agostino and Florence, showing early engineering and carpentry talents which he used during World War 2 when he was a foreman on bomb damaged sites in London during the Blitz.

Bunny's intellect, humour and natural empathy endeared him to all he met. Each of his 14 grandchildren continue to tell of the fun times they shared with him and of the skills that he taught them. The garden he turned into a play park with a pool, swings and a slide, and the unicycle he made, and rode round and round the garden, much to their delight.

He was a man of many parts, self-taught since the age of 13 when he took the responsibility for decorating the family home. And at that time, taken by his father as his apprentice in the trade of how to lay a parquet floor.

As toy production was suspended during the war Bunny began making wooden toys, scooters, dolls' houses and trucks when the war came to an end.

June Antoinette Necchi

The house we had lodgings in from 1945 to 1948 was lit only by gas light. Bunny wired the house for electricity and the word spread along the street. Soon Bunny was rewiring neighbours' houses, too.

And he didn't draw a line at using his sewing machine either, He made mine and my mother's clothes as well as curtains for our house.

He would sit for hours with his grandchildren modelling little figures in plasticine then bring them to life by filming them in action. As his grandchildren grew and had their own homes Bunny was the 'fixer' of everything, washing machines, bikes, cars and more…and chief babysitter.

I grew up with his example that I could achieve anything that I wanted to do. I have tried.

Drawn to challenges over his lifetime, his series of creative hobbies. sign painting, animation, glass blowing, photography, constructing over mantle fireplaces, designing and building house extensions, wrought iron work, and engineering satisfied his curious mind.

Working for a short time in the car production industry he was invited to Birmingham to be presented with an award for his contribution to the company to increase productivity with his time and motion study.

Using his skills as a cartoonist he was able to promote his interest as a fighter for social justice.

June Antoinette Necchi

In the last year of his life he designed and constructed, single handed, a beautiful loft room on the second floor of my home. He had the enthusiasm of a young man and used the experience to teach my 15-year-old son to build a staircase. Each day, as excited as a schoolboy, he'd arrive with a packed lunch eager to start work.

He was a youthful 75-year-old then, who we thought would be with us for many years to come. Sadly, he contracted an industrial disease and died a few months later. Indeed, Bunny was a one off…

DAD'S CLUTTER

Dad appeared at my front door one day. He looked worried "What's the matter, Dad? I can see something's wrong" "It's your mother". "What's the matter with her? What's happened!". "No there's nothing the matter with her but she's told me that she wants me to get rid of all my clutter. You know it's not clutter. It's all my hobbies, stuff and books".

"Oh, you should be used to Mum after all these years. You know how house proud she is. Remember when we lodged in that miner's house? We had two rooms. They were her pride and joy. Not a thing out of place. That little electric cooker gleamed and in the middle of the room, our dining table, polished so that we could see our faces in it. She'll never change. You know that. How about we appeal to her sense of domestic order and fine furniture. You know those recesses at the side of the chimney breast? Why not build shelves and cupboards?"

June Antoinette Necchi

Dad brightened up straight away. I'd hit the right spot! He loved a challenge, and ideas. "June, I know,! 'I've got that vintage wardrobe in the garage. Beautiful mahogany. Would make a lovely piece of furniture."

"And finish it off with some elegant brass handles. You know what Mum likes."

It was a bit like firing a starting gun. He made his way back home and I imagined him in his garage already busy at work.

I'd always been the main mediator between Mum and Dad when there'd been an issue about their differences, always easily resolved with some creative thinking! "Mum, what a great idea Dad's got for your front room. Just wait and see." So Mum, placated for a while, waited to see the finished result.

"Oh, Bunny, I love that beautiful, polished wood and brass handles," Mum told him as she admired the finished job. You must agree it's lovely now that your clutter's hidden away, isn't it?"

Domestic peace was restored once more thanks to Dad and me acting as 'partners in crime' yet again.

(A word in my ear a little later from Dad, "Never did think of my 'treasures' as clutter but at least Mum's happy".

June Antoinette Necchi

THE DANCE LESSONS!

"What are you doing there, Dad? "I asked Bunny, when I popped in one evening, as I watched him in his stockinged feet, outlining them on pieces of paper. "Well, your mother is insisting that I learn to dance."

Now we all knew that Mum's hobby had always been ballroom dancing, but I was surprised that at this stage of their lives, they were grandparents, she was confident that Bunny could at last be her dance partner. Always thoughtful, he was determined to learn some basic dance steps to take to the floor with my mother. "Gwyneth, look I'll lay them out on the floor. Give me a list of waltz steps to follow and I'll start practising." Mum knew that Bunny always approached a problem intelligently, and logically, though she was already imagining a robot like, one two together, turn, and repeat...

Applying himself diligently in his efforts to master dancing, he was confident enough, a bit later, to take my mother in his arms. "I'll put on a dance record. I think you may have the dance partner you have always wanted, Gwyneth. Let's go".

Somehow, despite his best efforts, he seemed surprised that he couldn't get the rhythm and the steps to connect. It was one of the few times in Bunny's life that he accepted defeat. "Gwyneth. I must admit it. I think I must have two left feet….."

June Antoinette Necchi

BUNNY LICHFIELD

It was Christmas 1990, after a lifetime of good health, Bunny, at 76, had surgery for bladder cancer triggered by working with a dangerous substance. It was a devastating prognosis for our family, unable to imagine a life without him. Within 3 days of the surgery in January of that year Bunny was entertaining other patients with his humour and stories.

By early May with his radiotherapy behind him Bunny was ready to 'hit the road' and begin campaigning on behalf of his objection to the Prime Minister Margaret Thatcher's proposed Poll Tax Community Charge.

A talented cartoonist, Bunny had drawn a sketch of a ship bearing the name of Titanic and heading for icebergs with Poll Tax inscribed on them. A caricature of Margaret Thatcher was at the helm holding a loudspeaker with the words "straight ahead boys!"

A small rowing boat was heading for the shore with a group of well-known politicians deserting the ship. I thought this an interesting political cartoon and filed it away.

Planning his first outing with me to a nearby small city, Lichfield, which was holding local elections, Bunny asked me to reproduce his drawing onto one of my canvases. With no blank canvas I decided to take one of my large painted ones, one on which I'd painted a head and shoulders of Christ and cover it with a white piece of sheeting on which I'd reproduced Bunny's cartoon, and the ship heading for disaster.

The canvas when attached to Bunny's car stood upright above the windscreen. It was certainly eye-catching! Arriving at the city, along a narrow one-way street, we spotted a group of candidates wearing blue ties and surrounded by a crowd of journalists with their cameras and booms who, when one spotted our placard, ran over bringing others in his wake.

Our car, whose side windows all displayed political sketches had obviously caught their attention and they were determined to get their 'story'. While Bunny didn't belong to a political party he was a courageous and active supporter of social justice. Opening my car window the journalists were confronted with this older driver in his woolly work cap, and myself with sunglasses, broken and at an odd angle on my nose.

"Who do you represent!?" they clamoured to find out. I adjusted my sunglasses. "My father is a one-man band and a fighter for social justice".

Clearly, the journalists were disappointed and couldn't be blamed for assuming that Bunny may be a crank, not knowing that he was a man of great intellect and creativity and prepared to put that to use as a fighter for social justice.

As they dispersed Bunny removed the Titanic canvas placing it to one side of a shopping centre entrance. This was in direct opposition to placards on the other side whose texts supported a right-wing party.

We drove around the city for an hour returning to collect our canvas and were surprised to see that it had been removed and placed alongside the right-wing groups' placards. Bunny walked over to collect it and was confronted by a man who shouted, "You are disgusting supporting that group". It was quite entertaining watching these two elderly men exchanging words and reverting to the street language of kids. "Don't dare call me right wing. I'll knock your bloody block off".

As usual I stepped in, calmed things down and off we went, satisfied with the events of the day....and then it rained. In fact, it poured. As the rain soaked through the canvas sheeting the painting of Christ's head underneath was revealed. Obviously Bunny had the Lord's blessing that day.

It was a Sunday morning in July when I arrived at Stafford hospital to visit my dad who sadly was in the late stage of cancer. Concerned at his deterioration I sat at the head of his bed with my arm around him. Did he wait for me to spend one last time with him? He had been my best friend, a father who found no fault in me, who encouraged me to take on challenges, and my 'partner in crime'. I simply said, "I'm here now, you'll be alright," at which he passed away.

Strange the things you think about at times like that… I cut a lock of his hair which I treasure.

June Antoinette Necchi

Shortly after his death a local headmaster came to give his condolences saying, "Your father was the greatest fighter for social justice that the town has known". And yes, I was, and still am, very proud of Bunny, my father.

June Antoinette Necchi

Bunny's political cartoon

June Antoinette Necchi

CONSCIENTIOUS OBJECTOR

Bunny was in his mid-twenties when the Second World War broke out and married with two young children. He was, and remained, a pacifist by nature, and had the courage of his convictions.

He defended himself in court when he pleaded that he was a pacifist and Conscientious Objector on the grounds that he would neither kill the brothers of his father, who was Italian, or the brothers of his mother, who was English. It was at the point in war when Italians were on the side of the enemy. Bunny told the court that he was prepared, as a carpenter, to do war damage work. He won his case and went on to be a foreman on war damaged sites, as well as helping build the pontoons for the Dunkirk invasion.

He wrote the following interesting letter to my mother telling her of a mid-war incident.

"I oversaw a Bomb Damage Repair crew. I was notified by my boss to get my crew together and report to a leather goods manufacturer at Kings Cross London. This was Saturday afternoon. A Doodle Bug had dropped the previous night and being a near miss, had removed the roofing tiles, all the glass, and some window frames as well as ripping the front door from its hinges.

I had a good crew of men covering most trades connected with building, and we all got 'stuck in' to make the necessary repairs. I, being the carpenter did

June Antoinette Necchi

the usual things of securing the front door by splicing timber where the hinges used to be, etc, whilst the roofers were covering the roof with tarpaulin sheets, others were covering the window cavities with roofing felt.

In general, all we could do because of the frequency of these 'incidents' was to make the building weatherproof and secure until such time as there was a lull in the bombing, when we would carry out Secondary Repairs.

Anyway, we worked hard and completed most of the vital jobs but decided that the details would have to stand until the next day as, after dark, no lights could be used because of Blackout Regulations.

We arrived Sunday morning and who should be waiting at the corner of the street 'Nobby' Clark the gaffer, red in the face. He greeted us with, "I thought I detailed your crew to do repairs on the leather warehouse. You haven't touched it."

I began to wonder whether we had repaired the wrong one, but no, there it was practically the same as when we had arrived on the previous afternoon …the roof off, windows and door out. The gaffer took a lot of convincing that we had in fact completed the job the day before. Only when I had sorted out the A.R.P. Wardens who told me that another 'Doodle Bug' had dropped in the vicinity and undone the work we had done the previous day. Was the gaffer fully convinced?

June Antoinette Necchi

Although this sort of thing was not unique, as one street in North London was subjected to bomb damage on three occasions…the same houses, at that.

June Antoinette Necchi

We began to wonder if we were wasting our time patching them up in case Hitler Demolition arrived the same night and ruined our handiwork.

The tenants of this little street always greeted us with lashings of tea, cakes and sandwiches all day long, and we became almost like one of the family".

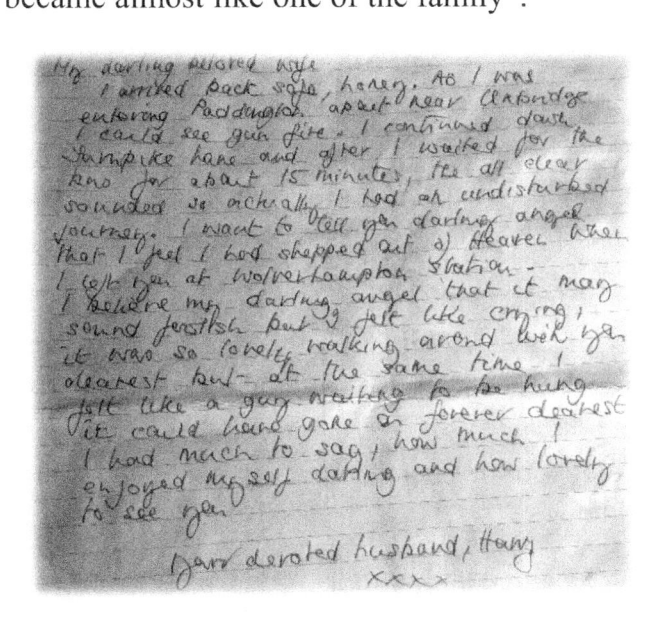

Wartime love letter Bunny wrote to mum

June Antoinette Necchi

END OF WAR

After the end of the war, and having returned to the family, Bunny's work usually involved anything to do with engineering or carpentry.

His hobbies were many. Engineering, writing, glass blowing, carpentry, and when he turned to wrought iron work he made gates, fire surrounds and a staircase for my new house as well as laying parquet flooring. His sewing machine found many uses, making my mother's and our clothes, and running up new curtains as well as alterations to the family's clothes.

In later years when in their own homes, Bunny was the 'fixer' of everything ….and the babysitter. His trademark fire surrounds with over mantles were installed in each of their houses, fire surrounds that were removed and taken to a new property when they moved house.

Bunny designed and built a wonderful room across the second floor of my house installing two Velux windows.

He had the enthusiasm of a young man using the experience to teach my 15-year-old son how to build a staircase. He was a youthful seventy-five-year-old who we thought would be with us for many years more. Sadly, he developed an industrial disease and died a few months later.

June Antoinette Necchi

Bunny made this amazing pool

Tracy, Donna, Jackie, Michelle, Nicola

Chapter 21

GWYNETH

My mother, Gwyneth, was a beautiful, elegant woman bearing the hair and skin colouring from her Romany grandmother. From the age of 14 she demonstrated a strong work ethic which was to form her character and life events.

During her career as a professional cook, she ran the family home like a tight ship, always organised with food for everyone, and an ever-open door to visitors. She had a great sense of fun and a gift for entertaining and organising social events in the hospital where she worked as head cook for many years.

Catering for 300 patients, some of whom were on special diets, she took great pride in serving up meals which she always told us "Have to be served up on hot plates and the food presented attractively".

Despite her busy life Gwyneth held tight to her hobbies of ballroom dancing, and horse racing.

From her early beginnings in the Welsh valleys, abandoned by her mother when only a toddler, and her leaving home to work in London, that tenacity

June Antoinette Necchi

coloured and influenced her whole life, and that of our family life.

June Antoinette Necchi

Bournemouth became the magnet for all our family holidays. Every year my parents made the trip, always accompanied by a variety of members of our family. They'd stay at a guest house and rent a beach hut for the week. Mum would naturally organise the picnic, and Dad the beach games. So many memories of Dad, looking like a pack mule fully loaded with enough food to feed an army, and his collection of games for the kids. Happy days!

Bournemouth had become an integral part of our holiday lives, so it was no surprise when Mum made the decision to buy a first floor flat there for family holidays. Of course, it wasn't long before it had the 'Gwyneth treatment', and along with Bunny's creative skills was a little flat ready to welcome friends and family.

A spare room was let out to a family friend, a hardworking young man I admit that Mum did mother him a bit, tidying his room and watering his plants.

One morning, sitting quietly with a cup of tea and a cigarette, Mum had a dreadful scare as she heard a crashing of the flat's main door downstairs followed by a charge of heavy feet on the stairs. "Where is he? Which is his room!!!"

What turned out to be three plain clothes drug squad men were set on finding the drugs they'd been given information about. I think at that time drugs to Mum meant medicinal....

Maybe because she was smoking they decided to search her handbag and finding no evidence of drugs then went to the lodger's bedroom door which proved to be locked. Mum had no option but to hand over the key. Seeing them removing the two or three plants she had been nurturing, she asked, "What are you doing with those?"

"And is that why three men had to frighten me to death for a couple of plants?" "They're drugs, Mrs Necchi. Cannabis "One of the squad, a Welshman recognising Mum's Welsh accent, kindly said, "Sit down Mrs Necchi and I'll make you a cup of tea. Here, I'll light a cigarette for you".

Mum took great pleasure in relating the tale to us later, "And to think I was watering those little plants daily" She also found it amusing when I suggested that there could have been a different ending had she been seen as an accomplice. "Mum, to think the front page of a daily would have a picture of you with the headline. *"GRANNY IN DRUG RAID"*. That appealed to mum's sense of humour, and she laughed.

THE BUTCHERS SHOP

"June, I can buy this butcher's shop. It will be a good job for you, and I'm asking George to manage it for me" "Do you think he will, Mum?. After all, he's been working at his present shop for years. And remember, he doesn't like change". "Don't be so negative, June. I'm sure he will like the responsibility".

June Antoinette Necchi

There was no stopping my mother when she had another investment idea and would always remind me of her successful boarding house where she was unfazed by the 20 Irish contractors, who couldn't wait to finish work to come back for Mum's huge dinners.

As a bonus, she shared their love of horse racing, discussing horses, jockeys and form over the dinner table.

My Dad had knocked two terraced houses into one, removing a staircase, and dividing rooms, which then easily housed the contractors.

Not to be deceived by Mum's image, that of a very elegant lady, she easily kept the fellows in line and ran a very successful business for a couple of years.

Any investment involving food always attracted Mum, after all she had worked as a cook for most of her working life, hence the butcher's shop idea.

As always, I had to be her intermediary, checking the shop's accounts, (which was to be my job in the event of the purchase going through!), the overheads, the suppliers, and dealing with the vendors.

I felt more despondent about my future employment as the weeks went by trying to advise Mum about the hold that supermarkets have over the public's meat buying. What was worse, the vendor began to visit me for updates. And now there was a face to the seller, I felt increasingly that I couldn't advise Mum against the

June Antoinette Necchi

purchase, but we were on the verge of completing when

June Antoinette Necchi

George had second thoughts and backed out of the job. (I love you, George!!) Mum, having no problem accepting defeat at the last fence, called me, "June, just let that butcher know that I've changed my mind". Just like that.

Left holding the baby, I called to tell the butcher the bad news. Within minutes he was knocking at my door piling pressure on me to complete the sale now we were at such a late stage. But too late..

My mother was a darling of a mother, and I did learn how to suppress some of her madcap ideas. Such was her enthusiasm and influence; I'd agreed to be a butcher's assistant. Funny she hadn't noticed that I had been a dedicated vegetarian for years.......

I have no photographs of my mother as a child, like many of us whose parents were born before photographs recorded their lives. But my mother's verbal memories, told to us over the years, brought her past to life in a way that photographs are not always able to.

her kaleidoscope of tales enabled me to see the little Gwyneth and her brother, Yanto, performing as part of the Bluebird's troupe, singing and dancing on stage for the locals in Pontlottyn in the Rhymney valley, and as a schoolgirl competing in running across Wales.

Left motherless at the age of three she was close to her father and brother, Yanto. With her decision at 14 to

June Antoinette Necchi

leave the valleys and work in London, Gwyneth couldn't

have imagined what turmoil the war would bring into her life.

Fast forward to her move to the midlands, now mother to three children, she worked at a local hospital as head cook for many years. Food was a constant theme in her, and our lives.

Her maths abilities in school years before might have indicated that she would have a 'business' head in years to come. Her strong work ethic enabled her to buy a property and open it as a guest house for workers. No takeaway meals there! Gwyneth's dinners ensured that her guest house never lacked guests. Her enthusiasm and energy never failed. Her ideas for making money were 'interesting', and sometimes paid off.

"June" she greeted me with when I walked in one day, "Let's go to the car auctions, and buy a car, cheap, then sell it at a profit" My heart sank. I knew nothing about cars, their engines, or current selling prices. Mum knew even less but did recognise a good-looking car when she saw one!

I did her bidding as usual, taking my young son with us. He was only seven but couldn't wait to drive! What a buying team we were. We wandered around what seemed like hundreds of cars on offer. Mum had her bundle of cash at the ready to bid for what SHE decided was a good buy. While I was desperately checking car prices in a copy of a car sales paper, Mum and my son grew excited as rows of shiny cars were

June Antoinette Necchi

brought in "That's the one! Bid for that one, June!" That one' was a hatchback Austin Cambridge. I lifted my hand to raise a couple of bids, but was reluctant to go further "Keep going, June, it's a lovely looking car".

With no time to argue we found ourselves the owners of this 'lovely looking car'.

Mum now had the bug, and before I could adjust to the idea that we had to work out how to get this car back home. Mum got excited, "Oh, look at that beautiful little blue car. What is it?"

"It's a Mini".

"Go on, June, bid for it" "But we've already bought one!" "That doesn't matter. This is a good buy". This from Mum who hardly knew one end of a car from the other...Like a lamb to the slaughter, I bid, and quickly found ourselves the proud owners of two cars. Mum wasn't interested in how we got them home, and my young son now also had the bug, asking when the next car rolled in, "Are we going to buy that one, too Mummy?"

A phone call to my dad brought him and a friend to drive our new purchases home. Was he surprised? No he didn't turn a hair.

Her love of following horse racing, each April's Grand National, always provoked the same conversation when I arrived at her home with my list of my chosen favourites, "What's the jockey's weight, his form, and does he like soft or hard going? And who are the trainers? "Sorry, Mum, not sure, haven't checked those". A bit of quick thinking on my part to change the subject," Mum, what's for dinner today?"

"June, "she replied in her soft Welsh accent, "Look, I bought a lovely rabbit for a casserole with rice. I'll save you some"

Such was her love of preparing and offering food as a gift, she'd put the rabbit on the draining board, skin, draw and wash it. My beautiful, elegant mother could always surprise me with her hands on cooking.

When it came to football she could be relied upon to know where in the league a team was at any given time, the team's managers, and the positions played. Her football mad grandsons liked nothing better than a football talking session with their grandmother.

Another memory of Gwyneth is, when following an accident, she lay on a stretcher in A&E aided by two paramedics. To them she was a lady in her 90's quietly awaiting a doctor, but she suddenly sat up, pointed to one of the paramedics, asking, "Which football team do you support?". He looked taken aback at this inquisition but told Mum his team "Their manager's no good, they'll never get anywhere till they change him!"

All three then embarked on a lively football debate! Being Welsh, rugby couldn't be ignored either, and so their sport exchanges went on until she was taken for X Rays.

June Antoinette Necchi

The surgeon stood at her bedside later, advising her of the surgery she would have. Gwyneth was surprised to be asked several random questions.

"What year was the war?". Confidently Gwyneth replied, "1914/ 1918!". Born in 1916 this was a reasonable answer….

Further questions, "How old are you? Where do you live? Who's the Prime Minister? Do you know where you are? She answered all the questions. As the surgeon walked away Gwyneth winked at me, "He was trying to catch me out, wasn't he!".

A few weeks later when in after care, she was approached by one of the team who began asking her the same questions. After three questions Gwyneth put her hand up saying, "I've already answered all of those and I'm not doing it again!"

One of Bunny's many ventures were when he indulged himself in the buying and selling business. I say indulged because of his lifelong interest in gadgets, big and small, from cameras to binoculars, TVs, as well as war memorabilia were all displayed in a small shop he rented.

It was a small friendly neighbourhood and word soon got around that he accepted, and sold, second hand goods. Knowing this, an old lady turned up at my mother's door one day saying, "Mrs Necchi, I'm in need of money. I wonder if your husband would like to buy my clothes and shoes here in this bag?".

June Antoinette Necchi

Now my mother wasn't a soft touch, but she had a heart of gold, so when the old lady offered her the bag of clothes, my mother said, "Of course", taking the bag from the lady who was clearly very happy to have a few pounds put in her hands.

After she left I watched my mother, who didn't look in the bag, walk to the back garden, and place the bag of clothes and shoes into the waste bin. The old lady's pride hadn't been hurt by a refusal and she went away happy.

Another elderly lady lived at the top of the road, isolated in a first floor flat with few relatives around and in the later stages of cancer she found it difficult to make food for herself.

Mum wasted no time in organising hot dinners for the lady taking her meals each lunchtime, often with Mum's specialities of Yorkshire puddings and roasts. And not only hot dinners but Mum entertained her with lively conversation and laughter, typical of her south Welsh character.

In 2012 my mother, tidying her kitchen, tripped over and fractured her femur. When discharged she was able to have an emergency care team in every day for six weeks which enabled her to get back on her feet and walk with the aid of a frame.

She formed a good relationship with the care team whose specific aim was to encourage mobility over the 6-week plan. Mum built up a good relationship with each of them enjoying their company, and they, her sense of humour and undemanding nature..

At the end of six weeks, they approached Mum to take part in a video which was to be used to advertise their flagship emergency care team, across the country. Mum gave a definite 'No' but would be happy to give her views the following day.

Next morning I was surprised to walk in and see Mum in makeup, wearing earrings, nails painted and a lovely scarf at her neck. "You've changed your mind then", I commented. "Well, they've been lovely to me, so I decided to agree. And I'm going to watch the video".

Showing no nerves she praised and thanked the team for getting her back on her feet and made amusing comments. She finished with, "Wait and see, I will be doing my own cleaning and shopping". And she did.

Unfortunately, another fall in 2014 left her immobile and needing 24-hour care. For a few months she lived in a nearby care home. She never got over the loss of her home and seemed to decide that she didn't want to go on, gradually withdrawing from life.

She stopped going into the communal lounge, then using her armchair preferring to stay in bed. She'd been an avid sport and horseracing fan all her life but lost interest and stopped reading or watching television.

This feisty mother who'd enjoyed her family and social life to the full had determined her own future and left

June Antoinette Necchi

the world in the way she'd chosen, just a few months later.

June Antoinette Necchi

It took a while for us to realise that life would never be the same without her, her dedication to her family, her sense of fun and the meal so she served up. She was the matriarch of the family, the Queen Bee and will always be missed and remembered with love.

June Antoinette Necchi

My mother wartime photo 1990 1

My Mother at 74

Chapter 22
EXPERIENCES

ERIC

One day while walking in the high street I was approached by a man who enquired, "Are you the local artist?". I had never seen him, before but clearly he knew of me. "Well, yes, I am but why do you ask?". "I wonder if you would be prepared to give me oil painting lessons. I would especially like to learn how to paint portraits".

A day and a time were agreed. It was to be after he finished work at his office nearby where Eric worked as an architect. This was a difficult time in my life as I had given up my job as an art teacher in a prison, a few miles away, to care for my daughter who had been diagnosed with a terminal illness. After she passed away I had taken over day care of my two young grandsons, and only when their father was home from work in the evenings was I able to give limited private lessons from home. I was pleased to take another student to help boost my income.

The following Monday, I was prepared for the arranged lesson which I was to give in my conservatory, after I had given my grandsons their

June Antoinette Necchi

dinner. When Eric arrived, I had already decided that it was not a good idea for him to plunge straight into oil painted portraits. "Eric, why not spend time discovering skin tones before you start oil painting? I think you will enjoy experimenting with pastels first. You can easily remove them by rubbing out if you are not happy with the colours. They are less daunting, and a sympathetic medium".

At the end of the hour-long lesson, I was impressed at how quickly he had produced some excellent skin tones even though I had only given him a summary demonstration beforehand. "I rather like these pastels" was Eric's first comment. "Ok, why not try out your first portrait in pastels, then?" He agreed, asking, "What materials should I bring along for next week?" "Don't worry, it will just be a taster so no need to buy new materials, so in case you find you are not keen, after all, and you may like to paint in oils instead".

One of the things that never fails to excite me is when at the end of the first lesson my student is enthusiastic and believes that it has opened the door into a fascinating new discovery and can't wait for the next stage of the journey.

I wasn't surprised when Eric arrived early for his lesson the following week. I'd laid pastels and pastel paper out on the table in readiness for his first subject of a young girl. It was a subtle picture with delicate facial shadows, and blonde hair tied in a ponytail with a blue ribbon.

June Antoinette Necchi

I asked him to select colours from the pastels which he would use for the portrait, and to set them aside. He clearly showed a strong sense of colour and was enjoying selecting the appropriate skin tones. He settled down to sketch in a light charcoal drawing of the young girl and when satisfied, began tentatively placing colour on the face. He needed only a little monitoring. He was a natural.

At his next lesson he had completed the portrait and breathed a sigh of relief. I held it at a distance for him to take an objective view. A smile spread across his face, and he commented, "I can't believe I've done that!". "And so, Eric, your journey of discovery has begun. It will prove to be exciting, frustrating and maybe obsessional. But I'm sure you wouldn't miss it for the world. It will open your eyes to the wonder of all that is around you and enable you to see things everywhere with new eyes as though through the eyes of a child. You will never again fail to see the dappled light falling around the trees in a sunlit wood, or the way that shadows and sun give life to paintings".

I had been teaching for some time and was aware that the relationship between teacher and student develops to quite a personal level based on their mutual interest, and a female teacher can become the innocent object of affection for a male student with a certain intimacy developing with sharing minds. Knowing this I was always careful to retain a teacher/ student relationship in my classes especially the one-to-one sessions. Eric was the perfect gentleman who did retain that distance.

One evening some months later, a close friend, Paula, arrived at my front door bringing with her the French student teacher who was staying at her house for a year. I too had a French student teacher, Sylvie, staying at my house, and a friendship had formed between the two young women.

I opened the door to my friend who was in tears. Her French student looked on sympathetically. "Can I come in?, asked Paula "Oh, look, I'm in the middle of a lesson. Maybe you can come back a little later?". "Please, June, I must come in. I'm so upset". This was typical of my friend who generally announced herself with a drama, however bizarre. "Ok, then. But take a seat in the sitting room and I'll be with you as Soon as my lesson's finished."

Once inside her sobs grew louder, her deep voice, carrying some distance as though on stage, had obviously been heard by Eric waiting in the conservatory for his lesson. Torn between consoling my friend, and returning to Eric's lesson, I was surprised to hear a knock at the connecting kitchen door. It was Eric, tentatively peering from the doorway. He asked, "Is everything alright, June?. Should I go?". To my embarrassment my friend answered saying, "Please don't go! June needs the money". Not content with that she went on to say, "June's told me all about you and how handsome you are". I had never said that, but my friend was really in theatrical mode now, and heaven knows what she would come out with next. Eric turned to me rather sheepishly at this 'revelation', his sweet smile

June Antoinette Necchi

indicating that he had no idea of my admiration for him. This was no time for denial so and not knowing

June Antoinette Necchi

what my friend would invent next; I asked Eric if he and Sylvie would go into the kitchen and make a cup of tea for us all..

The lesson recommenced after the tea was finished. Later, I settled down to go over the events of the last couple of hours. Sylvie said to me, "June, what is it about English people? When there's a crisis the answer always seems to be, "Let's have a cup of tea"'

It was only recently that I reminded my friend, Paula, of what she had said to Eric, and asked why she had said that all those years ago. "I thought he'd like to hear that"; she replied. Despite Paula's personal comment to Eric, which could have complicated the student teacher relationship Eric remained the perfect gentleman

My student Eric's pastel of my mother

June Antoinette Necchi

COLONNATO

The Lardo Mission.

Lardo! My Italian daughter in law became excited when I told her that I had booked a holiday in Pietrasanta just a few miles from Carrara in Italy. "Please would you bring some lardo back from Colonnato a village in the marble mountains of Carrara?"

I admit that I had never heard of lardo so I set about finding out more about it, and discovered that it is a type of salami made by curing strips of fat from the back of a pig, with rosemary, and other herbs and spices.

The most famous lardo is from Colonnato where it has been made since Roman times, and traditionally cured for months in basins made from marble from its mountains.

With three friends I booked a holiday in Pisa, a train ride from Carrara.

In bright sunshine we made our way to the station, rucksacks packed with lunches for the day out. From the station in Carrara a bus took us to the centre where we caught an old mountain bus to taking us up to the village where a halfway stop was made at a marble workshop. We bought the usual tourist memorabilia of

June Antoinette Necchi

wine bottle stops, olive dishes and key tags before setting off for Colonnato along the steep incline.

June Antoinette Necchi

We had failed to check the weather forecast, and found ourselves in a mountain deluge, the marble dust on the tracks, now sodden, and throwing up sprays of marble dust as the lorries drove by.

By now, unsuitably dressed in sandals and summer tops, we resorted to shielding our head with plastic carrier bags.

It was at this point that I said, "Let's forget it girls, with no village in sight I can't expect you to go any further".

I was surprised when they told me, "No! we're on a mission to find that lardo so we must keep going!"

Maybe 15 minutes later, rounding a bend, there in the distance we could see the roof tops of the ancient village!

There we found Colonnato, it's tiny piazza with a statue of a fallen hero and tiny houses along arched alleyways.

The view from the piazza was breathtaking! The summits of a range of marble mountains glistened in the sun which had just broken through. Were we on top of the world!

But where was the famed lardo? Hidden amongst the houses was one whose front window displayed the lardo! We had made it! And what an adventure it had been, and what memories it had given to us.

June Antoinette Necchi

In the airport on the way home, wandering around the airport shop, we spotted packs of lardo! We couldn't believe it, but all agreed that the memory of our mission could never be replaced with an airport shop purchase of the famed lardo.

THE CHINESE MOTHER MAI

I received an unusual request one day from the secretary of the local International School whose students were placed with me from time to time. It seemed that the mother of one of the younger pupils was flying from Hong Kong to see how her son was settling in and wished to stay in a private home or guest house close to the school. I was told that she didn't speak English, so I knew I would have to rely on hand and body language if I wanted to communicate with her.

Mai arrived at my door in a beautifully tailored outfit and immaculately styled hair. She had two pieces of luxury luggage and looked as though she had stepped from the pages of a high fashion magazine. We engaged by smiling widely at each other. I spread my arms in an inviting attitude and using my 'follow me' gestures, I led her to her bedroom, a twin-bedded room with its own staircase.

I had taken great care in choosing feminine touches when I knew that I was expecting a female guest. The effect of the matching embroidered bed linen and curtains, as well as the delicate vase of fresh flowers on a bedside table, created a welcoming atmosphere. Mai appeared pleased with it.

June Antoinette Necchi

Later, she had a meal at a nearby Chinese restaurant and retired early, obviously suffering from jetlag.

June Antoinette Necchi

The next morning, she clearly demonstrated that she would like me to go out with her so I thought that a nearby quaint coffee house would provide her with an insight into English culture, albeit a fading one! The black dress, the starched white apron and the white headdress of the waitress must have made quite an impression on Mai who politely accepted her drink. All ok, so far I thought to myself, but with half an hour or so to share our coffee I wondered what conversation would be possible? Then Mai surprised me. From her fine leather wallet, she produced a small photograph which she thrust into my hand. It was a photograph of a man. Since Mai had arrived at my home she had not uttered a single word of English but now unexpectedly announced, "Man. Divorce."

Needing to make a response I tried to shape the expressions on my face into a series of questions - When? Why? Etc. Understanding each other as only women can regardless of any language barrier, Mai managed to convey to me her pleasure at being divorced and her low opinion of her ex-husband.

And so began our nonverbal relationship that was to last the two weeks of her stay in England. By some means she let me know that she had her own business, apparently in the property market, and the quality of her clothes, jewellery and luggage indicating that she must be reasonably wealthy.

She easily developed a routine, shopping in the mornings, visiting her son's school later, and a siesta

June Antoinette Necchi

between 4 and 6, after which she went to the same Chinese restaurant staying until the end of the evening.

About a week into her stay a call came from a man who was coming into the area to supervise extensive motorway maintenance 5 or 6 miles from my home and wanting to know if I would have a room available in the coming weeks. I assured him that a room (Mai's) would be available soon.

A request from him to come and have a look at the room that evening couldn't be refused, so when he suggested 5 pm I agreed knowing that I would somehow have to uproot Mai from her room, from her siesta, for my potential guest to have a look.

At 4.45 I knocked on the door to Mai's private staircase and a few minutes later she appeared at the top, sleepy. I beckoned her to come downstairs. She looked at me with a blank expression on her face and remained at the top of the stairs until I beckoned her down, more furiously this time........ I had little time before the new guest arrived.

Indicating the digit 5 on my watch and using one of only two English words she knew, "man", I pointed upstairs gesticulating a sleeping mode by cupping my palms together against my cheek and at the same time closing my eyes and faking sleep. Mai looked a little bemused but nevertheless came down into the sitting room to wait for the arrival of the 'man'. I greeted him at the door as he arrived on time and took him up to

June Antoinette Necchi

Mai's room which he booked for the week after her departure. I breathed a sigh of relief that a potentially awkward situation had been neatly avoided......

That evening Mai invited me to join her at her favourite Chinese restaurant where she had formed a relationship with the owner who greeted us, eager to serve tasty food from her menu.

Shortly after she and Mai engaged in what appeared to be a serious conversation, a look of consternation crossed Mai's face as she began talking quickly and anxiously. The owner turned to me saying that Mai was worried about something. "What's that?" I asked. Can I help?" "Mai understands that there is a man who is going to share her bedroom, and sleep in the other bed". So much for my body and hand language! I had failed to convey to Mai that the 'man' was only approving of the room, and only when she left would he move in!

The two weeks of her stay came to an end and as we gave each other a fond, farewell hug, she said, "Hong Kong!" and gestured that I would visit and stay with her. "Thank you". I replied.

Later, thinking about the whole encounter, I realised that despite Mai's anxieties about the prospect of a male bedroom companion she hadn't packed her bags post haste and found alternative accommodation……!

PETER

Are you the art lady? "Large dark brown soulful eyes stared out of an angular face. A mop of thick black hair

June Antoinette Necchi

and an almost ludicrous gaucho moustache all combined

June Antoinette Necchi

to surprise me. Peter standing over 6 feet tall and with an athletic frame looked the picture of good health and fitness. He was wary, now, standing back, letting his mother speak for him. "Peter's been drawing for years, always animals, but now he wants to do something different, and use oil paints too".

I asked to see some of his drawings which Peter carefully reached from a portfolio on the other side of the room. They were all large 30"by 20", and, yes, they were all animals, mainly of the big cat family. Though the colours drawn with coloured pencils were crude and flat the pictures had been painstakingly drawn and showed his love of wildlife.

Today though, the picture he wanted to copy was of a Cornish seascape It was a wild scene with gigantic waves crashing against menacing looking rocks beneath a threatening sky. Each year the family spent weeks at a time in their large mobile home sited close to the Cornish coast where Peter had developed a love of the sea, and its coastline, in all its seasons, and now wanted to capture it in oil paints.

It was a superb subject, but the precision of Peter's animal drawings and the loose brush strokes needed to paint the seascape in front of us, contrasted sharply. My heart sank. It was a challenging painting even for someone well practised. I was uncertain how he would cope with the pressure of a change of direction in his paintings, and the use of oil paints. For a beginner who

June Antoinette Necchi

had done only structured drawings it seemed impossible,

even setting to one side his learning difficulties that his mother had described when first she phoned me. "Peter had a brain haemorrhage as a six-month-old baby which triggered severe epilepsy, and later, problems with learning." She hoped that private tuition would enable him to improve his skills and widen his interest in art. Knowing this I set about demonstrating how to mix oil colours, take care of brushes and make the first steps in preparation for a painting. He enjoyed this, listening earnestly and working quietly.

At the end of the second session, with the rock shapes and horizon drawn in, I suggested that he paint in the light and shadowed areas as an underpainting for the rock forms. Encouraging him to try his hand at these effects created problems for both him, and me. He tentatively tried to follow instructions to use contrasting tones to give the rocks structure, to achieve a 3-dimensional effect, but he was lost. The subtleties of form are notoriously difficult to reproduce but for Peter it was beginning to look impossible, and I was concerned that he might be losing confidence.

My teaching methods had always involved sharing my enthusiasm and ideas with students as well as having a strong social aspect. I found that challenges, however small, focused interest and opened doors to confidence and skill building. I was already concerned that this was a challenge that Peter would not be able to meet

When Peter's mother had initially contacted me I had looked forward to having the opportunity to help him develop what talents he might have. It was not going to be 'special' teaching to a student with learning difficulties but a journey overcoming obstacles along the way, thereby lessening the fears of them. It would be a journey of discovery. Each student has his or her own pace and I hoped to tune into Peter's pace of learning, and in doing so, help him to move forward.

Now, attempting to teach a flamboyant style of brushwork to create the wildness in nature in the sea and the sky, we were both held back by his naturally precise approach and the ensuing insecurity of leaving it behind.

That evening, I left his house aware that I could not press him into a style that was not his. But what was the alternative? The next morning, I paid a visit to the art section of my local library and discovered a book which I could hardly wait to show Peter. It was an oversized beautifully illustrated book of paintings of polar bears in their natural habitat. There was page after page of these lovely creatures, each one demonstrating the painter's infatuation with the bears. I was elated. Here was a man who was quite single minded about his choice of subject, repeatedly painting the polar bear and clearly never tiring of it, seeming to me that each painting revived his interest The conversation I had with Peter in the lessons had been dominated by his obsession with the big cats, describing in endless details the coat markings of the various breeds.

June Antoinette Necchi

At his house a few days later, I announced my arrival by simply putting the polar bear book into his hands. I watched intently as he turned the pages, stopping only to study the details of the fur and the natural settings in which the bears had been painted. He was entranced. I explained, "Peter, if this painter can spend his entire life painting these animals he loves then you can do the same! Let's start now!"

"I'll never be able to paint the sea anyhow", he said.

Now I had my direction and could lead Peter along a road that had no ending. I explained, "First, I'll show you how to do grid drawing to get the shapes of the animals exact, then we'll learn how to make the coats gleam and show off their markings. There's a lot to do come on, Peter!"

Peter entered the spirit of it enthused by the idea of reproducing his favourite cats, and in the process learned more about art.

As the weeks went by he grew more confident with his drawing and at the same time revealed a character that was sensitive and funny. We developed a good working relationship, each week sharing our ideas for his work as well as mine. We were artists together and Peter loved to spend his time talking about tones and techniques. He was very respectful but teasing me sometimes confirming that he was at ease with me. His mother was a constant companion serving tea and giving me updates on family news, so we too became friends.

June Antoinette Necchi

Peter spent 3 days a week at a local centre for people with various disabilities and always took his drawings along with him. After some months he came home one day saying that one of the carers wanted him to paint her cat.

That was the beginning for Peter and the commissions began to grow. As one was completed he often had another waiting. Peter had started to make decisions for himself.

He decided to paint a picture of the centre's old dog and to present it to the manager. He was very proud to see it hanging in a place of importance there.

His communication skills improved as he was always happy to talk about his pictures, show them to anyone around as well as to give them away. As his confidence grew so did his popularity lessening his sense of isolation which had been quite marked when first I met him. His increased knowledge of how to achieve the effects he wanted enabled him to accept commissions for other animals, cats, dolphins and eagles. His store of pictures grew as he worked daily on them.

About 2 years later I suggested that he might like to have an exhibition, not as a commercial venture, but simply to exhibit his works for public viewing in the local library.

Nervous at first he asked his mother what she thought and when she readily took up the idea, Peter was happy to agree. The 'exhibition' now became the focus of his attention. There was an air of excitement in Peter's

June Antoinette Necchi

house for weeks before the exhibition was due to begin.

June Antoinette Necchi

The whole family became involved in their various ways, proud that Peter was using his talents, and it became a project for them all. They were delighted to support him. They bought and made frames for his canvases, planned an opening mini ceremony, and contacted the local press.

A flurry of activity led up to the opening day. The paintings were hung and rehung as we tried to achieve the right balance. At last, they were all in place and satisfied that we had got it right we opened the door to local visitors. The steady stream showed their appreciation of Peter's skills, the Press arrived taking photographs of him standing alongside his paintings, and we all toasted him, and his one man show.

Peter, delighted in talking about the animals he loved, sharing his knowledge of their habits and habitats with those who'd come to see his paintings. His parents stood to one side watching with pride their son who had achieved so much despite a disadvantaged beginning.

That day, Peter was acknowledged as a talented painter whose artistic views were valued not only by his family and his social circle, but by those who had visited his exhibition. He seemed to grow in stature as his confidence grew and I felt that this young man had come a long way since the day we had first met, and he had expressed a wish to paint.

June Antoinette Necchi

Chapter 23

PONTREMOLI ADVENTURE

I should have accepted the offer of a lift to the train station by my hosts on that wet, windy and overcast day in Pontremoli, Italy. Travelling from Pisa earlier in the day I was on a mission to find more about my Italian heritage. Research had revealed that Pontremoli, in the Tuscan area of Italy was the home of a doctor with my family name, and I had his address. Maybe he would fill in some of my ancestry gaps….

With a local map in my hands, I headed for the distant hills close to the address I was searching for. The impressive house, its balconies spilling out trailing flowers, stood in large grounds. It seemed strange to have come so far to see a nameplate engraved with my family name. 'Dottore Luciano Necchi' The doorbell's response was a woman's voice asking who I was. My response was "Signora Necchi da Londra". There followed an invitation to join her on the first floor. There, with us both speaking in broken English and Italian, I heard more about the family history.

Her father-in-law had sailed with my grandfather from Italy in the early 1900's, and together opened a

June Antoinette Necchi

restaurant in Villiers Street London. After the Depression in the 1920's her father-in-law returned to Pontremoli where he opened a restaurant overlooking the river.

I was happy to decline a lift to the station as I was keen to take a different way down to the main road, an opportunity to get to know the town better. Maybe 25 minutes later it began to dawn on me that the route was rather longer than the one I'd taken when leaving the station and peering through the rain it seemed there was no end to the road.

Dusk was falling, it was a Sunday, and I assumed that the locals were home for the night, and no one to ask for directions. I admit to a rising panic, and made up my mind to stop the first vehicle that came along.

A large army vehicle carrying troops rounded the bend, I took a deep breath, ran into the middle of the road waving my hands. They greeted me with smiling faces while waving and responded to my question, "Dove la stazione?" (where is the station?) What a relief! At least I now knew the way. Apparently the road had gone off at a sharp angle taking me a mile or more off course.

Arriving at the station I'd missed the train and had a two hour wait. Bedraggled and hungry, I spotted a lit-up coffee shop across from the station and headed straight for it. Through the low lighting and heavy cigarette smoke I realised this was a man's bar, typical in Italy where they gather to play cards, smoke and

June Antoinette Necchi

socialise. I had a choice to make, a two hour wait in an isolated station, or overcome my nerves, stay in the men's bar and order a coffee. I had no option but to strike up conversation with the males who I suspect didn't quite know how to handle this situation, and who stood silent when I was at the bar. A handful of them responded as we exchanged conversation. My limited Italian saved the day.

Was this the first time a female had crossed this threshold, I wondered, since these old coffee shops are the hideouts for males of the older generation whose daily pleasure is playing cards, smoking and drinking?

MY LITTLE ESCAPEE

When I received the results from my doctor that I was pregnant with my third child I was thrilled. Already with a son and daughter, aged 10 and 7, I naively anticipated that my new baby would share with its brother and sister their same temperament, and same sleeping patterns. Wrong!

My first two babies were textbook babies, so why wouldn't my third be? I must admit my surprise when at 7 months, Matthew, insisted on standing up in his cot at bedtime, flatly refusing to lay down. I had already made concessions. His siblings had, uncomplainingly, been put down to sleep each night at 7, but allowing for different sleeping patterns, baby number three was given one and a half hour's 'furlough'. 8.30 seemed to me a reasonable extension of time for this lively little one. Despite this, the noisy

June Antoinette Necchi

protestations coming from his bedroom couldn't be ignored and my maternal instincts responded by going backwards and forwards, offering a dummy, a cuddle, but to no avail.

Having tucked him in for the umpteenth time, before I reached the bedroom door he was standing up again. For greater effect he developed the ritual of continually banging his head against the cot. This was a bit like a game of chess....my move next. So, I padded the edges of his cot with cushions bound around with a pair of tights to prevent him hurting himself. I quickly realised, though, that he was, in effect, in a padded cell!

My weekly visit to the baby clinic would surely come up with an answer. They did. "He's hyperactive. Put his name down for a nursery as soon as possible". No fear! The mother hen in me rejected this advice out of hand.

Clearly, baby number three had his own agenda which by day was fine. With his brother and sister in school he and I became daytime companions. He was a fun, adventurous baby who couldn't wait to walk. So, from 10 months old he'd scamper down the garden, dig in the sand pit, then bored, would try to burrow under the fence.

One day, I panicked when he was nowhere to be seen in the garden. Surely he hadn't scaled the fence! And then to my great relief a smiling little dusty face peered from the coal bunker.

June Antoinette Necchi

His biggest dash for freedom came when, again missing from the garden at the age of three, I spotted him running down the middle of our busy road, a packet clutched in his hand. I kicked off my shoes to make the most of my sprint after him, chasing down the road. His feet must have had wings because I couldn't catch up with him. Lorry drivers seeing this woman, barefooted, arms flailing, running down the middle of the road, had no idea that I was trying to prevent the little figure, disappearing into the distance, from being run over. Just before the bridge, Matthew, turned into the left which is where I caught up with him....in the office of the local Waterworks yard sharing out the biscuits from the pack he had been clutching.

I knew then that this was going to be a very interesting journey with child number three. And it has been.

CEDRIC'S SECRET LIFE

Cynthia heard the key turn in the lock of the front door. She glanced at her watch. Half past ten. Cedric was home late tonight.

Ever since he had decided to have a dog, a few years earlier, Cedric had made a habit of leaving the house at 8 o'clock in the evenings to walk Monty across the nearby fields.

Cedric was a stickler for routine, and it had begun to pervade all areas of his life.... his time keeping was faultless arriving on the stroke of 9 at his office each morning. Strange really, Cynthia thought, as he was his own boss, running a successful telecommunications company. He had no need to go in early, if at all, some mornings.

Predictably, his appearance was always smart with his bespoke suits, Saville Row silk shirts, quality ties and leather shoes. Cynthia was bemused when she saw both men and women show Cedric a certain deference as though he was a man of substance and status. Cynthia was thinking that a little vanity in a man wasn't a bad thing, but Cedric was taking it too far with his nightly trawling of the internet searching for prestigious shirt and suit makers. Maybe his time would be better employed by nurturing his relationship with her.....

She was increasingly irritated by Cedric's focus on his self-image. It really was getting out of hand. Concentrate on the positives she told herself.... he's a good provider and a faithful husband.

Cedric shuffled into the lounge looking flustered and dishevelled. "Good heavens, what on earth is the matter?", Cynthia exclaimed. "What's wrong, what's happened?". "I don't want to tell you about what's wrong", he replied, anxiously.

"Look, sit down and I'll make you a nice cup of tea then you can tell me what it is you don't want to talk about.". "Now", Cynthia said, "What is it you don't want to tell me about?" Cedric took another sip of tea and blurted out, "I've been seeing another woman for years. Ever since we had Monty. She walks her dog, too". Cynthia's face was expressionless. "You mean you have a dog walker mistress?" "Yes, and I'm glad

June Antoinette Necchi

you know now". "Well, Cedric. I think we had better sleep on this. It's late now. I'm going to bed to think about what you have just told me".

The next morning it was as though nothing had happened and Cedric, as well coordinated as usual, went off to his office.

Cynthia made another coffee before reaching for her dressmaking scissors from the cupboard. Upstairs, opening Cedric's dressing room doors she was momentarily impressed by the array of his fine suits and shirts. She understood why Cedric created such an impression wherever he went, and whoever he met. One by one she removed the suits and shirts from their hangers and laid them on the bed. She began, expertly, to remove the sleeves by carefully cutting along the seams and the trousers to knee length. A smile crossed her face as she mused that at least Cedric would be pleased with her precise, even professional, dissecting of the sleeves.

She was surprised to find that the pieces filled two bin liners...In the garage she took down a large tin of white gloss paint and eased the lid a little.

With the boot of her car loaded with the bin bags, and the paint, she drove to Cedric's business premises whose plate glass windows overlooked the parking area. She could see Cedric's pride and joy, his gleaming black Mercedes.

Parking her own car alongside, Cynthia took out the contents of the boot, placing them carefully on the

June Antoinette Necchi

ground, then removed the paint lid. The white paint fell in blobs onto Cedric's car's bonnet then dribbled down the wings and lights as Cynthia upended the bin liners contents onto the paint covered bonnet creating what Cynthia, a talented artist, thought was an interesting collage.

Mission completed and with a look of smug satisfaction she spotted Cedric through her rear mirror, his arms flailing as he ran after her. She mused as she drove away that revenge is best served on a cold dish.....

AMNESTY

At the end of Mass one Sunday morning, I was idly looking through the week's Church news' sheet when my eye was caught by the following.

'There will be a meeting of Amnesty International on Thursday of this week to form a group of supporters in the local area. Would you like to come along?'

This had instant appeal for me as I had always wanted to know exactly how International Amnesty worked to release religious or political prisoners of conscience.

Arriving at the meeting there were probably 2 or 3 dozen in the audience and 3 speakers. I was fascinated to hear of the dedication of its members in the cause of supporting and releasing those imprisoned for their beliefs. I had gone along, curious to know how the system works, and to possibly help by writing letters to heads of governments, prisons etc., to pressurise them into reconsidering the imprisonment of these individuals

as letters of protest are at the heart of the work that Amnesty International do. I was therefore surprised when during the usual routine of electing individuals for certain roles I found my name being suggested as Media person. Despite me shaking my head, it was seconded by another, much to my dismay. I asked the panel what duties this role would bring and was told that I would represent Amnesty when required for interviews for TV, radio or the Press.

"Oh,, I couldn't possibly do that", I said, "I'm more of a back-room person but will happily write reams of letters if necessary".

Unhesitatingly, the speaker informed me, 'Don't worry. Only when a prisoner is released would you be interviewed, and we haven't even got our own prisoner yet. It will be a year at least before we have one".

"That's fine then. I'll happily accept that role".

I then settled into hearing about the case of a released prisoner, released because of the letters written by Amnesty International.

The prisoner, a husband and father, imprisoned because of his religious beliefs had become a non-person in prison, was simply a number, no name and no clothes of his own. He had been imprisoned for some years when letters from Amnesty began to arrive to the Governor and Heads of State. It was several hundred letters later that he was given his name back,

June Antoinette Necchi

and finally his own clothing. In time he was released and left his country for the UK where he was reconciled with his wife and children and settled in London.

I left the meeting in awe of what had been achieved by peaceful negotiating means and looked forward to being part of that letter writing.

I vaguely remembered a mention at that meeting that the twenty-fifth anniversary of the inception of Amnesty International was coming up soon but didn't connect that fact with a phone call I had from local radio 3 or 4 weeks later.

The caller said, "I understand that you are the Media representative for Amnesty International" "That's correct", I told him.

He went on to say, "As it is the twenty fifth anniversary of Amnesty we are doing a live program on Sunday and would like you to come along for a discussion".

"Oh, I can't possibly do that as I am a very new member with no experience".

"That will be no problem for you as the area member Dr. X will be leading the discussion. There will also be another member there, too".

Still unsure, there didn't seem to be a good reason not to attend. "Ok. Can you tell me where and what time then, please?"

Having accepted the invitation, in other words having committed myself to making an appearance, an

June Antoinette Necchi

unexpected phone call 48 hours before the program was

to go on air threw me into a quandary. "Mrs Necchi we are looking forward to you appearing on our program raising the awareness of Amnesty International but just to let you know of a minor change. Doctor X, the area leader, has unfortunately fallen sick and is unable to attend. Nevertheless, I can assure you that the program is still going ahead.".

"Oh, dear, I'm quite worried now as I have scant knowledge or experience of Amnesty, nor do I like public speaking".

He tried to reassure me saying, "As I told you a few days ago there is nothing to worry about as another representative will be there".

How could I refuse and leave a lone interviewee at the radio station? Gird up your loins and go for it, I told myself.

I had to have a plan of action! Write a script for myself and take it along to the studio just in case I was asked for a few words.

It was a miserable rainy, and windswept evening as I arrived at the radio station, a gaunt solitary house shrouded by trees at the end of a long driveway. It could have been the setting for a ghost or horror movie.

The door opened automatically in response to my bell but there was no sign of life in the stark reception hall. The eerie silence was broken by the shrill sound of a telephone on the desk ringing. It echoed around until I felt obliged to pick it up anticipating that it was my interviewer calling.

"Hello".

The voice at the other end.." D'ya know what the footie result was between Arsenal and Everton??"

"Sorry, I don't. Can you call back later?" Obviously as a local radio station the public expected that sports results were readily available to its listeners. I was only too happy in this spooky building to speak to another human, albeit one probably miles away.

Eventually a man appeared and asked me to follow him through narrow black painted passageways to a small studio at the top of the house. In the middle stood a black painted octagonal table with a series of microphones evenly attached around the edges.

Now a friend, who knew I was paranoid at the idea of coming face to face with a microphone, had reassured me that modern microphones are tiny and concealed on the skirting boards. Another fright or flight situation but no opportunity for flight now. I felt trapped in an upper dark chamber. A surreal situation.......but remembering the notes I'd made clutched in my trembling hand I took a seat at the table joined by the second guest who had just arrived.

I told him, "I'm so glad you made it as I'm a new member and not really the right person to be interviewed".

June Antoinette Necchi

He answered, "I've been a member for only 3 months".

We both fell silent, and as directed by the interviewer watched the enormous clock on the studio wall tick the minutes and seconds to the start of the interview. Quick as a flash I placed my notes on the table.

"Sorry, Mrs Necchi. Please don't use notes as it takes away the spontaneity".

As I watched the last seconds tick away I had some understanding of the prisoner awaiting the hangman......

The bright voice of the interviewer announced, "Can I introduce Mrs Necchi who has come along to speak to us on the 25th anniversary of Amnesty International. Mrs Necchi, can you tell the listeners why you joined Amnesty?"

All I could do was to speak from the heart, remembering how impressed I had been by the letter writing which had achieved the release of a prisoner.

I began. "I have been a member of Amnesty for a very short time but can relate to you why I decided to join." I repeated the story I had heard at the meeting about a prisoner of conscience who was held captive for years, and who after hundreds of letters, was released. I ended my piece by adding that, "The power of the pen is mightier than the sword."

Driving home I couldn't believe that I had survived what for me was an ordeal Maybe ridiculously, I had

June Antoinette Necchi

thought I might even have a heart attack in the studio, so it was

June Antoinette Necchi

with great relief that I went home to my two waiting sons. Expecting those to be equally relieved for me, I walked in the house saying, "Well, was I alright?"

The boys, engrossed in a TV programme, looked up absentmindedly, "Sorry Mum we forgot to listen"…..

A DREARY SUNDAY AFTERNOON

The dreary overcast Sunday afternoon trip out to search for a recently converted barn into a craft centre, somewhere in the countryside close to my home was rapidly turning into a wild goose chase. My sons in the car were impatient to return home.

In the village lane nearby, bent over with a pooper scooper, accompanied by an ageing Labrador dog, was the frail, quaint looking figure of an elderly woman. Now, completely lost in our search for the newly established craft centre, I stopped my car and opened the window to enquire about the way. A friendly, intelligent and effusive response from the lady invited me into her house nearby to check with the Directory Enquiries phone line for the recently opened craft centre.

Her house, maybe three or four hundred years old, appeared imposing and incongruous, surrounded as it was by large detached modern houses. Its appearance was grey and gaunt. The stately, old gates shut behind us with a bang and were locked…..suggesting a finality. The grounds of the house spread out before me with a miscellany of small straggling rockeries, potted

June Antoinette Necchi

plants in disarray, an assortment of ivies rambling over faded garden sculptures, with trees and shrubs dissected by an endless bower stretching the length of the grounds and trained to create a piece of Nature's architecture. A dusty weathered hayloft and run down garden buildings were surrounded by abandoned agricultural machinery. Everywhere I looked were winding paths, trickling water features and curiosities, all overgrown.

My attention was attracted to the woman's persistent command, "Come here, Robert, come here!".

Robert, a heavy old tabby cat ambled up and nuzzled his mistress's legs. Turning towards the house, she beckoned me saying, "Follow me. Follow me".

Inside the scullery, what could have been the first gas stove ever made, stood against one wall on a floor of quarry tiles with a scrubbed top table against the other. The entire scullery was devoid of any modern equipment, large or small.

Excitedly, my newly acquired companion demonstrated the use of the antique bread oven built into a wall at the side of the inglenook fireplace. Pointing to a tiny window above the oven which looked onto a clock face on a nearby church, she said, "See, they would time the bread by checking by that clock over there!".

I was fascinated by this world I had stepped into as the gates had slammed shut behind me, and by this lady who was so eager to share her home. I followed her

June Antoinette Necchi

through a door which opened on to a long, narrow vaulted-ceilinged room, its wall dotted with yellowed photographs, large dark oil painted canvases, and framed needlepoint embroideries. At the table at which some 20 antique chairs were set was a dazzling array of dishes, serving bowls, cut glass, gleaming cutlery with candelabras lining the centre of the long table.

This centuries old building and its contents had combined to place me in a past era, and its table setting with an expectation of guests about to arrive to be served a meal, resembling a banquet. The owner encouraged me to follow her through a low arched tunnel-like a hallway linked to a larger reception hall. She stopped briefly to point up to a hidden original salt cupboard set in the wall at eye level, "That's where we keep our valuables!".

The three imposing and elegant doors leading off were closed, while a small, recessed area was cluttered with tumbling books and a telephone. This genteel and charming lady pointed to the phone saying, "There you are, check the Directory Enquiries"

On enquiring I was told that the number of the new Craft centre had not yet been listed as the business had only recently opened. Now I was back to square one, so I thanked the owner for offering to help me.

"Come on, come on I'll show you more", this lady commanded, and began walking up a magnificent, panelled staircase leading to a spacious landing with doors on either side. She opened one of the doors revealing what could only be a laboratory crammed

June Antoinette Necchi

with instruments, test tubes and mountains of paperwork. At

this point she informed me that she was a retired optical consultant and her husband, a radiologist, whose eyes had been adversely affected by his work with radium.

I couldn't help but think that this dreary Sunday distraction was becoming more fascinating by the minute....

As we climbed a narrow staircase to an upper floor, open doors revealed furniture, artefacts and more books stacked on floors.

How much further, I wondered, and what exactly were her reasons for this protracted journey? I must admit a little shudder of anxiety remembering the heavy gates which had closed with a resounding noise behind me....and then of being beckoned into an inner sanctum.

One reads some weird things. Could this be one of those?

Why on earth do I need to be taken to the top of this centuries old house? Hadn't we already established that there was no telephone number, or even an address for the craft centre?

Well, I thought, philosophically, I will soon find out..

An open heavy ornate door was at the end of the winding landing, and I could see from where I stood that the far wall was lined with bookshelves, and in front of them a huge antique bed. On a table under a

June Antoinette Necchi

window to the left of the room was a comprehensive selection of breakfast cereals Standing in the doorway I looked around and saw an extensive range of 'things', dark furniture, artefacts, paintings and books scattered across the floor. And then my eyes came to rest on a tall, hunch-backed figure of a man leant over an old carved desk littered with paraphernalia. Lost in concentration over a huge screen in front of him, this elderly man struck an imposing image.

A few minutes later, after an introduction by his wife they both became very animated pointing out their various antiques before leading me into the next room, a disproportionate room, high ceilinged and narrow.

"We have installed our own fire escape system from this window here as we are on the second floor and need to have means of getting out of the house if there is a fire down below. Let's show it to you!"

A ladder was in place beneath the small window over the wash basin and I was asked to climb up and look through to the heavy-duty rope ladder attached and hanging from the high outside wall. This was their only escape in the event of a fire! They assured me that they had tried it out by climbing out of the window above the sink and reaching the ground by means of the rope ladder!. I was astounded that this couple in their 70's had devised and were relaxed about using this means of escape, if necessary.

Moving the ladder in line with a loft opening they urged me to climb up in front of them. By now the whole experience had become surreal. I admit to

June Antoinette Necchi

asking myself would I get out of this alive …but did as they asked.

June Antoinette Necchi

The attic, several linking rooms running the width of the roof of this ancient house held memories of their lives, photographs, newspapers, coins, letters and all scattered about in strategic places, on beams, under beams, recording the many years that they had lived in the house.

By now I thought I was wandering through a never-ending dream....... yet there was more to come..

Back downstairs I was ushered into a far room whose walls were hung with more old paintings. This was clearly the activity room complete with billiard tables, bookshelves and half completed embroideries on stands, with pieces of antique furniture filling the spaces. The wallpaper and paint colours dated from previous eras as did the richly patterned threadbare carpet.

This remarkable couple, living an equally remarkable life in this old house, and insisted that I see one more room across the hall. Elegant, beautifully carved, gilded and embellished furniture filled the room with heavy dark drapes hung at the windows. The whole scene took my breath away, "This is an incredible collection", I told them. "All of these came from the Paris Exhibition of 1851", they replied, ending an intriguing tour of the house.

Finally on the way out I thanked them for their hospitality, for the fascinating experience, and for opening their doors to me, a perfect stranger. I told

June Antoinette Necchi

them that my sons, who were still waiting in the car for me, would love to have been here at which they promptly invited us back, with family, the next Sunday.

Returning a week later we were served a traditional afternoon tea in the kitchen, my sons were shown the old machinery in the garden, the Aladdin's cave of a house and told tales of the couple's careers when working in the medical world.

The entire experience had been easily exchanged for a visit to the craft centre...... I never did find that.

MISTER JOE

Throughout my time living in what was my third home, since my marriage, a variety of Polish ex-prisoners of war lived in the adjoining house. The original owner was someone who I came to know as Mister Joe.

His wartime experiences as a teenager had left him traumatised and fearful of 'the enemy' who he suspected lurked around every corner. This fear developed encompassing every area of his life.

He paid his mortgage monthly into the local bank, over the counter. but in time his suspicions grew about the honesty of the bank clerks he resolved it by walking 10 miles each month to a city bank.

When he could no longer cope with his suspicions he resolved it by selling his home to a resident fellow Pole, Peter, who when he got married was grateful to Mister Joe for remaining there to monitor the security of the house.

June Antoinette Necchi

Visiting him I would wait patiently while he unlocked the complicated locks he'd installed on the kitchen door.

It was only on one of these occasions that the extent of his trauma and phobia became painfully clear. In whispered tones he asked. "Did you hear those stones thrown at the roof last night? It was the enemy that came to find me. But I had locked all the doors".

I was overwhelmed with sadness for this man and what he had endured as a boy who had worked with his father on their farm when the Russians took him prisoner at the age of 17.

A few years later Jeannie arrived from Poland to become the wife of Peter, my next-door neighbour, a lovely lady who seemed happy to be in England but experiencing difficulties as she had no knowledge of the English language.

This became a problem, when later with two children, she needed advice about them. Fortunately, Mister Joe had a good command of English and was able to act as translator for Jeannie, when needed, often arriving at my door relaying questions from her. Having children of my own I was, of course, ahead of the game! I hoped that I could help.

Mister Joe was a very respectful man, always treating his requests with almost a political-like seriousness each time addressing me as 'Madame Prime Minister'!

June Antoinette Necchi

Answering the door one day, Mister Joe, looking very agitated, told me "Madame Prime Minister, please come quickly. Jeannie said her baby Peter is dead" I knew that the baby had been ill with bronchitis but with this news I hurried around next door where Jeannie was in tears.

Running into the bedroom all I could see was a huge duvet on the bed, no baby. I was filled with dread for what I was about to see. Jeannie pulled back the duvet only to see the baby's twinkling blue eyes looking up at me. Yes, his cheeks were very rosy, but wouldn't they be lying under the weight of the duvet in an overheated room?

Exchanging conversations with Mister Joe over the garden fence he'd often told me of his life back in Poland on his father's farm and of how one day he would like to have his own little piece of land in the country to grow his own vegetables and keep chickens. He told me that he would grow enough to take them to market, and this was an oft repeated dream of his. As welcome as he was made in Peter and Jeannie's household it was a far cry from the life he once had and which he longed for. Every day I could see this man aimlessly wandering about as though waiting for his life to change. But how?

And this is how I came to be studying the property advertisements where a cottage deep in the heart of Shropshire would perfectly mirror Mister Joe's young life.

A smile spread across Mister Joe's face as he read the advert and told me that he would like to see the

June Antoinette Necchi

property. A phone call to the agent quickly secured an appointment for a viewing but came with an apology that since he, the agent, was at a function that evening would we be able to pick him up from the venue and together drive to have a look at the cottage.

The agent himself was wearing a dinner suit and was very old Etonian, Mister Joe in his daily garb of heavy shapeless, dark, peasant like clothes, and ourselves, a young couple. This motley group squeezed in our little car painted a surreal picture.

We left the main roads behind driving through winding lanes until we reached a track about half a mile long. There at the end in absolute isolation stood a centuries old cottage surrounded by a piece of land whose perimeter wasn't clear due to odd bits of broken fencing. The cottage itself was almost medieval with small winding stone stairs leading to two tiny bedrooms. All the ceilings were wattle and daub with heavy oak beams. The kitchen, primitive with a brown stone sink, and an ancient gas stove.

Mister Joe appeared to be very happy and able to imagine himself living there, enthusiastically describing what vegetables he would grow, and where he would erect some chicken pens.

As this was to be a cash sale it should be an easy transaction which would have made the disruption to the agent's evening worthwhile, especially as this property would only attract few buyers. He was quietly confident as we got into the car to return him to his evening out, that was until Mister Joe suddenly said, 'I

June Antoinette Necchi

will buy a gun to kill the enemy when they try to rob me'. The agent looked aghast, and a little fearful. He quickly left the car with scarcely a backward look. Sadly, Mister Joe was unable to start a new life, too damaged by his past and realising that the only security he could cope with was living with the family who had in a sense become his family.

LIFE PAINTING

I had a call one day from a young man called Steve. He asked would I paint a picture of him to give to his girlfriend.

I said, "I'm happy to do that. The painting is head and shoulders, 20"x 16". Is that ok?"

"Actually, I want a full-length painting for her".

This was the first time I had been asked for a full-length, so I was curious as to why.

"Are you a military man or sportsman?"

No I'm a bodybuilder. I want this painting for my girlfriend's bedroom wall"

(I'm averse to pictures of body builders but this was business, so no option).

"Can you send me two or three photographs, then, please?"

"I would like to pose for the painting if that's ok with you".

June Antoinette Necchi

I tried to talk him out of that, but he was insistent, so, reluctantly, I gave in.

I was completely taken aback when he said, "I would like to pose in the nude. Would you be happy with that?".

With my eyes fixed firmly on my income, and as we know life painting is part of art, hesitating I said, "I'm not too sure".

(Funny how you can be taken along a conversation path, one which began with a request for a commission, and which had gradually turned into the possibility of a strange man named Steve, posing naked in my dining room).

And before I could say anymore there was another question "What will you be wearing, June?".

"Pardon !!!!"

"Well, I will be embarrassed if I'm the only one without clothes".

I think you will believe me when I tell you that I ended the conversation abruptly....

Now, each Saturday my mother would visit for a morning coffee, an enjoyable activity. The phone rang while we sat chatting.

Breathlessly, he said, "Hello June, this is Steve, I would like you to.................... There followed the most ridiculous crude suggestions as to who did what to the other.

I responded, "I've never heard anything so funny!".

That taught me a timely lesson.

The whole experience had been a learning curve for me carefully vetting clients before committing myself to commissions.

I remembered then that Steve had told me during his request that his girlfriend had finished with him and that he hoped to win her back with this painting!

THE LITTLE RED BEETLE

It was a rainy, cold night when I viewed the little red Beetle, and though it shuddered and rumbled at the owner's repeated turns of the key, I was not fazed, after all we all know that dreadful weather conditions can affect the performance of an ageing car. Not only that, but as the owner explained, the car had been standing unused for a while since his purchase of a replacement.

Now, I'm regarded in my circle as a pretty 'savvy' person but also as a bit of a romantic, so I chose to accept the explanations as I had always dreamt of owning a Beetle, and this one came with a price tag of only £500! There was a practical reason too. As my old banger which ferried myself and my niece, Maria, to our cleaning jobs in outlying villages, had given up the ghost that morning, we needed an immediate replacement.

June Antoinette Necchi

The Beetle advert in the evening newspaper seemed to be the answer to our predicaments so I happily handed over the cash and got behind the wheel..........I didn't realise how noisy these dear little cars were once on the road. Still, all part of the character of Beetles....

I was in for a shock when the morning light the next day revealed customised wheels on my dream car. How could I have missed these even in the gloom and rain of the night before? They were big and they were ugly, and so at odds with the little Beetle's image and character. Not only that, when I was behind the wheel it became a source of sniggers, and pointing fingers no doubt wondering why this grandmother had turned into a boy racer! Another surprise awaited me..... it guzzled petrol. Why had I assumed that a little car only needed little to 'drink'? This added expense was going to eat into mine and Maria's cleaning wages.

More was to come. Driving into a multi storey car park the Beetle came to a sudden halt. Getting out to check what was the problem, I found that the customised front bumper couldn't cope with the gradient of the entrance road. This car had now become a liability explaining why it had stood in a dry dock in its owner's garage for so long.

Well, I had no option but to hang onto it until I could find some young person who like me, was, or should I say, had been in love with Beetles, and could raise, say, £350 to take it off my hands.

I must admit that I was becoming increasingly nervous as to what I might discover was yet another problem with this hasty purchase. I didn't have to wait long....

One early evening I hastened to my front door answering loud knocking. My neighbour was frantically pointing to where I had parked the Beetle though I was unable to see it through clouds of blue smoke. My teenage son ran to the car, opened the door and partially disappeared inside. I ran after him pulling him out as he shouted, "Mum, it's on fire under the back seat!".

"Leave it!" I shouted, dragging him away.

Quick thinking neighbours had meanwhile called the emergency services with a fire engine and police car turning up in minutes.

Nearby neighbours were advised to not leave their homes until the fire was under control, but didn't seem to mind too much as they stood around in small groups discussing the potential dangers of car batteries under back seats, as well giving them a chance to get to know each other.

My little dream car had come to the end of its adventures and was destined for a car- graveyard.

Had I learned my lesson on car buying? I thought I had.

DOCTOR HARWOOD

"Doctor Harwood here", the voice briskly announced.

June Antoinette Necchi

I'm not sure why I was taken by surprise at this response to my query to a mobile phone number advertising an old car for sale, but I expect that I assumed the owner of a small old Fiat was probably a young vendor or possibly an older person who had decided that the time had come to give up driving.

The advert was 3 days old, so I was surprised, but pleased to hear that the car was still available, but as though to explain why it was still unsold, the doctor told me, "I have been away for a few days and forgot to take my phone with me. There are several calls on my phone, but I will give you the first refusal. The car belongs to my daughter who works in the local hospital with me. I'm a heart surgeon, and she's a nurse. She is going to nurse troops in Afghanistan for 6 months and doesn't need the car any longer."

Now normally one would be wary of buying old cars, not wanting to buy a 'dud' from a con man, but clearly I had no concerns with these vendors. Why would a doctor risk his reputation with the sale of a dodgy car?

I was happy to ask if I could go and have a look at it and was surprised when he suggested bringing it around to my house. I assured him that was not necessary as I would come to his home. He demurred at this insisting that it was no problem. I thought that this was quite gentlemanly of him.

When I phoned my son Dan to tell him that a doctor was bringing the car to me, he warned me, "Mum you

June Antoinette Necchi

don't buy a car from a man at the door". But, Dan, I reasoned, "he's a professional, a surgeon, for goodness' sake. If we can't trust him who can we trust."

Why was there a little voice in my head asking me why he called himself doctor when he answered the phone? I thought that a surgeon's title is Mr.….

Doctor Harwood pointed out the new seat covers as I looked over the neat little car, as well as the cleanliness, and the gleaming dashboard, saying "my daughter bought it three years ago from her best friend", and then hastily asked me, "What do you think about it?"

"Well, it looks like a nice little car, but of course I would like my son to have a look as I know nothing about the mechanics. Naturally, I need his opinion"

Meanwhile, Dan had phoned his brother, Matthew, telling him of my proposed purchase.

I invited the doctor back into my house to discuss arrangements for an inspection of the car and could see that I had an email from Matthew asking the car's details registration, etc, which the doctor gave me. We then had a very friendly conversation, the doctor assuring me that he had driven the car down from his daughter's home in Norwich, the day before, and there had been no problem with the trip of nearly 200 miles. Oops, I thought he told me that his daughter worked as a nurse at the same local hospital as him, a hospital about a mile from my home. must have misheard, I decided.

June Antoinette Necchi

The doctor wore, as you would expect from his station in life, quality clothes, fine leather shoes, with his hands revealing neatly clipped nails.

I was surprised at an obvious cigarette burn on the front of his sweater. He'd mentioned his wife, and I had a niggling thought.... why wasn't a wife of a professional man more solicitous about his appearance? Oh, well, maybe not.

By now the conflicting information he had given me about where his daughter lived, as well as the title, doctor for a surgeon, was stacking up in my mind. I even wondered was it because I had once worked in a prison, that I was suspicious.

An email from my son responding to the information we had been given, listing the car's year and make, and its current selling price. This was considerably lower than the asking price of the little Fiat. I had no option but to show the doctor the information, but he seemed unfazed by this reminding me that it had been driven by two females for years proving to be reliable and a positive selling point. Before he left we set up and inspection for two days later, by Dan.

I was happy that I might get a reduction in price of the car once Dan had checked it over. I had kept a copy of the advert showing a picture of the car with the mobile number. Looking again at the photograph had been taken against the backcloth of a building of beautiful architecture including arched windows. Was this a familiar building? I thought about it for a while and had a Eureka moment. It was a local chiropractic college! Why would he do that? Ony for one reason to enhance, somehow the value of the car. Could this be a con man? Surely not, as he wouldn't risk his professional standing for the sake of a car worth less than £2000?

The second thing I'd noticed that there had been a code after his mobile number. Was I getting paranoid now, I asked myself, when I saw the code.

I rang and asked Matthew, "Why this code in the advert."

"The code is used for commercial adverts", he told me. "Don't worry, I'm going to ring him now."

Not long after he rang me back saying, "He certainly sounds genuine, and told me because he renovates machines and advertises commercially, is the reason why a code was attached to his number.

I mumbled something like, "Gosh, then he renovates machines as well as hearts".

Dan was not easily convinced. He also rang the doctor to arrange the inspection, and again was told that the car would be brought round to my home, but Dan insisted that he would go to the doctor's home.

The doctor then made the apology that he was staying in a flat now as he was renovating a family house he'd

June Antoinette Necchi

bought. So now a renovator of hearts, big machines and

houses! Maybe my prison work had served me well after all.....

Dan's intention was to find the truth, so he arrived at the flat in a slightly run down area. Dan himself, was dressed in his usual hippy outfit with a colourful trilby on his head, flowered shirt and ripped jeans. I guess the doctor seeing him thought that this designer son of mine would be a walkover. But would he have guessed at his engineering skills?

I was interested later to hear Dan relate the story. He suggested that he test drive it, walking around the front, and surreptitiously touching the bonnet. Doctor Harwood's first mistake... he had apparently warmed the car up in anticipation of the inspection. Dan noticed too a new accelerator cover, and a glove box well scratched from probably some passenger's shoes. He lifted the bonnet.

"There's three oil leaks here". "Oh, I know nothing about engines", responded the doctor who 'renovated big engines.

"Ok, can I see the paperwork, please?"

Apparently this caused the doctor to try to bluff his way round facts when Dan pointed out that it was in the name of a car sales garage, saying that they hadn't done a change of ownership.

(Hold on, been in your daughter's name for 3 years?)

June Antoinette Necchi

So much for my 'dream little car'. Needless to say, I didn't buy it.'

Who exactly is this man? We were soon to find out who he wasn't!

Aweek later coincidently, I was at a dinner with a friend of my family, a nurse, who worked in the local hospital, and who told me that there is no heart surgeons based there and that her sister worked in the hospital theatre. She telephoned her there and then and confirmed there is no such person on the staff as Doctor Harwood.

My son found out later that the 'doctor' regularly advertises cars for sale in a national car sales newspaper, Exchange and Mart. I rang our local paper to warn them of Doctor Harwood's deceptions.

EMIL

The evocative strains of Polish folk music played on an accordion drifted from my neighbour Emil's bedroom window, in the house adjoining mine. The music was at times, lilting, at others, melancholy.

Not much was known about Emil's early life. Word had it that he had arrived in England at the end of World War Two from Poland having been captured by the Russians when he was barely 20 years old. He had begun work in the local coal mines, as did many ex-prisoners of war, and noted for their work ethic, chose to work on the coal face blasting their way through the

June Antoinette Necchi

underground rock. It was dangerous and tough work, but the pay was better.

June Antoinette Necchi

He became a well-known figure around the town centre, always carrying an old, small attaché case, greeting and stopping to speak with the locals. He'd wave to them across the street, always with a smile on his young, handsome face.

He became a popular character around the local marketplace attracting people to him with his sunny, gentle nature, smiling face, and vivacity. Stopping to have a chat with him, as many did, he would reel off the names of all those he had met over time in his adopted home, keeping a notebook of people's names in his attaché case. He'd produce it sometimes to demonstrate the number of friends he had.

"Emil, what a lot of friends you have!" We'd exclaim.

"Yes, I can remember all their names. I will never forget."

Few of us wondered if Emil's irrepressible nature hid an inner pain, a loss of family, home and country as a very young man. Was Emil making a determined effort to attach himself to people, to create a new family and put down roots? No one knew, they could only guess what lay behind Emil's ever smiling face.

One afternoon while taking my baby son for his daily outing I spotted a small group of people in the marketplace gathered around the local newspaper seller's stand. I moved closer.

A placard showing the headline carried a stark announcement,

June Antoinette Necchi

"LOCAL MAN KILLED BY LORRY."

Curious people queued to buy the paper and find the details of the tragedy.

The front page read,

"A MAN WHO HAS YET TO BE IDENTIFIED WAS INVOLVED IN A FATAL ACCIDENT THIS MORNING".

A witness told the police,

"He was standing at the pavement edge. He seemed to wait for a lorry to approach and then stepped out in front of it".

The police statement said, the victim had an accordion on his back and an attaché case lay nearby. We expect to identify him from a list of names found in his case."

I suspected from the description that it might be Emil, and the following evenings newspaper revealed that it was the lovely Emil,

I was young with small children at the time, whilst having great sympathy for his wartime experience, I had not the maturity, or worldliness to realise he needed to seek psychological help.....One of my lasting regrets.

THE RED SKIRT

My friend, Jan, and me booked into Trastevere, an old part of Rome over one of the many bridges across the

June Antoinette Necchi

Tevere river. A few months earlier I had seen a photograph of the narrow-cobbled streets, the washing

June Antoinette Necchi

hanging between the ancient buildings, and tiny coffee houses with their chairs and tables spilling out onto the alleys. A statue of the Trastevere poet, Trilussa, who wrote poetry in the Roman dialect, stood in the piazza named after the poet.

We booked accommodation close to the river walk which leads to Vatican City or crosses one of the bridges into central Rome. The location proved to be a great choice with our evenings spent in Trastevere away from the main tourist areas.

The first morning, the river walk took us to Ponte St Angelo bridge. While crossing the bridge I pointed out to Jan, two ladies whose outfits were beautiful and in the style of the 1930's. We weren't really surprised with Italy being the home of fashion but seeing two or three men dressed in clothes of a similar era, we looked around to find that we were caught up in a large group of period dressed individuals. At that point we were approached by a man who turned out to be a film director." Scusi, this is a film set, we are filming the life of Tulissa, the poet".

For us it was a happy coincidence.

One morning we decided to walk into the city centre to visit the Colosseum and stop for a drink in a quiet side street. Choosing what to wear on an exceptionally hot day, I chose a little red cotton skirt.... not knowing then that it would be decision I would be glad to have taken.

June Antoinette Necchi

As the morning grew hotter it was hard to refuse the friendly owner with his offer of a seat at an outdoor table. And harder still to refuse when he showed us a food menu. There's nothing quite like relaxing under the awning of an Italian eating place with local food, and a glass of wine. Enjoying the meal, we commented on what a lovely way of life Italians had.

Ready to leave, Jan went to the powder room while I paid the bill and went outside to wait for her. I was surprised a few minute later to see Jan beckoning me from the doorway. I was even more surprised when the owner told me. "You haven't paid your bill".

I was surprised at how aggressive he sounded.

"Yes, I have", I said, sounding apologetic."

"Where is your receipt?" he demanded.

Gosh. I was a bit taken aback at this.

"Well, I wasn't given one. Sorry".

"Show me who served you then ".

I couldn't believe where this conversation was going.

He continued, "It wasn't me or my wife so show me who it was".

I had to rule out a middle-aged waiter leaving only two Middle Eastern young men, but I couldn't for the life of me remember which of them. I assume I had looked at the cashier for only a few seconds.

The owner put his arm around one saying, "He is like my brother!". At that point the 'brother' emptied both pockets suggesting his innocence. Despite more pressure to point out the cashier, I told the owner, "I don't know which one took my money, so I can't tell you".

"I will call the police then".

He was angry now. Poor Jan was so embarrassed, and told me, "June, I'll pay. Just let's go". I dug my heels in.

"No Jan, this is a matter of principle".

Suddenly, the owner came up with an idea. "We go to the video. It's under the stairs".

Squeezed into the small space with the owner and me, was the waiter he had described as his 'brother'. My heart dropped as the video began with its blurred screen. I could see only shapes, no details. The video ran on until a flash of red. My skirt! There I was handing over my money to his 'brother'.... who at that point turned tail and fled down the street.

The owner offered me a bottle of wine which I refused, telling him quite simply, "I'd like an apology, please".

In retrospect, I had brought this on myself as I discovered later that it is a legal obligation to take a receipt from a cashier.

I can't remember whether I had an apology.......

June Antoinette Necchi

ALLEN THE SCULPTOR

One evening I invited my cousin Allen Necchi to come along to a monthly Arts Society meeting in my local library.

We always had interesting evenings with a demonstration of painting by a visiting lecturer. At the end of the demo drinks were served while art works by the members were placed on a table, inviting comments.

Allen's interest in woodcarving as a boy had continued into his teens, carving small pieces which I thought showed the seeds of a natural talent which was the reason I invited him to accompany me, and bring some of his work with him.

I'd guessed that Allen might feel a little out of his depth as a young lad amongst the more mature members, but I was fairly determined that his work be seen by others.

At the interval he was reluctant to include his work for general viewing, but I managed to persuade him. Taking the pieces from a plastic carrier bag he placed them on the table.

What followed next became history.

Seeing his pieces the lecturer asked who they belonged to. Taking Allen to one side she asked if he would mind giving her his phone number, saying "My

June Antoinette Necchi

husband is head of Stafford Art college, and I think that he would like to see your work".

She had spotted his talent.

There followed a three-year sculptural course at the college which inevitably opened more doors for Allen.

This unassuming young man, now a father and grandfather made, and continues to make a successful career doing what he loves

A cabinet maker, my father's favourite wood was oak and I'm sure that when Allen carved his gravestone in the traditional way that my father would have loved the oak leaves and acorns that Allen incorporated.

Headstone carved by Cousin Allen

June Antoinette Necchi

My cousin Allen's restoration work

June Antoinette Necchi

Chapters 24

HOLIIDAYS

FRENCH HOLIDAY

"Who's Mag? "I asked Joyce, my friend who had just invited me along to a holiday in a French gite in which Mag was staying.

"She's a fellow teacher. Is spending the last week of her summer holidays in Brittany. Her family can't stay any longer. Asked me along with a group of friends to share the roomy gite. You can come. Only got to pay for your ferry. Mag'll pick you up from Roscoff port. Me and my sis are biking to Plymouth. Will meet you at the Youth Hostel. Stay overnight. Get the morning ferry. We'll bike down to Brittany.

See you there."

I loved this blunt staccato style of Joyce's but needed now to know a little more as Joyce was careless with detail.

"You say Mag will pick me up? I've never met her; how will I recognise her?"

"Easy, she has red hair and spots".

June Antoinette Necchi

"Oh,, come on Joyce, this isn't good enough. Can I meet her before?"

"Don't need to. I'll take your photo. She'll recognise you then. Give me a photo album".

I tried to object to the photo she pulled out, showing me in a wedding guest outfit, telling her that at the port awaiting Mag I would be wearing walking breeches and boots bearing little resemblance to my rare glam appearance. Typically, she swept this objection away reminding me as she usually did that I was being over cautious.

I was at least a little surprised when the next day she returned the photograph to me.

"Why didn't you leave it with her? It's a good 6 weeks away and she will have forgotten".

"Course, she won't", was her only reply

My parents, encouraging me to take a break from raising my two sons alone, had kindly offered to look after them in my absence. Six weeks later I boarded the train with a friend, Ann, who was to make the number up.

Arriving in Plymouth we quickly located the Youth Hostel there, dropped our bags off and went looking for Joyce and her sister who were due to arrive on their cycles. After a night in the Youth Hostel, we all set off for the ferry due to leave for Roscoff at 7am. After

June Antoinette Necchi

boarding I settled into a lounger where I hoped to catch up on my sleep.

June Antoinette Necchi

Minutes into sailing I was violently sick and had no option but to spend the next seven hours sitting blanket-clad ion a deck chair at the front of the ferry keeping my eyes straight ahead to avoid my old enemy of travel sickness.

Seven hours later Roscoff came into view and as foot passengers we were able to embark before the vehicles. We waved goodbye to Joyce and her sister, promising to meet them at the gite deep in the heart of south Brittany. Checking my watch, I saw that we had an hour to spare before Mag was due to pick us up from the port so suggested to Ann that we go to the cafe, buy lunch and practise our French. It was then it dawned on me that I had left all my responsibilities behind in England and had one whole week of freedom. Was I too relaxed I wondered?

Everything had gone according to plan so far and glancing at my watch less than an hour later I said to Ann, "Let's go and wait for Mag, now".

"Ann, look out for a red headed lady with spots. That's what Joyce said, and red hair isn't that common so we shouldn't have any trouble spotting her. I doubt that she will remember me from my photo!".

I was starting to become a little nervous after a while with dwindling numbers waiting for lifts. After an hour I asked the staff to put out a message for Mag on the intercom though it had already dawned on me that the plans might have gone awry. And they had. The answer lay on the waiting room clock which was

June Antoinette Necchi

continental time.... one hour ahead of my watch. Mag must have been and gone while we were happily lunching.

By now it was early evening, and we had nowhere to bed down for the night. I sprang into action and headed for the nearest telephone box. With a list of Roscoff youth hostels in my handbook I began ringing around asking in my schoolgirl French for a room for the night for two females.

A nearby bus took us into the town where with great relief we found what was to be our home for the night, a small whitewashed old building whose reception was on ground level and the hostellers' rooms, two of which were bedrooms with another for a bike store, in the basement. A drinks food preparation room and a washroom with 3 basins and two toilets completed the basement.

We were shown to our room, a small one with a bunk bed either side of the door, and a metal bed on the floor beneath an old French window. I chose that one and Ann was happy to have a bottom bunk.

Later while having a hasty game of snooker with Ann, I spotted a man coming out of what I thought was our room.

"Which room is ours, Ann?" I asked her.

"That one number 2".

"There must be a mix up. Let's go over to sort it out"

June Antoinette Necchi

There were two men in there. I checked the beds and on both top bunks were ruck sacks.

"I'm sorry", I volunteered, but I think you have made a mistake………."my voice tailing off when my mind recalled that French hostel bedrooms were mixed sex.

There was no turning back now but where on earth were we to undress with a shared bedroom and shared bathroom!

I was quick off the mark making a swift change into pyjamas as they left the room. Ann, on the other hand who had come only with a baby doll nightie, forgot, and leant over her bed unaware of the watching males..

Before I left for France I'd told my teenage son not to worry about me as tight plans were in place for me to arrive safely. I now sat in bed writing him a post card.

"Hello. Matthew, would you be surprised if I told you that I am sharing my bedroom with two strange men? Don't worry about me, I'm ok". Love Mum. X

At that point one of my bedroom companions, a French man eager to learn more about the intricacies of the English language, leant down from his top bunk, and quizzed me on some of the grammar complexities of our language. Normally more than willing to help those who were eager to learn, this was a request too far given that I had been up at 5 that morning and I was struggling to keep my eyes open. After about 15 minutes of breaking down particles of speech and listing phrasal verbs I called an end to the 'lesson'.

June Antoinette Necchi

With the lights out I had an uncontrollable fit of the giggles, the rusty springs of the ancient bed rattling, reflecting the bizarre situation I'd found myself in and wondered would my son panic and alert the French Gendarme after reading my postcard?.

The next morning, we caught a coach to the Brittany town near the sea, but not before we had bought crusty bread, cheese, salad and wine to take with us in our search for the holiday gite. It's not an exaggeration to say that the taxi we'd taken from the coach spent an hour scouring the lanes in an effort to find the gite. Driving down a track I spotted a farmhouse with a modern block on the same ground and two bikes leant against the wall. "That's it, I think", I called to the taxi driver, grabbed our rucksacks, paid him, and went over to where the bikes were.

"But wait a minute", I said to Ann, "They are heavy looking bikes like Joyce's but what if they're not hers?".

A peek inside the window revealed on the fireside chair, knitting needles and a ball of wool. "Joyce goes nowhere without her knitting." "Yes! I'm sure they're here! Let's open the wine and celebrate! "

Happily, we were able to share the wine and food with Joyce, her sister and Mag when they turned up shortly afterwards. Now the holiday could begin….

June Antoinette Necchi

DISCOVERING PIETRASANTA

Never drawn to package deal holidays we located a family-owned holiday company in Manchester specialising in Italian breaks. One in particular that interested us was that of coastal holiday villas in Pietrasanta. Its mediaeval small city was a short distance away, inland, at the foot of the Apuan Alps.

Researching the area, we discovered that it was long famous for attracting artists. This description convinced us to make a booking there.

'Imagine yourself breezy and carefree in one of those dream-like summer evenings with the music of top-class performers, and the sweet scents of seasonal flowers wafting as you enjoy a drink surrounded on all sides by centuries of culture and ambience.'

Pietrasanta's piazza was just a few hundred yards from the station and was used annually to display sculptors' works. Seeing a collection of superb sculptures, and curious to find the name of the sculptor we were surprised to find that they were the work of Gina Lollobrigida, the famous Italian film star! We hadn't known that she had an art background. What a talented lady.

From there a taxi took us to our villa, a old building set in a garden surrounded by tall pine tree close to the beach and local shops. The first thing we did was to hire cycles and enquire as to the whereabouts of the nearest hospital.

After the excitement of planning and booking the trip, we had a medical emergency when my son, Dan, then aged 11, caught his finger in a door at home the day before we were due to fly. Doctors in A&E were concerned that we were leaving for Italy the next day, and were unsure if Dan may lose the end of his finger. Only when we promised to take him to the hospital in Pietrasanta for daily check-ups where we given the go ahead.

We looked forward to the cycle rides through a forest up to the hospital each day, collecting fresh food from the market before returning home. The cycles became our main mode of transport, discovering the villages and towns around Pietrasanta.

Cycling up steep roads from Viareggio a coastal port about 3 miles away, we were thrilled to stumble on the home of the late Puccini, and the Puccini theatre built on the side of the lake Lago Di Massaciuccoli. His home, Villa Puccini, built in 1900 overlooks the open-air theatre. Another discovery of one of Italy's gems.

A fifteen-minute train journey from Pietrasanta through luscious countryside, its roads lined with marble workshops, took us to Carrara, a small town at the foot of the famous marble mountains. The views of the white marble sparkling in the sunshine was spectacular. The slabs of marble on the mountainsides resembled chunks of cheese, and the heavy vehicles, like Dinky toys and the roads that had been constructed up the mountainside to access the beautiful marble for Michelangelo's David. This made it a very special visit.

June Antoinette Necchi

We caught an old mountain bus to the workshop part way up the mountain where we browsed the collection of marble memorabilia, taking home wine bottle stoppers, olive dishes etc. The holiday would have been worth it if only for this Carrara experience.

One evening, celebrating my son's birthday at a nearby restaurant, the following conversation took place with a couple at the next table."

We thought that we were being clever when at the end of our holiday we booked a 3 am train to Milan. We reasoned that few would be travelling in the night, allowing us to have sleep undisturbed on the long journey combatting the crowds we'd experienced on our journey there.

The direct train ran from Viareggo, a main station with beautiful, marbled floors. We were surprised to see other travellers taking the night train, all young women in scanty clothes and knee-high boots, lolling around the station's seats. There seemed something odd about the scene,...naivety on our part comes to mind.

We'd chosen a middle of the night train expecting to have the train to ourselves. It was a corridor train, and with the help of the guard's torchlight, an opened carriage door revealed males spread out sleeping across the seats. He demanded that they move over to make room for me and Slavica, who like me was horrified and fled to the open space by the exit doors where we spent 4 hours with my sons sitting on our luggage

June Antoinette Necchi

The ladies of the night we had seen on the station platform paid visits to various carriages. What a friendly

June Antoinette Necchi

train! What a variety of situations you experience on independent holidays.........

SWITZERLAND ITALY

"Ooh, can we have a ride in it?", asked the children, excited at seeing our first car, a newly acquired 8-year-old Morris Traveller, sitting on the drive. I didn't mind that we still hadn't a fridge, because the car I thought, was going to serve us better. It was going to take us on our first holiday overseas.

We lost no time in planning a trip to Riccione on the shores of eastern Italy. There were to be three families, and between us 5 children. My friends, with their small daughter were to travel in our Traveller with us and our two children. Seven passengers in all!

Young, in our 20's, the world was ours to discover now that we had a car. And with the optimism of the young we were completely unfazed by either the journey across three countries with 7 on board, or the fact that we had no insurance cover for the car in the event of a breakdown. In fact, checking our journey on a European map, we were thrilled to find that in order to cross from Switzerland to Italy we had to drive two thousand metres up to the Simplon Pass, a tunnel made through a mountain. We couldn't wait!

"June let's make a list of all the stuff we need to take on this camping holiday", said my friend, Maureen, who had good organisational skills.

June Antoinette Necchi

"We've got two tents. You can have one. There's a lovely new one and an old bell tent. Look, to be fair, you choose as we are going in your car".

So tents sorted, a list was made of essentials for a 3 week camping trip.

"Ooh, we didn't realise how much we'd need", we both echoed as the list grew longer, airbeds, bedding, towels cooker, table, chairs, tinned food supplies, and clothes for 7.

At that, John, Maureen's husband, intervened, "We've forgotten the blow-up boat. We can't go without that!".

This was an obvious point as we had planned to camp on the beach in Italy.

A quick decision at the last minute was made when it became obvious that the car and roof rack couldn't take any more... so we abandoned the chairs. Why did we need those refinements anyway, we reasoned.

It was the start of the summer's holiday as we piled into the loaded car to make the journey down to Dover to catch the ferry, and there was a sense of holiday fever in the air. It was all new and exciting, the sight of France in the distance, our attempts to practice our schoolgirl French, and the kids, eyes opening wide on hearing a language they couldn't understand.

Leaving the ferry port at Calais, we stopped briefly for a roadside snack before driving to Lausanne where we were to pitch our tents at a mountain camp.

June Antoinette Necchi

"Are we nearly there?" kept ringing out from the back seat of the car from the kids perched on laps.

Chugging up an unlit steep track up the mountainside really tested the old car, but we made it. Now the kids could run about and stretch their legs while we set up camp and inflated the boat to go on the manmade pool, the planning and long journey behind us.

The basic washing facilities, enormous stone sinks with only cold water, sheltered under small canopies, with wonderful views across the mountain range, were a world away from our little hometown.

This though, was the first stop on the way to Italy. After a two day stay the tents came down, everything packed away and off we set for the Swiss Simplon Pass tunnel.

You may say that we were a bit foolhardy to attempt a 2000 metre climb in an over loaded car, but I promise you that it felt exciting, that was until my friend's husband sent out a warning, "Watch out, check the dial, the engines overheating!". And it was. Seriously.

Never doubting that it would eventually cool down, we all sat at the roadside where the mountain views more than made up for the 'minor' inconvenience.

Once on board again, we had our most challenging journey in front of us.... through the tunnel, down the other side into Italy and around Lake Como, heading for Milan.

June Antoinette Necchi

Did we really camp for one night on the intersection of two motorways in central Milan? We did, and we actually cooked a giant spaghetti meal for us all with squealing of brakes, motor horns, and the roar of motorway traffic all around ….as we bedded down for the night.

It was bliss the next day to arrive on the beach in Riccione where, once more, we set up camp, the intention to stay for a couple of weeks.

Camping, eating and sleeping on the beach of a Mediterranean tideless sea may sound perfect, until you find that the sand burns your feet, and that your 7-year-old son refuses to come out of the sea spending all his time on his Lilo bed.

Two days later I horrified my friends by saying, "Let's go back to the mountains".

Oh, dear, we had come over a thousand miles in 5 days and now I was asking them to go back. Credit due to my friends, they agreed, and we set off. Sometimes in life you have to make difficult decisions but returning to Lausanne gave us a wonderful holiday completed by the most spectacular thunder and lightning storm bouncing around the mountains lighting up the skies.

I never held it against my friends that the 'new' tent they had loaned us, let in water…

June Antoinette Necchi

PAINTING IN PIETRASANTA

Had we known how steep the climb was to our holiday home, a medieval stone cottage in the Apennine Mountain range, we would have taken the rattling little bus up to Capezzano. A three quarter of a mile hike appealed to us as a start to our two week stay in this tiny village overlooking the piazza of Pietrasanta, the sculpture centre of Europe, little known to most visitors to Italy.

The holiday home had been offered to me by the Manchester company, who were planning to add painting courses to their holiday attractions. I was there to check out the area, and its opportunities for painting students, and to plan an itinerary to include travelling to local attractions for painting sessions. A main line station was minutes from the gates of the piazza with trains to some of Italy's gems ….. Cinque Terre's three villages, Monterosso, Vernazza, Corniglia, and Riomaggiore, Manarola, clinging to the mountainside, linked by both a mountain path, and by their small stations.

The small town of Carrara whose marble mountain range dominated the area, and whose marble was that chosen by Michelangelo for his David sculpture was a short train ride away from Pietrasanta.

Lucca, the beautiful walled city just 20 miles away was another perfect location for art students. Yes, I was excited at the prospect of summer painting holidays in Italy and couldn't wait for them to materialise.

June Antoinette Necchi

At the end of that first climb to the village, the cottage awaiting us stood at the edge of a wooded area, with its old church only a few steps away. On our doorstep was a small basket with new laid eggs, a gift from the villagers whose home stood at the level beneath ours. We would enjoy getting to know our new neighbours over the next two weeks!

After finishing an evening meal, and with darkness having fallen, we opened the door to the sound of wonderful orchestral music. But where was it coming from? We followed the sounds along a path, drawing nearer and nearer to the music. There, in a clearing, whose trees were lit by fairy lights, was a full orchestra, musicians surrounded by the villagers who were entertained with the music of Benjamin Britten. Looking back on that memory it still seems like a dream!

The next morning, Sunday, the bells of the nearby church were pealing calling the villagers to morning Mass. I hadn't realised until then what a special experience it is to hear the echoing around the mountains of a church's old bells.

A week later we attended the church celebrating the First Communion of the local children and followed their procession around the village, joining in with their families.

The next two weeks allowed me to put together a painting holiday by taking trains to the chosen locations. I had settled into the daily routines in the

June Antoinette Necchi

marble mountains and found it difficult to leave behind but

looked forward to returning with groups. But that never happened.

Shortly after arriving back home, we had the terminally ill diagnosis on my daughter who was to become the focus of my life........

THE SWISS OBERLAND

The North face of the Eiger! Why did those words fill me with excitement and hold so much magic for me? Was it because it seemed to me to be the ultimate challenge to climbers? But yes, magic and romance, both.

Was the Swiss Oberland an unlikely holiday location for two small families which included 4 young children and a 14-month-old toddler? Not such a challenge as those attempting to climb the Eiger, I reasoned, and so January found us, a detailed map spread out on the sitting room floor, planning our journey for that summer, by car.

Interlaken! Yes, that appeared to be perfect as a base from which to explore the lakes and mountains of Switzerland.

Finding suitable accommodation proved to be a little more difficult but a bit of creative thinking would allow us to rent the first floor of a typical Swiss chalet, creative thinking as much as the chalet's beds catered for 4 adults and 3 children, and seemingly no room for compromise. What was wrong with taking our own spare beds I reasoned with my friends? How about lilo

June Antoinette Necchi

blow up beds? Better not to discuss this with the owners who may not like the idea, and in fact may not have the floor space for it. Would they turn us away after a trip of hundreds of miles? I doubted it.

My friend, Anne and I had thought that a crash 6-month course in German, the language of the Oberland, would be helpful when engaging with the chalet owners. After all they lived on the ground floor and no doubt we would bump into each other.

Planned down to the last detail the itinerary involved a ferry trip to Calais, then an early morning run through to the French Swiss border, followed by a field stop to cook the ingredients for an English breakfast over our camping stove. The planned stop in a rural part of France, we thought, would be an ideal place for our breakfast picnic.

Back on the road we would travel around the edge of Lake Geneva bound for the Swiss Oberland arriving, we estimated, mid evening. The timing was crucial if we were to arrive at our chalet before its owners retired for the night, so sightseeing along the way was off the agenda.

Arriving at a delightful chalet quite close to the town of Interlaken set the children jumping excitedly in the car, and ourselves overawed by the storybook chalet overshadowed by the surrounding mountains.

A rosy cheeked lady with a kindly face came out to greet us but as nine humans poured out of the cars her

June Antoinette Necchi

expression changed as she head, counted, then shook her

June Antoinette Necchi

head speaking quickly in German and indicating that there were too many of us. Now to communicate my creative thinking that are the extra beds, the lilos. In desperation I resorted to miming, by suggesting blowing up with my hands, then pointing to the car and indicating the beds inside. Surely this lady would not turn away these 2 families at her door. With a resigned expression she led us up the external staircase to the rooms upstairs with their magnificent views overlooking Mount Niesen which stood at 11.000 feet. The kids excited, at first, ran around the rooms exploring, but soon settled into the beds, the cot and on the blow up lilos.

How welcoming were those rooms! The ambience created by the wooden walls and floors along with subdued lighting created the perfect setting for the bottle of wine we shared after the children had gone to sleep, but not before I had grabbed my German English dictionary and run downstairs to attempt to communicate with our hosts to find out where the fuel was to light the wood burner. Meanwhile, my friend, Anne, took responsibility for sorting out the waste and where to deposit it.

We couldn't resist, on that first day, a journey on the funicular railway to the summit of mount Niesen. Looking up from the base the sun shone from a bright blue sky, but as the train climbed higher the temperature began to drop until we reached the snow covered peak when we found ourselves in a different climate totally unsuited to our light clothing. My 14-

June Antoinette Necchi

month-old toddler son was determined to wrench from
my grasp to reach

the fragile piece of rail at the topmost peak, and his little hands tried to disentangle from mine. With him in my arms I went into the small nearby cafe and was given a piece of rope. I still carry that little scene in my head of a securely roped toddler happily peering over the edge of this 11,000 ft mountain.

The next day we set out for the famous Lauterbrunnen waterfalls which we viewed from a shelf cut into the mountainside while the waterfall, a torrent, poured down only feet from us. We still remember it as one of the most spectacular sights in Switzerland.

And then the Jungfrau Mountain beckoned as it overlooked Lauterbrunnen. We headed for the funicular railway but were disappointed to see a heavy mist descend as we grew closer cancelling any trips to the top. Nevertheless, the Eiger and its north face still awaited us.

Grindelwald, set in the lower hills of the Eiger, proved to be yet another fairy tale village. We bought lunch at the cafe there before making our way along the track encircling the base of the mountain. I looked up in awe and was entranced by that sheer north side. How was it possible to climb it? To me it was a magical sight that I had dreamed of for so long. I will never forget that moment.

Whoever would have thought that four adults with 5 young children could have had such a memorable 2 week stay in the Swiss Mountains?

June Antoinette Necchi

PIETRASANTA

Few know that Pietrasanta, a tiny medieval town at the foot of the Apennine mountains in Tuscany, is one of the sculptural centres of Europe. The town has Roman origins, but the modern town is named for its founder, Guiscardo Pietrasanta who built it in the mid thirteenth century as part of the republic of Lucca.

Bronze and marble workshops are tucked away at the back of shops, restaurants and bars encircling the Piazza Duomo. The white marble cathedral of Duomo di San Martino stands proudly in the piazza attracting artists and visitors from around the world. The Bozzetti museum nudges against the cathedral and exhibits sculptures and sketches. Pietrasanta is an important centre for working marble and was used as a source by Michelangelo. It is set against the backcloth of the Apennine range of mountains which rise immediately from the Piazza.

On my first visit, and delving into the history of the area, I came across the information that Michelangelo's sculpture of David was made from some very special white marble found in the marble mountains above the town of Carrara, just a short train journey away. In fact, a road had been built specifically for the purpose of bringing down the marble for the David.

I had visited the area a few times in the past so when a couple of friends asked if I would accompany them on an Italian holiday I jumped at the chance. They were keen that I work out an itinerary. I brought out maps describing the areas that I thought they would appreciate visiting, suggesting we stay in Pietrasanta. And so, the die was cast, and travel and accommodation plans put in place.

A taxi ride from Pisa airport took us to our home for the coming week an apartment along a narrow-cobbled street lined with colourful fruit and vegetable stalls and tiny restaurants immediately off the Piazza Duomo. Checking my map and train times, I lost no time in inviting my friends to join me on the trip.

After just 15 minutes we arrived at Carrara where a short bus ride from the station brought us into the town centre. We picked up some local information from a small bookshop there and discovered that we could catch a bus up the winding road, stopping along the way at marble workshops.

Waiting at the foot of the mountains for a bus to arrive I was overawed at the natural magnificence of the towering mountains clothed in white and glistening in the sun. So that is why Michelangelo chose this marble! At nearly 2000 feet this range of mountains was breathtaking, and a sight never to be forgotten.

The huge heavy machinery perched on mountain ledges, used for slicing through the marble, appeared like Dinky toys from where we stood. Trains carried chunks of marble, cut like wedges of cheese, down the mountainside, while lorries, loaded with smaller pieces, rattled down spraying the white marble dust onto the road.

June Antoinette Necchi

Before we set out on the bus to the marble workshops I felt transported to an earlier century when Michelangelo discovered this precious white marble which would in his hands be transformed into the now world-famous David.

The bus carrying villagers to their homes in the mountains stopped off at the workshops where we were able to see the hundreds of pieces of marble, from tiny wine bottle stoppers to pieces of sculpture, all created from the majestic mountains surrounding us. As so often happens when we have that moment of absolute objectivity about our place in the world, confronted with the wonders of Nature, the details of our personal lives diminish.

Catching a train back to Pietrasanta later we had a lively discussion as to where to celebrate a friend's birthday that evening. An open-air Trattoria appealed to us as it had no menu! You simply ordered whatever you fancied. The setting was beneath trellis work carrying foliage lit by tiny lights, and nearby, a beautiful life size sculpture, was sure to give my friend, Jan, a birthday to remember. We dressed up for this last night in Pietrasanta and were in high spirits as we arrived at the restaurant.

"We are celebrating my friend's birthday tonight! What wine would you suggest?". The evening had started well. The waitress returned with our glasses of wine, telling us, "The Signor at the next table has sent these for you, A birthday drink"

June Antoinette Necchi

With my sparse knowledge of Italian, I nevertheless felt it only polite to thank him, so joined him at his table, briefly. No language problem as he was an American, a sculptor, by the name of Joseph Shephard, who had lived in Pietrasanta for many years.

Unfortunately, we had missed his exhibition of paintings in the piazza museum, paintings which depicted the horrors of war. The exhibition had ended the day before we had arrived on holiday, but the beautiful sculpture close to where we sat was a piece of his own work. Our choice of restaurant had made Jan's birthday special and memorable.

We spent 8 days in Italy visiting Cinque Terre, Lucca, Viareggio Forte Di Marmi, Florence and the very special Torre del Lago 'Villa Puccini', the home of the late composer, and the open air lakeside theatre there.

In the evenings, sitting at Pietrasanta's bars, we did people-watching from the piazza whose backcloth of the hills rising to the mountains was magical with twinkling lights weaving through the trees.

It was a week crammed with memories....... memories which no one could take away.

THE WELSH HOLIDAY

How to plan a break with my friend plus an assortment of our various children with a couple of their friends thrown in ? The first decision had to be where. That was easy. Wales. Pop down the M5 from Birmingham, and onto a reasonably quiet road.

June Antoinette Necchi

It was decided to put the two teenagers on the train from Birmingham and meet them at Llanelli station 3 miles from the cottage we had rented in a hamlet set in a picturesque landscape.

My car, before child seat regulations came into force, would carry 5 little passengers in the back, my friend and myself in the front. My friend's 8-year-old daughter complained about having her 3-year-old brother on her lap, constantly repeating, "He's your child, not mine".

What to take for a week's holiday presented problems. Change of clothing for us all, plus entertainment for the kids...this included a portable gramophone with records, card and box games all roped onto the car roof rack.

My friend and myself were determined to have our space so entertainment was essential for them all, the teenagers both boys 14 and 15, were to have other ideas......

We arrived in driving rain, picked up the key from the owners who lived in a garden caravan, then quickly unloaded the roof rack to let the kids have a run after their journey.

Later the pile of our sodden clothes lay in a corner ready for drying out in the sun next day, but there was no sun the next day, or the next.... not even for the remainder of the holiday.

June Antoinette Necchi

It was at this point that the owner's wife turned up and stood in the kitchen complaining about her abusive and alcoholic husband!

June Antoinette Necchi

Pat, my friend, became neurotic thinking that he may attack us, and when later that evening he knocked our door and came in, we really did think that he'd overheard his wife complaining about his abuse and had come to confront us. To our relief he left after a few minutes leaving us somewhat unnerved.

Later, serving hot food cooked in the cramped damp and cold kitchen, we were more than ready to settle the little ones in bed and leave the others to play music, but the kids' bedtime was a nightmare with my 6 year old son refusing to sleep with Pat's 3 year old despite having promised to.

The three girls were no problem as they played records and sang and danced around the cottage, while the teenage boys sat with miserable faces repeating the mantra, "We're bored. It's boring here. When can we go home?"

"Look lads, we've only just arrived. Tomorrow we'll find something for you. What would you like to do?"

"Go to a disco".

"Ok we'll go into Llanelli in the morning and see what we can find".

My prayers were answered when we discovered that a disco was to be held there that night. I was happy to drop them there making tight arrangements to drive into Llanelli to pick them up at midnight only to find my son's friend, the elected messenger, relayed the message, "As we want to stay 'til the end can you give the money for a taxi, please? "Well at least they'll arrive back safely, I thought.

My concern grew as 2o'clock, 3 o'clock came and no sign of the boys. Their arrival at 4 having walked through lonely countryside from the disco convinced me that the most helpful thing I could do would be to put them both on the train home at the earliest opportunity. Two happy boys!

Now we could settle into our rainy holiday, but another problem reared its head the next morning.

About to leave the house for another rainy walk, the owner arrived on the driveway astride a big motor bike. My machine mad 6-year-old Matthew wanted to investigate and was delighted when he was offered a ride on the bike. I was, of course, horrified, making excuses to both my son and the rider. How could I ask the owner, "Were you drinking last night? Are you safe to take my son?". Short of having a physical struggle with my son it was impossible to stop him getting his own way and before I could say or do anymore the rider had lifted him onto the pillion and disappeared around the bend in the lane. I still remember the relief I felt when he was returned in one piece.

After a wet and windy uneventful week, we set off home after stopping off along the way at Neath Co-op to buy a plastic cover for the roof rack. I managed to rope all the roof rack luggage together protected by the new cover.

June Antoinette Necchi

Driving along the M5 Motorway my daughter in the back seat cried out, "Mum, the roof racks come off the car!".

And it had! It was sitting in the middle of the next lane!

I indicated that I was stopping on the hard shoulder when my friend, hysterically, shouted, "Don't stop! We'll be hit by passing cars or lorries!"

I had to ignore her fears. I couldn't just continue driving home and leave the contents of our holiday sitting on the fast lane, So I stopped abruptly on the hard shoulder, raced across to the rack trying unsuccessfully to drag it complete with the pushchair, record player and luggage. My main concern was that of triggering a multi car crash as the cars hit this obstacle. Miraculously, as I ran back to the car, a van pulled up behind its sign emblazoned on the side, *'MOTORWAY MAINTENANCE'*.

The roof rack safely removed from the motorway lane and stored on the van; we followed behind ending our journey in the maintenance yard.

Pat's husband, Martin on hearing a phone request from her, "Can you drive down and pick our luggage up from the M5 maintenance yard, please?", understandably, wanted to know what we were doing in the maintenance yard, but that explanation could wait.

June Antoinette Necchi

Chapter 25

KEEPING A ROOF OVER MY HEAD

PROBUS

I like a challenge, so when I had a call from a member of the local Probus group, a group of professional and businesspeople, I agreed to give a talk and demo on oil painting as a leisure pursuit.

I was aware that Probus welcomed speakers as a one-off, but my bank statement reminded me that I should accept any earner offered to me.

I must admit that I was prepared for a daunting experience, but at least I am enthusiastic about my subject, which generally enables me to overcome initial anxieties.

The group of 12 would be mainly men, suggesting to me that I include a few technical details without compromising the creative aspect of the oil painting journey. In fact, I took along only a few materials, canvas and a selection of paints to demonstrate the variety of colour that can be achieved by mixing.

June Antoinette Necchi

After sharing coffee with them I introduced the subject of light and shadow which at first hearing may seem a little obvious, but an actual demonstration proved to be quite revealing to them provoking lots of, "Never noticed that before!", and "That's exciting!".

The demonstration involved me standing with sunlight slanting through a window to my right hence throwing my left side into shade. Though I was wearing a black top they could easily see, once pointed out to them, the effect of the light on the folds of the cloth threw a strong shadow into the folds.

Then when I explained that to paint a garment one needs at least three shades of the original colour, that is, the actual colour and the effect of light on that colour, as well as the effect of shade. Now they were intrigued, saying, "But we would have painted a black top, black!".

"Now think about buildings, pieces of fruit, flowers, in fact everything. Your tones of light and shadow produce a three-dimensional effect. "You have now made an exciting discovery about the magic of oil painting".

I was happy to have shared my enthusiasm with them. They thanked me, then out of the blue I was offered 6 teaching sessions

We agreed on a two-hour weekly class when they would bring along small canvases, and a basic selection of oil colours and brushes.

June Antoinette Necchi

Over the weeks I encouraged them to decide what subjects appealed to them, and bring photos or prints to

June Antoinette Necchi

copy from. I had always found that this is the best way for beginners to approach painting in the early days as it retains their interest and builds their confidence.

They always arrived early, eager to get started on the lessons, while relationships, based on their shared art interest, flourished. As their initial anxieties faded so they took on more painting challenges, and when the sun shone they invited me out of doors to teach in the museum grounds. What fun we had!

I was now offered indefinite sessions with them. As their ideas grew bolder they asked would I be prepared to travel with them to spend a day in the grounds of a country mansion and share with them a buffet lunch. The grounds were quite extensive, and in retrospect I think I should have taken my bike to ride around the grounds checking them all out!

The lunch was quite a sumptuous one served by waiters in the magnificent dining room of the mansion, now an educational centre in the Shropshire countryside.

We left there after afternoon tea and a request from them for me to award a star prize to whoever I thought deserved it. Certainly not my cup of tea but I did, awarding it not to the best painter, but to the one who had progressed so well despite his earlier difficulties. His career had been as an architect, but he had learned how to exchange his detailed style for that of loose painting, culminating in a wonderful moonlit snow scene.

The initial offer of a 6-week teaching session came to an end 3 years later due to my personal circumstances.

The members of Probus had risen to the challenge, had created paintings using various media, and exhibited them in the museum…. paintings they could be proud of.

FAMILY PLANNING CLINIC

Janet, my neighbour, often shared a morning coffee in my kitchen. One day she told me that a mobile Family Planning service was to be provided for the public in outlying villages. Janet, who worked with medics, had wind that an urgent situation had arisen…..that of the driver having a medical emergency and unable to work for the foreseeable future. She knew that I was on the lookout for a job to fill out the few hours my children were in school and nursery, hence her urgent call.

"June. I've got just the job for you but better be quick. You'll need to start tomorrow. I've got an interview for you this afternoon."

"That's a bit out of the blue, Janet but I knew you were on the lookout for me. How did you hear about it?".

"Well working for medics I've always got my ear to the ground. You'll manage it easily".

"Manage what?", I asked

"Driving an ambulance".

June Antoinette Necchi

"Stop there, Janet. You know I've never driven an ambulance, and not only that I've only held a driving license for a year!".

"You've had a few goes in your dad's minibus, so you'll be alright".

"Oh, not sure, but if it fits in with my hours then I might consider it...".

"Get going, June. You're the only one yet to have an interview so you stand a good chance.".

The cat seemed to be in the bag, and the job mine when Janet told me of the working hours which seemed designed to fit in with school and nursery hours.

Losing no time, I met the Family Planning Chief that same day at the local clinic. She told me that the post was only recently established but that the driver had left suddenly due to ill health.

Today was Monday. By tomorrow the driver had to be ready for the Bridgtown run. She told me, "It's imperative that a new driver is installed within the next 24 hours", adding humorously, "otherwise the population of the village could dramatically rise in the next 9 months".

I usually find in life that assumptions can lead to misunderstandings, and this is the mistake we both made in this hurried interview. I happily accepted my new job without hesitating...and then she dropped the bombshell.

June Antoinette Necchi

"You have towed a caravan before, haven't you?".

June Antoinette Necchi

Have you ever had the feeling that your wires are crossed?

While I was discussing a job, she seemed to be discussing holidays. It took a little while for me to piece together a few words that made sense, and when I did I discovered that the ambulance I looked forward to taking on to the highway would be pulling a caravan. And not any old caravan but a purpose-built clinic 20 feet long! Now I had to try to come to terms with the fact that this time tomorrow I could be an articulated vehicle driver, or in transport terms, an 'artic driver.

Already in a panic at the thought of becoming an artic driver overnight made me break out in a sweat. Take the easy way out, I said to myself. Resign before you've begun.

"I'm sorry" I told her. "I hadn't realised this job involved towing a clinic. And I must mention that I do have a bit of a problem with sort of directional dyslexia so would be concerned about reversing etc".

"Oh, please. Do try it as we are desperate to fill this place.".

Never one to resist a challenge, a thought crossed my mind. If someone can give me instructions I will have a go.

A couple of phone calls and ten minutes later the die was cast. A mechanic who had serviced the old

June Antoinette Necchi

ambulance ready for the road agreed to meet me for one hour's tuition before I set off tomorrow.

June Antoinette Necchi

That was it! The patients would be waiting at Bridgtown and so would I!

My heart raced as I waited apprehensively in the local ambulance station for my instructor to turn up. Was this fear that I found this challenge exciting? I had no time to work this out as my instructor turned up, climbed into the driving seat of the ambulance, and invited me to do the same. The steps were high, too high for me, so taking hold of the handrail I pulled myself up, manfully, into the passenger seat. I was already getting a feel of the job.

I'd hardly dared to look at the clinic attached to the back. It was considerably wider and higher than the ambulance. It even dwarfed it. I really had to stop thinking about it. First things first. I had just one hour in which to gain enough confidence to drive it to a couple of villages a few miles away.

The instructor drove about 3 miles passing through heathland and forested landscape as we left the town behind, and then we stopped, swapped seats, and I hit the moment of truth! Once you've driven one vehicle it's said you can drive them all and I think that's possibly true, So I surprised myself by slipping quite easily into it.

The difficult part was shuffling across the seat, first this way, then that, to use the gears or my wing mirror, and since the ambulance had been taken out of old stock, it was not power assisted. That first and only

June Antoinette Necchi

lesson I became familiar with the controls, and doing the

trip, under supervision, I was quite relaxed. Back at base my instructor deserted me.

In retrospect I'm sure that I must have taken leave of my senses to even consider taking these vehicles a few yards along the road, let alone a round trip of 20 or so miles over the next week through rural roads I never knew existed

It was then that I dared to turn to have a look at the clinic which loomed over the back of the ambulance. It was a fight or flight moment but there was no option but to wait for the doctor and nurse who were to be in attendance in the clinic.

A car pulled up and I met my new colleagues for the first time. A nurse and a male doctor. Like lambs to the slaughter with no idea of their driver's limitations they boarded my ambulance and off we 'sailed'

As I wasn't privy to the locations I needed to ask my passengers for the address of the first stop, which a "Well drive to the main road and we'll direct you from there.

I was fairly relaxed driving along the main road until I was told, "Turn right here." I felt a frisson of fear at this. Not yet acquainted with right hand turns, I wondered could I position the clinic to make the turn avoiding damage to either the clinic or to the substantial wall to my left, as I turned the corner.

But my luck was in, I straightened up my vehicles read for the climb up the steep hill in front of me. With what

June Antoinette Necchi

I thought was quiet clever use of the gears, or maybe beginners luck, I was relieved when the road levelled out, and I guessed that I must be nearing my first location.

"Now you have to turn left somewhere here", the nurse informed me.

"Oh, this might be it. Try here"

Suddenly, things began to go wrong. How many times have you turned into a road only to find it's a dead end?

Ok, inconvenient if you're driving a car, but at the 'helm' of this great ship with 20ft of treatment room grimly hanging on behind, it's the stuff that nightmares are made of.

Now, I like a challenge but presented with this situation with two wordless strangers at my side waiting for me to make the right decision to get back on course, I couldn't think clearly. My mind had already changed gear into the get-up-and-run-away one I was suffering from silent hysteria. The trouble was I couldn't anticipate what direction those far off back wheels would take even at the lightest touch of the steering wheel.

The clinic seemed to have a life of its own. In a mindless way I just ran the gamut of towing/driving permutations, hoping against hope that one of the moves would, in this narrow cul-de-sac, point us in the

June Antoinette Necchi

right direction before I demolish the wall, or even worse, ploughed into a house.

June Antoinette Necchi

I suppose I must have looked demented by now, red faced and sweating, I saw faces of house holders in the nearby houses. Maybe they thought it was a new form of street entertainment…my bizarre driving must have resembled that of a six-year-old let loose at the controls.

Aware that my audience grew every minute, I relied on the law of averages to solve my problem.

To this day I have no idea what combination of moves brought my articulated vehicles into the exit position without jack-knifing Vowing never to bite off more than I could chew again, I left the cul-de-sac.

The adrenaline was really flowing now, and despite my hair-raising experience, a glow of satisfaction was beginning to spread over me. It was difficult to believe that after this first mornings work it would all be plain sailing. And of course it wasn't

About a couple of miles away I found my patients waiting at a lay by close to a row of neighbourhood shops waiting for the clinic.

The anxiety that I had been feeling earlier had faded by now, and I was beginning to think that maybe that this was not such a bad job after all, as I spent the next hour growing familiar with the knobs and dials in my cab.

My next port of call was to be a junior school playground in a nearby village, Bridgtown.

June Antoinette Necchi

Learning from experience and wanting to anticipate problems, or to be wise before the event, lead me to take a trip in my own car out of hours, to reconnoitre the area. No more assumptions for me. This time I would be in the know!

The school yard proved to be a sizeable playground with ample room for a variety for a variety manoeuvres of the Mobile clinic in fact a perfect place to practise my driving.

The entrance approach was good. A wide a sweep from the right and I could complete a full circle, and head for the entrance, with the clinic at a perfect right angle.

Does this sound too good to be true? I thought my luck was in. But there was a catch......

The gates opened onto an attractive, especially narrow bend of a surprisingly busy road. The houses opposite were charmingly sited on the pavement......a strong hint of times gone by. Some hundred yards up the road this narrow highway culminated in a broad junction which received traffic, buses, cars and lorries, from every direction. The large school playground seemed like a haven set apart.

I envisioned this fortnightly stop would enable me to come to grips with the many complexities of towing-driving. In my mind's eye I was seated at the great wheel swinging the mobile to the left, and to the right, reversing, and then forwarding. I'd set myself exercises on this great expanse of school yard, satisfied I couldn't come to grief. Clearly, I could see the day

June Antoinette Necchi

when, like dancers at one with each other, the mobile clinic and I would perform on cue as required. Whatever the road situation, we would meet it. This was the answer... practise to develop mastery!

Looking back, it's amazing that I felt so detached from the ever-changing traffic problems along the road at the busy junction, even unaware of them.

Perhaps my driving experience, which consisted of daily trips within a 2-mile radius of my home to deliver my children to nursery and school, had not exactly prepared me for my new career. It has been a little more than one year since I passed my driving test. Obviously, the all-powerful feelings of my success persisted and still caused me trouble. One, that I didn't recognise my driving limitations, and that I saw no connection between the busy junction 100 yards up the road and the peaceful school playground where I would be parking the clinic once a fortnight.

The weather on the way to Bridgtown was clear and bright with ideal road conditions. With my staff safely on board I made my way to the village. As we grew nearer to the school, and in good time, I indicated a left turn into the gateway. At this point instinct told me to swing out to the right, just a little, to achieve a good straight run into the entrance. This failed hopelessly because of the 'timeless' houses perched picturesquely on the edge of the right-hand pavement.

'Only a matter of a few extra swings', I said to myself. The next swing left the driver's cab dangerously near to the gatepost.

June Antoinette Necchi

Starting to get worried, I reversed a few feet and tried again to locate the opening. This time I almost removed my side of the cab. By now the Doctor and his assistant were beginning to shuffle uncomfortably. I really had the bit between my teeth now and was determined to 'take' this gate on. But whatever manoeuvres I made just got me into a bigger mess.

Locals were gathering around watching intently. I seemed to have wedged the two vehicles at a crazy angle straddling the road, and the clinic looked as though it was on the verge of the dreaded Jack knifing..

What was worse, the traffic had been brought to a standstill and was lining up along the road on either side. I can still remember a coal man in the driving seat of his lorry, looking down on me, and smiling.

The limit of my 'artic' knowledge was unbearable. Should I just take the bull by the horns and charge at the opening? A ridiculous thought, but seeing other vehicles unable to get past me, and unable to turn back in this narrow street, the solution must lie with extreme measures. Maybe I thought, wildly, should I run to the nearest phone box and call my father to help me out.

It was at this point that the school caretaker appeared. He looked quite annoyed that he had been called out for something that was a non-school matter... After all, I suppose he couldn't care less about Bridgtown's future population.

June Antoinette Necchi

I wasn't sure what he could do to help. As far as I could see the vehicles were at such an odd angle to each other, they could never be straightened out again.... unless of course the small houses that were in the way, were hastily demolished.

The growing traffic problem in the street around the stranded 'arctic' was turning the whole situation into a pantomime with everyone enjoying it except me, and of course the caretaker.. ...Now, he came up with an idea. Striding up to the gates, he lifted them off their hinges, and stood back sure that I would soon clear the road. With all eyes on me, I tried again, determined to bring this farce to an end. It was no good. By now it seemed that the caretaker had, to my embarrassment, proceeded to remove the metal supports of the gates giving me a precious few inches.

I triumphantly drove through with only an inch or so to spare on my right side. I'd done it!

I almost received a standing ovation from my audience. There were smiles and waves from the queues of drivers as they drove on. It was beginning to occur to me that my fleet and I were being regarded as a travelling comedy act.

The clinic's session came to an end with me driving my vehicles through a wider alternative entrance to another playground, one which I hadn't been advised of at my interview.

June Antoinette Necchi

As I drove back to base, and safely delivered my staff I couldn't have guessed what lay in store for me....

I must admit that I hadn't even thought about the parking of the clinic as all my anxieties had centred around the complexities of towing and arriving safely at my destinations, but here I discovered that parking presented another problem.

Parking has never been one of my strong points, and another thing I'm not good at is being caught in the crossfire of opposing forces. But now the parking experience was to bring together these two personal weaknesses.

The mobile clinic was stored in the yard of the local ambulance station. How was I to know that an ongoing dispute between the local Station and the County made the clinic, or should I say, its driver, the target for their complaints beginning with not wanting to store the clinic at their base?

I had spotted one empty parking bay and was heading for it when the ambulance Chief came running from his office, his hands held in front clearly sending a 'stop now 'message.

I suppose I could be called the pawn here, and my initiation into this new 'game 'began when the Chief, red faced and angry, told me,

"We never wanted that here. It's not our problem. It's the County's".

June Antoinette Necchi

While the staff couldn't turn it away, apparently they could make it difficult for it to stay. Creating a few practical problems would make the 'County' sit up for a start. He gave me precise warnings about where I was not allowed to park.....just about anywhere as far as I could see.

At last, now heading towards the yard's own petrol pumps he was saying, "Turn left at the fuel pumps and there's your parking space". It was, too. It looked about 2 feet wider than the clinic itself and was a scrubby piece of land wedged in between the ambulance bays and the fence beyond the petrol pumps. It looked as though it served more than one purpose...it was a coke store too!

If I'd thought that navigating the clinic was the ultimate in challenges then I'd run into the problem of wrong assumptions.

What sort of conundrum was this? Where was I to start? OK, I accepted that it had to be reversed because given the location of the fuel pumps, the alternative of reversing out was pretty mind blowing, it was painfully clear that to pull off this feat entailed me combining a sharp right turn missing the pumps by inches and with a near perfect timing in braking to avoid Jack-knifing.

I could see there was no option but to attempt to deliver the back end of the clinic into the overgrown, coke storage area awaiting it. A moment's lost concentration could result in fracturing the main corner

June Antoinette Necchi

support of the entire bay structure, to the right, or worse, flattening the fuel pumps to the left.

June Antoinette Necchi

My mind was in overdrive. Disaster seemed inevitable, sooner or later. It was just a matter of time.... As the Chief listed his complaints against 'the County', I got a funny feeling that the present problems caused by the dispute would shrink by comparison with those yet to come.

Right now, I was overcome with cowardice. I had to reluctantly acknowledge to myself that it needs a miracle for me to park the vehicles without causing major destruction on the first day of my new job.

Using my feminine charms and the helplessness of my skinny form I enlisted the help of a burly ambulance driver to settle my fleet for the night. As much as anything I needed to see that it WAS possible to park the mobile in this miserably small and obscure spot allotted to it, and my total lack of understanding of the many directions involved in reversing an 'arctic' must have aroused the driver's fatherly feelings. He was my Good Samaritan when I needed one.

He climbed into the cab, took the wheel and safely tucked the vehicles into the space allotted to them. Driving home I tried to be objective about the whole day's experience.

Yes, it was clear that I was not suited to the job therefore I must resign as soon as possible allowing the County to find a replacement driver. With this thought in mind when I arrived home I immediately made a phone call to the County.

June Antoinette Necchi

As so often with official departments there was a waiting time for a response. And it was that waiting time which jolted my mind. Why not give it one more day, then resign? With that thought I wasted no more time and put my phone down. The time hadn't yet come to throw the towel in.

Self-punishment as usual, the old familiar lines were forming in my head, 'if someone has done this before then so can I'

One of the stops I had to make sounded interesting. It was a residential mobile home site located up a steep incline near a woodland area.

Unfortunately, there had been a blizzard during the night before I was due to take the Family Planning service to the residential site. Arriving at the ambulance station the windscreen of the ambulance was white over with frost and snow. Climbing onto the bonnet to scrape the screen I couldn't help but think that I hadn't been prepared for this eventuality.

Finally, I was able to ask the doctor and nurse to board the ambulance ready for the next run. As we set off my mind was in overdrive preparing for the icy climb up to the caravan site.

It took a few false starts, sliding backwards, and gear changing but I was relieved to make it to the top, accident free.

Parking up, I found that the ground was uneven which could result in a patient rolling off the examination bed

June Antoinette Necchi

unless I levelled the clinic on the ground! Remembering the instructions given to me I levelled it ready to receive the patients.....safely.

I was beginning to get the hang of this clinic thing but not enough to make a career of it. I sat in my cab while the patients filed into the clinic still disbelieving that I had found myself in charge of what amounted to an articulated vehicle, something I had only ever connected with muscular men.

The movements of the Clinic around the district became the subject of much speculation. Acquaintances, and near strangers alike, having spotted me at times towing the Clinic would cross the town when I was out shopping, and question me about my job.

In a small-town rumour and guesswork flourish forming fascinating conclusions and are passed down the many local grapevines. Curious and bemused spectators always seemed to appear from nowhere minutes after the mobile Family Planning clinic had descended on their village, the unmarked vehicles unfailingly raising many guesses......" I think it's a new mobile chippy, Elsie".

"No, it's not. I bet its door-to-door groceries,".

Customers queued for fruit and vegetables only to discover at the door that we dealt, not in salads and spuds, but in caps and condoms!

June Antoinette Necchi

One day, a rosy faced, slightly muddled, though cheerful lady in her mid-80's, insisted that the doctor give her, "My regular supply of Durex".

The doctor wondered if this was a world phenomenon, then paused for a couple of minutes before replying gently, "I don't think you need worry about Durex anymore, my dear, but maybe I can give you diuretics for your water?"

No I didn't throw the towel in, I worked on the clinic for a further three years! The on-board team was replaced by the head of family planning services, Dr B. who had interviewed me for the job. and what an interesting lady she was!

She was very practical having a car boot load of tools used for servicing the Royal Navy's small boats. These came in handy when we decided to transform the back of the ambulance towing the clinic into a waiting room for those patients awaiting their consultations. Hitherto they had waited outside, often in dreadful weather conditions.

We put the two-hour lunch break to good use by Dr. B. taking out the stretchers with the use of her boat maintenance tools which we replaced with cushion topped chairs and tied back pretty curtains to the windows creating a charming and welcoming waiting room.

June Antoinette Necchi

On board we carried a detailed map of the area showing hidden tracks and lanes. Sometimes it required a bit of

June Antoinette Necchi

ingenuity to reach out of the way places to stop for lunch, but we explored some wonderful countryside in the three years that I shared the experience with my copilots!

My pregnancy heralded the end of the job. Maybe not a good advertisement for a Family Planning Clinic.

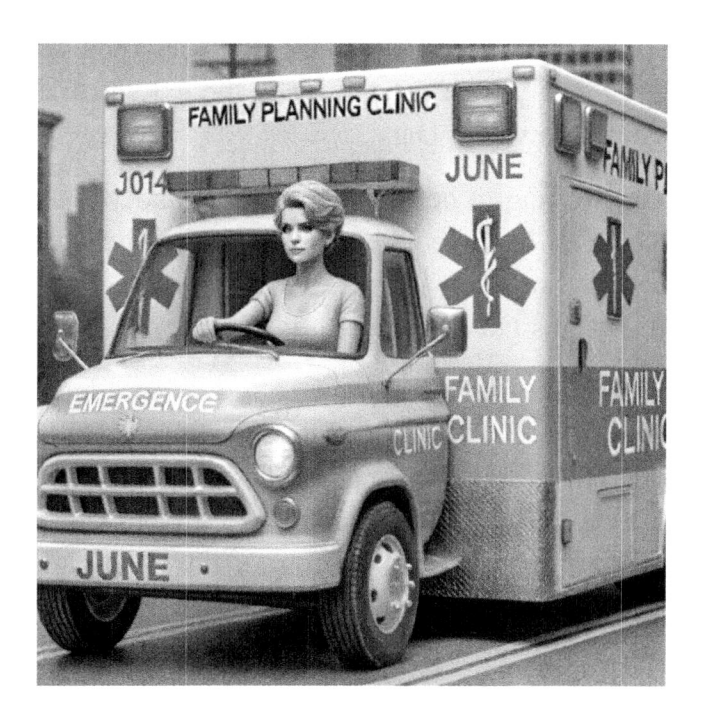

An impression of the clinic

although mine was much larger

June Antoinette Necchi

INA

The information from Ina when requesting a yearlong stay in my home was.

"I live in Germany but moved there from Russia with my parents. I am 21 years old. My main hobby is kickboxing.".

The diminutive, pretty girl who presented herself at my door fit no preconception of her! She was a joy to host, engaging easily with my family to the extent of falling in love with my son, Dan.

Ina was proving to be full of surprises, and yet another was soon to be revealed, not only was she an Elvis Presley fan but she was obsessed by him, his music and his films. This gave me a great idea.

Just a couple of miles from my home lived a lady who ran the Elvis Presley fan club and who was a well-known character. celebrating Elvis's birthday and death anniversary each year by placing remembrance messages in the personal column of the local paper, as well as putting on events at her home to mark the occasions.

Over the years the media turned up in full force with the local papers and local television news publicising the event. This seemed to be a golden opportunity for Ina…… maybe even a once in a lifetime experience.

June Antoinette Necchi

Aware that the TV cameras would be there, I advised Ina to wear something eye-catching in the hope that the cameraman would film her, giving her a great memory.

Looking as pretty as a picture without makeup, her natural curly blonde hair tumbling over her shoulders, denim jeans, leather boots and a cowboy hat, the picture was complete as we set off for the event.

As usual a crowd of locals and fans filled the garden and house from which the voice of Elvis drifted out singing his well-known songs while fans peered into the antiquated pink Cadillac parked in the drive and admired the life size gilded figure of Elvis dominating the front garden lawn. A mass of smaller Elvis's memorabilia was spread around the garden and house whose walls had screens showing Elvis films.

Ina was captivated by this over-kill though, and I'm convinced that she left with stars in her eyes. That evening we sat waiting for the TV news and it was no surprise to me that the cameraman had spotted Ina and filmed her. This was undoubtedly the highlight of Ina's stay with me and memories of her stay in England, as well of course of her falling in love with Dan who despite visiting Ina at her home in Germany sensibly decided that long distance relationships held little hope of survival.

SUZANNE

One Sunday, my day of rest, while I was relaxing by an open fire in my sitting room, an obscenely outsized suitcase and an assortment of plastic bags announced Suzanne's arrival. I was aghast!

She'd left her home in Europe 4 weeks before for a teacher training placement locally. Apparently, her first student accommodation had not worked out and she had heard along the teacher's grapevine that I let rooms to students.

Reluctant as I was to let my remaining spare room, a room I used as my study and my sanctuary from student life, I bent like a twig in the breeze to the formidable will of Suzanne.

My main argument had been that the room was too small to accommodate a bed and a year-long stay of luggage.

"No problem", Suzanne had said, "I bring little to England".

I wondered if she had said she was bringing a friend to stay, too.... surely something must account for this tumble of bags, big and small as well as the monstrous case.

Whilst groping for a way of putting the question, "Who do all these belong to?", I lost sight of her as she struggled into the kitchen heading for my freezer armed with a collection of plastic bags." I must put my frozen food in your freezer, NOW!", she commanded.

"But I don't think there is enough for all of those...".

June Antoinette Necchi

The words froze on my lips as she systematically removed my items, replacing them, neatly stacked with her's. Mine, she squashed in, piled hastily on each other, where she could. At this point I was desperately working out how I could reverse my decision for her to stay with me.

The 'I'm on a mission,' Suzanne, was on her way into my sanctuary and was already reorganising the room... with no consultation. Not one hour had gone by, but already she had left her mark on the household and showed every sign of riding roughshod over everyone living there.

I could only imagine the reaction of the two student teachers already harmoniously settled into my little nest.

Suzanne was cautiously welcomed by Yvette and Linda, who had arrived at my house a month before. Yvette had made up her mind at the age of thirty-four to take up a teaching career and left the family home in Portadown to train in England. Her shy nature had prevented her leaving before, and her nervousness when she arrived at my home had been obvious. She quickly bonded with Linda, a friendly and grounded sports teacher who though ten years younger, quickly became her confidant and mother figure.

The new guest had, by the next morning, asserted her new position in the household. She hogged the bathroom with incredible disregard for others, and at the breakfast table dictated exactly what healthy foods they should be eating first thing in the morning. Yvette

June Antoinette Necchi

and Linda were clearly in disbelief, and like me, must have been wondering what else lay in store for us all.

June Antoinette Necchi

It was unfortunate that Suzanne, when she asked for a room, had neglected to tell me that she would be in school only 12 hours a week leaving her with time on her hands, and more importantly, much more time in the house with me....

I began to feel driven out of my own home, as predictably, she took over my sitting room. It was beginning to feel like an onslaught, but I just hoped that time would improve things.

By the end of the week, we had developed some avoidance tactics, and however inconvenient, it made life more bearable.

A week later, Suzanne had disappeared mid-morning into the bathroom. Hearing a considerable amount of activity up there, I wondered what exactly she was up to. I soon found out! She made her way downstairs, half hidden behind a huge pile of bathroom towels and mats.

"I must wash everyone's towels and flannels", she announced.

In no mood to resist her taking control of my home I meekly nodded assent.

Suzanne's confidence was breathtaking, and I needed to consider a campaign to take control of my home and my life again, a campaign which didn't involve confrontation which I considered would be water off a duck's back, anyway.......

June Antoinette Necchi

The first opportunity to lay down some ground rules came when I arrived from work early one day. Suzanne was in the kitchen making dinner for herself and her fellow countryman who was sitting with his feet up on my dining table.

He was quite unabashed when I said to him, "Would you mind taking your feet off the table?"

I put it to Suzanne, after he'd dined and left the house, that in future I would like her to ask me if it's convenient to invite someone for dinner.

It wasn't only the towels she seemed to have a fixation about, it was also washing clothes. One heavily raining, bitterly cold day she decided to put on the washing machine and encircled the fire in the dining room with swathes of clothes on airers, leaving Yvette and Linda huddled over the dinner table wearing their outdoor coats. Suzanne objected when I asked if she would take the airier away while the others were eating, and to dry the clothes later, telling me, "I have to dry my washing".

One day I was preparing lunch for a friend and myself in the kitchen when Suzanne came in and physically took over the space I was working in.

The final straw came when she interfered with the timer on my boiler telling me that as she was home most of the day she needed the heating switched on all day.

June Antoinette Necchi

Much to the relief of us all I managed to find her alternative accommodation!

June Antoinette Necchi

SARAH AND MIRIAM

Sarah, who after graduating from London's Royal College of Music, had accepted the offer as music teacher for a year in school in my area. It was an easy host guest relationship. With Sarah's interest in art, she joined the painting group I ran at that time. She alternated her weekends between my home and London with her boyfriend, Glenn, who like her had graduated from the Royal College of Music. Glenn, a saxophonist, was appearing in the long running Five Guys Called Mo.

"June, how about coming to London, and I'll take you to see my show?" Glenn asked.

"I'd love that, Glenn!", I told him.

I had never been in a theatre performers' bar before which made an interesting start to the evening with Glenn introducing me to other players. It was a brilliant performance, and I easily understood why the show was so popular, even travelling abroad.

A host never knows where a simple host guest arrangement can lead....

Miriam, a Special Needs' teacher, also came to stay for the same year as Sarah, and she too had an interest in art, so lots of art sharing went on that year.

Miriam was the daughter of the Head gardener of Powis Castle, a medieval castle in Welshpool, and keeping it in the family, her husband to be, Michael,

June Antoinette Necchi

was also a head gardener at the Rothschild's estate in Oxford.

Miriam was a gentle, unassuming young woman, and like Michael, interested in the great outdoors, particularly mountain climbing. She used to tell me about the home in which she was born and grew up.

One weekend, me and my mother were invited to travel with her to meet her parents and see the gardens in the castle grounds. My mother was as thrilled as myself to see the beautiful well-kept gardens, and to share afternoon tea in Miriam's parents' old home located in the grounds of Powys Castle.

At the end of the year all three of us had bonded and continued to meet up from time to time.

I visited Sarah and Glenn in their home in Shepherds Bush and saw their family grow with three musical sons. Miriam and Michael with their two daughters live in the midlands where Michael became Head of Gardens on a Staffordshire estate.

PRISON LIFE

I jumped at the chance to teach in a Young Offenders' prison a few miles from my home. It was a good rate of pay and would boost my income especially as my teenage son was still at home.

My initiation was a 'mug shot' followed by the handing over of a thick black leather belt strung with several keys.

June Antoinette Necchi

I sat nervously in the staff room, and since non-smoking rules were not yet in force, there was already a heavy

June Antoinette Necchi

fug of cigarette smoke in the air with one of the teachers telling me that a 'fag' first thing in the morning was essential to face a 3 hours' unbroken session trying to teach and control the inmates. (I could see that, as a non-smoker, I was going to have to get used to this smoke-saturated staff room.).

I took my seat in what was to be my classroom and waited. I heard the march of the lads as they made their way from their cells along the landings to the staircase bringing them to the concourse where the classrooms were situated.

An officer told me. "At the end of the lesson make sure you've got all the tools back in there, we don't want any of those finding their way back into their pads"!

I was already wondering how I could persuade or convince an inmate to hand over, say, a Stanley blade, if he was reluctant....

A steady stream of young offenders took their seats after I'd registered them. Most took out cigarettes, lit up, and sat back.

"Miss, will you bring some Munchies in?" "Miss, can you draw Roger Rabbit for me and put a spliff in his mouth?". "Miss, can I show you how to hot wire a car in seven seconds!".

Always lots of questions, personal ones as well, "Miss, d'ya have any sons?". "Yes, three". "Which prisons have they been in, Miss?"

June Antoinette Necchi

They laughed when I told them, "None".

"Go on, Miss, you're kidding".

I discovered that there is such a thing as the 'prison grapevine' hence inmates with experience of other prisons, handing down info about officers and teachers.

One morning a new inmate presented himself in the doorway to my room, legs astride, shoulders braced and hands on hips.

"Are you the f…..g Miss who draws faces?".

I replied, "Good morning", and with tongue in cheek, said, "Please don't swear at a lady". "That's not swearing, Miss!".

What could I say? "Yes, I do draw faces".

"Can you draw one for my girlfriend, Miss?".

"Of course. You do some work for me today and I'll do it at the end of the lesson".

The promise of charcoal portraits helped build relationships with the lads, but also gave me a bit of control.

June Antoinette Necchi

An impression of Prison Life

June Antoinette Necchi

CANNABIS LEAF

A couple of years later I found myself overseeing a holding group of about twenty new inmates, each awaiting their turn to be ushered into the office of the Head of Education when they would choose the lessons they wanted to attend.

The atmosphere amongst the new arrivals can be very tense with the potential for a 'kick off' amongst old rivals who have served time in the past. For newcomers to the prison system, particularly the 16- and 17-year-olds, it can be a bit of a shock, and they can appear withdrawn.

I anticipated that with no prison officer in the room, and the possibility of old feuds being reignited. I needed to engage the lads in some sort of joint activity.

But what activity? How could I get the attention of a motley group of young offenders? I had an idea!

Drawing a cannabis leaf on sheets of pastel paper, I handed one to each lad along with green pastel pencils. I must say that they were enthusiastic about colouring them in to take back to their pads and stick on the wall.

At the end of the session, they took their rolled cannabis posters into the Head's office. I had thought that focussing the inmates' attention on a subject that held their interest may prevent disruption, but it seems the Governor had other ideas.

June Antoinette Necchi

At the end of the session, he sent a message with an officer, "Tell Mrs Necchi not to draw cannabis leaves for the inmates".

So much for what I thought was my positive thinking.....

There was just one potentially difficult few minutes in the room that morning when an offender who had had his sentence increased after an incident in my art room a few months before, stood at my desk. I felt quite nervous remembering the incident.

I'd confronted him when he took coloured pencils from a puny 14-year-old who had been busy colouring in a TV character. Asking him to return the pencils to the youngster, he denied he'd taken them, then walked out of the classroom. I had no option but to call him back and return the pencils.

Taking control is essential in that setting or the teacher becomes putty in their hands. I tried to hide my nervousness as this offender was almost 21, big and strong and the,' cock of the north' in the prison setting.

On his return to the room, and handing over the pencils, he was ridiculed by another prisoner who evidently was happy to see his 'put down.'

Angered by this, he threw a punch, and a fight broke out when tables and chairs were upturned. Within seconds it had become a free for all. I ran to the alarm bell on a far wall, panicking when I thought it was broken as I could hear no alarms going off. ...that was

June Antoinette Necchi

until I heard what sounded like an elephant stampede and the heavy clanging of the gates on the prison landings followed by a rush of a dozen officers who grabbed the main offender who'd thrown the first punch.

As they lay him face down on the landing, his hands behind his back, the mother in me pleaded, "Don't hurt him!".

Later, an internal court was held where I was called to give evidence about the 'kick off'. I found that difficult but had to be honest though it did result in the offender being isolated.

But now he stood before me at my desk in the incoming offenders' room, what will his reaction be to me? I took the bull by the horns and asked him, "You were in a funny mood that day. "I was moved by his reply, "Miss, I'd had a letter to say that my auntie was dying of cancer"

VULNERABLES UNIT

When I was offered a teaching job in the Young Offenders' prison some 3 years earlier, I thought that it might give me an insight into the problems which might trigger a young man to be in involved in crime.

Many had spent time in care homes when young or had been brought up in dysfunctional family homes. Of course, there were others who despite good family influences were drawn into crime, mainly through drug taking, or getting into the wrong company.

June Antoinette Necchi

It was at this time that another teaching schedule had been added to my workload.... that of working in the 'Vulnerable's Unit', a room set aside on the landing where the cells were located, so named because the inmates who attended lessons there had committed crimes which put them at risk of attack by other prisoners, crimes usually involving children or the elderly.

It was at one of these sessions that I met a young boy who looked about 12 or 13 but was in fact 18. With about a dozen of these lads in the room he chose to sit at my table separating himself from the other lads. Within minutes he asked me the question, "Miss, how long does it take for the pain to wear off from an injection?" Apparently he had taken the metal lid from an old Vim container and scored his chest and had received an injection to prevent infection.

This information had rapidly spread across the prison grape vine, and now the other lads clamoured to inform me that he was a devil worshipper, which he denied, (he later confided to me that when young, his mother would take him and his brother to centres around England for devil worshipping).

Asking me could I draw a picture from the sleeve of a cassette for him to colour I was aghast at the image of a skeleton arising from a grave and declined to do it. His next request was that I draw a large circle for him which I was happy to do …..that was until he told me that he wanted to make a Ouija board, the last thing this disturbed boy needed to be involved in.

As an aside from the other inmates, he told me that he had been in care, then adopted to a family who not long after placed him back into care. He hadn't seen his birth mother for years until the day he appeared in court. This poor lad told me, "She must love me, Miss, because she turned up at court".

As the lesson ended he was the only one to stay behind and help move the chairs and tables. I was touched when he put an arm across my shoulder and said, "Thank you Miss for this afternoon."

The following evening, I saw the headlines on the local town bandstand, 'Man of 18 found hanging in the local prison'.

The 'man' was this tiny tragic figure who I last saw in the Vulnerable's Unit the previous afternoon.

I was saddened at how this young lad's life demonstrated the devastating effect that the lack of family bonds has on an individual's emotional wellbeing.

THE WEST INDIAN CULTURE COURSE

A break from teaching under 21-year-old prisoners came as a welcome surprise when I was asked by the Head of Education at the Young Offenders' prison I worked at to run a West Indian culture summer course at the adjacent prison, one for the over 21's.

It was generally known that I had shown an interest in West Indian culture and so it was presumed that I would be able to put together a week of the various aspects of its history, music, food, religion, etc.

I felt uncomfortable with this offer as one of the teachers on our staff was in fact West Indian and I felt, naturally, that he was the person who should be offered the weeklong session. There was no arguing with the Head who simply told me, "You are the teacher I want to deliver this course". (No pressure then!).

The initial excitement I felt at the challenge quickly evaporated and left me wondering what I could possibly build on my scant knowledge to present a whole week of 'interesting' entertainment and exchanges.

That weekend I hotfooted it to a well-known bookshop in the heart of the West Indian area of Birmingham to do some fact finding. Armed with a selection of books I hurried back to do my homework. I realised that the week presented a daunting challenge, but I found in those books a richness of their history, it's music, religion, it's characters and a wonderful variety of food. Now I was on a mission, and I couldn't wait to begin

The evening before the course was due to start I considered what might be appropriate to wear in class,

June Antoinette Necchi

and anticipated the first reaction as the prisoners came into the room, panicking when I realised that their expectations would be of a black male or at the very least, a black female waiting to greet them as they arrived.

To describe myself I am white and fair, hardly the image these men would expect of someone running a course for West Indians. Wear something colourful, I told myself, something that may be seen on a Caribbean beach, and so I took from my wardrobe a sundress scattered with full blown flowers in vivid colours, one I found in a charity shop.

I sat in the prison room, behind a Formica table, only my lively patterned dress relieving the scene's formality. Waiting for the men to appear I began to shake. What on earth was I doing accepting this offer? When would I learn to question ridiculous challenges? Was it too late to back down?

A thought teased me......I could excuse myself and just disappear. But then I would be letting these waiting men down as well as myself. I knew then that I had to stay the course no matter what it cost.

The first prisoner came through the door and stopped in his tracks as he saw me. He looked perplexed. I took in his appearance, a tall man with dreadlocks down his back. Other inmates were lining up behind him, all seeming reluctant to come into the room. My thoughts were that the die had been cast, there was no turning back. I had no idea where it would all go from here but having accepted the challenge I had to go for it.

June Antoinette Necchi

"Please come in, gentlemen, and take a seat".

About a dozen prisoners of all ages took their seats, silently.

Still in the fight, or flight mode I had nothing to lose by addressing what I saw as their problem.... the wrong person taking the class.

Taking control of my nerves, I began, "Now you must be wondering what a white woman is doing here to talk about our culture, our West Indian culture?". "Well, first, I would like to know more about it from you as I think that it is a spiritual, passionate and heartwarming one. Now, I may appear to be white, but I too have mixed blood, Italian, Welsh and a drop of English"

From that point on I took my cue from the men who responded to my suggestion to tell me about the history and roots of their culture. It was fascinating to find out about the trials and slavery in the earlier years whose details seemed ingrained in the men despite having been born in England. I found this fascinating and embarrassing.

As the day went by they gradually opened and talked animatedly, apparently happy to share the richness of their culture, leaving me humbled at the experience.

Music was the theme the next day providing us with the opportunity to hear and talk about the wonderful, lively and happy Caribbean music and their instruments. I hoped that a day immersed in music

June Antoinette Necchi

would lift their spirits and bring them a sense of camaraderie.

June Antoinette Necchi

At the end of the day, smiling, the men offered me the 'high 5' as they left the room. What a breakthrough despite my worst fears!

The subject of religion the next day demonstrated the natural strong spiritual character of their race often found in their music as well as their ease to discuss spiritual matters.

We arrived at the fourth day to talk about food, and it came as no surprise to discover that there were a whole range of spices, colours, vegetables and exotic drinks. Given the prison diet of basic foods their enthusiasm mounted with an idea I had, that they put a menu together which I would present to the Governor asking if I could bring the food in and perhaps cook in the prison kitchens as a way of ending the week. That was to be the icing on the case so to speak.

When the Governor agreed that I could buy the food in, and with 3 handpicked prisoners, prepare and cook to celebrate the end of the holiday course, I was delighted.

In the nearby town I was able to find all the ingredients at a speciality shop, ingredients which the inmates were looking forward to preparing.

The colours and the tantalising smells from the food, loaded onto the prison trolley. Was a special time for these men, some of whom had spent years in prison.

June Antoinette Necchi

The evening before, I had packed throwaway plates and cups as well as a carving knife, forbidden for me to take into the prison, but essential to cut the large crusty loaves. I hid it in the cardboard cylinder inside a kitchen foil roll.

It was high summer, August, So I raided my loft to unearth some Christmas decorations to decorate the stark Formica prison tables and to create a party atmosphere, doing justice to the celebratory food.

Wheeling the food laden trolley into the room we laid the food and drinks out and wound the Christmas decorations around the dishes. I stood at the head of the tables ready to cut and butter the loaves and to slice the cheese into portions and hand out to the waiting men. The atmosphere was already resembling that of a Caribbean gathering! Then, without warning a large group of men, non-blacks, burst into the room demanding food. My men began calling out to them, "You haven't been in June's class this week. This is our food!".

They were besieged by angry responses and aggressive demands for food. The air was drowned out by the angry exchanges, and I knew I had no chance to be heard above the shouting, but as the situation was becoming volatile, and with no prison officer to hand, I had to do something, and quick.

I grabbed the heavy carving knife I'd secreted in and brought the handle down with a clatter on the nearest table. It had the effect of distracting the 30 or so men and silencing them for a few seconds. Now I had their attention, and I had to seize the moment.

Speaking quietly so they had to strain to hear, while holding my hand up in a calming gesture, I said, "Gentlemen, please. Let's be fair, these men have been in my group all week and have planned this meal. I promise you, you will all have some food and drink but it's only right that this group eats first".

Losing no time, I took a little of everything and placed on the plates of the first group of prisoners, adding slices of the crusty buttered bread with cheese, as well as the colourful vegetables. I realised that portions of bread and cheese were going to be considerably less for the latest visitors, but I felt that if they each had something they would be happy. And they were. Though I ran out of plates and then butter, I carefully handed them pieces of bread with small portions of cheese, apologising that I had no plates, but would they mind too much if I simply gave it straight into their hands. They received them politely much to my amazement, and then left.

After the meal one of the inmates climbed onto a table and produced a piece of paper saying that they had put together a message of thanks to me. He read out, finishing with the words, "Thank you, June, for your heart and your warmth this week" ..... they hadn't realised that it was those who had taught me to open my heart to them.

They told me that they had one last message. "We have written to the Governor and asked him if he would consider you coming in on a weekly basis. Those first

June Antoinette Necchi

tentative steps in the prison classroom, sharing time with

the long over 21 serving prisoners were rewarded by the Governor who agreed and invited me in to sign a contract 2 days later.

Unfortunately, I had to break the contract within days as my daughter received the results of her MRI scan which revealed that she had a brain tumour.

I'll never know if the Governor passed this message on to the inmates. I hope he did.

FARM CLEANING

Gwyneth, my mother was rather surprised that I accepted a cleaning job offered to me by a friend of a friend, after my marriage ended. Always considered by her to have no interest in domestic stuff being more interested in sewing, dancing and being with friends.

The hourly wage was poor but easily balanced by the farm's beautiful setting amongst the trees on land which was once a Royal hunting ground.

The farm itself had ten bedrooms inhabited by a late middle-aged couple, their son, his wife and two young children. They had a big stock of cattle as well as free range chickens.

The list of jobs I was required to do were many and interesting. The rooms were all around six or seven metres wide by maybe five metres. I was invited to look around the house while the farmer's wife listed the work to be done in each room……it was considerable.

June Antoinette Necchi

In the drawing dining room, I was surprised to be told that I was to remove and clean each piece of artificial coal from the electric fire. I wondered if this came under the term of 'cleaning' but kept my mind fixed on the additional income I would have. When I commented on the beautiful eighteen-seater table, the farmer's wife said, "This has to be polished with beeswax every two weeks".

In the farmhouse kitchen a large wooden clothes dryer hung from the ceiling which was about ten feet high. I was a little anxious when she pointed to a stepladder and told me that the dryer had to have a monthly scrub, and that the steps would allow me to clean the windows, too.

Taken into the kitchen where red quarry tiles were laid to both the kitchen, and it's adjoining equally large utility room, I was thinking that a mop and bucket wouldn't take long to clean the areas. My thoughts were interrupted by the mistress of the house, "When I was a girl we got down on our hands and knees to clean the floors. I would like you to do the same. You will see how lovely they come up".

By now our conversation had revealed that she was brought up in a home with Victorian standards which obviously she had brought into her own home. This then was to dictate my cleaning role there.

But there was more to come. The size of the huge circular bath in the bathroom upstairs would need me

June Antoinette Necchi

to stand in it to clean, AND it was the colour that all cleaners dread, …deep maroon.

June Antoinette Necchi

Is it possible to complete all the cleaning requirements in the four hours allotted to it, I asked myself.

I was coming to the realisation that I had possibly bitten off more than I could chew with accepting this job. But there was no going back now. I needed the extra income.

My first experience of cleaning the two quarry tiled floors for the farmer's wife, before she left for market, began with her reminding me of how to clean them. By the time she returned she praised my cleaning, not knowing that in fact I'd used my own method of mopping!

What the eye doesn't see, the heart doesn't grieve over.

The other half of the farmhouse had the same number of rooms, but the young couple were modern minded, and I could see that cleaning there would be a pleasant experience.

My mother was surprised to hear that the farmer's wife had recommended me to another farm …this time a five bedroomed one.

It was inevitable that I would bring an end to this job, and the moment came when the farmer's wife asked me to clean the farm labourers' toilet and bathroom, a large room whose floor was encircled by water pipes covered in Verdigris. "June, will you take a Brillo Pad and clean all those pipes please?"

June Antoinette Necchi

I'd worked there for three years by then and knew my time had come to an end. I gave up my farm cleaning job but not before the farmers commissioned me to paint family portraits for them.

JOERN

After receiving detailed arrival arrangements from Joern a 25-year-old German trainee hospital administrator, I wasn't really surprised when he arrived at my house at exactly the time that he had predicted. This polite young gentleman was to be part of my household for the next eight months while he received training in the local hospital.

From the beginning it was clear that he would benefit from a home that was carefully time-tabled beginning with his time slot in the bathroom each morning.

Joern was always considerate and aware of others in the house. In fact, I would say he was the perfect guest.

The first evening he tapped at my sitting room door asking would I mind if he joined me in there as he wanted to improve his English. A discussion followed about television programmes with Joern asking me if I watched soap operas. I told him, "When you've lived here long enough, Joern, you will find that living in this household is one long soap opera!"

Life settled into a comfortable routine with Joern enjoying his new position in the hospital and making friendships there. A lady a psychiatrist, thirty-eight years old, and a mother of four appeared to take Joern under her wing.

June Antoinette Necchi

When she invited him to her birthday party held at her house, a mansion, set in the countryside about 20 miles away, Joern was pleased to be making inroads into the English society.

On arrival he was shocked to find that he was the only birthday guest, while her husband, a wealthy man, was abroad on business.

Joern appeared to be quite an innocent man and though surprised didn't suspect her intentions.

On another occasion she offered him to visit, with her, the family holiday home in London. On hearing that neither her children, or husband would be there, Joern declined.

Early in January on his birthday he received a gift through the post. On opening it he dropped it back on the table, shocked, as it was a very expensive watch from his female admirer.

He returned it straight away but found it difficult to continue working alongside her for the rest of his stay as she stalked him.

He was relieved when he was ready to return to Germany but found a red rose under his windscreen wiper as he was about to drive off.

While wishing him a safe journey, I said to him, "Joern, do you remember our conversation about soap operas the evening you arrived? I told you that when

June Antoinette Necchi

you have lived here long enough you will find that living in this household is one long soap opera? What you didn't know was that you were going to be the star performer!"

I visited Rendsburg, his home in Germany, a few months later when he told me that his admirer had turned up at the family door pleading with him to live with her!

CAMBRIDGE

Carys was the English name this little 16-year-old Chinese girl had chosen when she came to stay at my home in readiness to begin studying at a local international school. The only child of her parents, both doctors, she had lived a very sheltered life protected by her parents and never allowed out unless with them.

She was indeed a treasured child sent to the UK to study English and hopefully be accepted in Cambridge university one day, the ultimate dream of many Chinese parents for their children.

I wondered why the school had accepted Carys in the middle of June as the other students were taking end of year exams putting their learning year to the test. Carys was at a loose end unable to take exams or yet to begin her autumn studies. She filled her time with various activities both in school and in my home.

One such day she brought home 2 white mice bought from the local pet shop. I needed to know that they wouldn't multiply when safely sharing a cage on her bedroom cupboard. She assured me that they were both

June Antoinette Necchi

boys so no problem there. To be truthful I wasn't keen on sharing my home with them but if they would help

June Antoinette Necchi

Carys settles in then I was ok with that. That was until a week or two later

I noticed the swollen abdomen of one of them and, yes, a little family of mice would be joining it's Mum and Dad in one of my bedrooms. With no time to spare I walked with Carys to the pet shop to complain that they had sold mice not fit for purpose. Carys didn't mind as she had already become bored with them.

She had arrived in England with thousands of American dollars and like many of her Chinese student friends, couldn't wait to go on a spending spree...... Now she wanted a cycle.

Since she had never been on a bicycle I was concerned for her safety and thought her parents would expect me to advise her against it, but all the advice fell on deaf ears. She turned down my offer of taking her to a second-hand cycle shop saying she wanted to buy a new one. She handed over £220 pounds for an attractive cycle but refused to buy a safety helmet despite me telling her that her parents would expect me to take responsibility to advise her that she should wear one. She refused point blank, So I had no option but to buy one for her.

The next morning, I watched from the window as she tentatively mounted the bike and wobbled dangerously along the road..... with the helmet hanging on the handlebars never to be worn.

June Antoinette Necchi

Each Saturday I'd go out of town shopping leaving Carys to invite friends who preferred to get away from their boarding school and share some leisure time in a normal home.

Arriving home one Saturday I found a group of about 7 students, all teenagers. I did sense an air of secrecy about the room and was soon to find out what it was afoot!

Early Monday morning, the first day of the autumn term, instead of preparing for school Carys informed me that she was going to Cambridge with her friends for the day to take the Cambridge English exam to be accepted into a senior school there. Apparently she and her friends had assumed that once in a school it would be almost automatic that they would go to the acclaimed university. That these seemingly unsophisticated youngsters had organised the whole mission had taken me by surprise. It felt like a fait accompli.

I learned that they were disillusioned with the school, its lack of promised activities, and of the broken promises that there would be a majority of English students in class enabling the Chinese youngsters to learn English and socialise Whatever my views I couldn't influence her, just simply insist that she return that same day ready for school the next.

What I hadn't taken into consideration was that the school would have been aware that 8 students weren't in class and that the Head already had wind of the

June Antoinette Necchi

'plot'. When he phoned me to ask about Carys I had no option but to tell him the truth that she had gone to Cambridge and promised to be back later in the day. He became quite irate as all the scouting for students in China was in vain if some absconded and warned me that he was coming to confiscate Carys's belongings as her autumn school fees had not been paid yet and were overdue.

When I hesitated to say, "I don't really think I can let you do that", he responded saying that he would bring the police to my house to carry out the collection. This was a tricky area for me as I relied on the school to support my income but on the other hand I knew that the students were getting a raw deal.

"I'm sorry", I told him, but I'm concerned about my legal position because if I allow anyone to take Carys's things I am at risk of being charged with theft. You see she told me that she has £7000 hidden in her case".

I was relieved that he accepted, probably not wishing the whole situation to be publicised.

"Look, when Carys returns I will phone you". He reluctantly accepted that.

Knowing that the students' plans were like a train out of control I guessed that neither me or anyone else would be able to persuade them otherwise.

Nervously awaiting Carys's return, Joern, the mature German young man who had been staying with me arrived back from work and listened carefully to the predicament I was in. He had developed a protective, fatherly attitude towards Carys and offered to help in any way he could.

June Antoinette Necchi

She arrived shortly after saying she was booking a taxi immediately to the 100 or so miles to Cambridge, and to a room she had rented there, and planned to study in Cambridge. Joern was horrified that this young girl was being thrown to the wolves and insisted that he take her and see her safely into the room she had found.

My close friend, Anne, had been privy to this whole episode quite enjoying the 'entertainment' the various activities and experiences my life and my home attracted. Always helpful, she suggested that she would be the 'lookout' standing along the street watching for the appearance of the headmaster. I knew that I could rely on her to be on the ball.

Joern, working against the clock rushed up and down stairs with Carys's luggage, packing it tightly into his car, even finding space for her dismantled cycle. Ony one item remained... an outsize blow-up teddy bear in the shape of a chair. It refused to deflate but Carys was determined that it would travel with her. There was last minute panic... Joern and I struggled to get Teddy onto the front seat, Anne beckoning wildly to get a move on before the Head made an appearance. Finally, Carys was sitting atop Teddyon the front seat as Joern leapt in the car and sped off down the road as the headmaster's car came around the corner narrowly missing collecting the school fees.

June Antoinette Necchi

Joern returned with the story that Carys's room was squalid with no wardrobe or drawers, and that there were several small children living with their mother.

Carys sent me messages saying that she was given pasties every day for dinner and had left to set up home with other Chinese students in a flat there.

Did she ever achieve her parent's desire and be given a place in Cambridge university? I will never know.

Despite my questions as to whether her parents knew about her moving to Cambridge, she refused to answer.

A month or two later I was invited to his home in Rendsburg where he told me of the final chapter of his 'romantic' interlude. The lady in question had flown to Germany and turned up at his door! It was the home of his mother who lost no time in sending her 'want to be 'daughter in law, packing.

Five days later at the airport, I turned to Joern, "do you remember the reason I said that I didn't watch soap operas? That living in my home was one long, ongoing soap opera".

Joern laughed, and said "I didn't believe you, then, did I?"

"You didn't, nor did you know that you were going to be the 'star' of our soap opera!

MARIA WAGNER'

I hosted some interesting foreign students. Maria Wagner, from Germany, replaced Joern at my house along with two more students. She had given me very little information about herself simply that she was to be a student teacher. Nor did she give me details of her

June Antoinette Necchi

arrival. I made a hasty supermarket trip with my friend, Anne, hoping that Maria didn't turn up in my absence.

About to drive home I spotted a lone figure crossing the car park. Her head was wrapped in multiple colourful layers, and on her back, a huge rucksack. Turning to Anne, I said, "I've a strong feeling that may be my new student". And it was.

She came to my door and was fairly wordless.. She was an attractive girl who appeared to play it down.. She quietly went to her room to settle in, then joined us at the dinner table, though seemed uninterested in her companions. She wasn't exactly aloof, but I guess a private person, though on occasions she sat with the others, then quite suddenly, without a word, leave the table and go to bed

There was never any drama with Maria, and she moved silently about the house, though I would often feel a bit spooked as I'd turn around and find her at my shoulder. Or any one of us would leave the bathroom to trip over Maria who was sitting on the floor outside. I was unconcerned by this, just finding Maria different with no spacial awareness.

Arriving home one afternoon the kitchen floor and surfaces appeared to have been hit by a snowstorm. Maria was busy kneading bread, obviously oblivious to her surroundings.

"I am making bread. I Have made 7 loaves. I will put them in your fridge".

"That may not be possible, Maria, "I countered, as the fridge is pretty full of everyone's food".

It was clear that this hadn't occurred to Maria, again the unawareness of others, and in her own world.

"I know Maria, put one in the fridge, seal the others in an airtight bag, and put them in the utility room. It's cold there. They'll be fine.".

Maria seemed not to mind this suggestion at all. It was becoming clear that my stove was a source of attraction for her. We got used to seeing her bent over the stove testing her latest recipe out.

Reluctant to draw a line over her culinary activities, I had no option when, one day, Maria had been peeling and slicing apples which were in the oven when I came home. They were on a very low setting.

"Maria how long will the apples be as I need to cook the dinner?"

"I am drying them out. They will take 24 hours".

When I had first seen Maria crossing the car park on her way to my house I was, I admit, intrigued by this lonesome figure, and still equally intrigued by her personality on the day she left for home. I had come to realise that hosting students was rather like watching actors crossing a stage, mixed characters, and all playing different parts........

June Antoinette Necchi

ROYCE AND KAREN

Hosting students can be an interesting way of earning an income from home. Students, all individuals', all with their own stories, create for the host a patchwork of cultures and personalities, all of which fascinate me.

The picture I had of Karen, a northerner and trainee French language teacher, was of a fairly solid, maybe conservative young woman, and her appearance at my house seemed to bear this out.

Karen, dressed for hiking, wearing no makeup, and heavily built, presented an image of someone unsure of herself. I normally find it quite easy to break down social barriers but sensed a hesitation in Karen. Before I could take her to her room upstairs, my 17-year-old son came into the house. On seeing Dan, a look of anxiety crossed her face and before I could introduce them she asked, 'But I thought you said that your son was in college?'

'Yes, he is. He attends the college in the town centre'.

"I thought you meant he lived away from home!"

And now a look of absolute panic as she raised her voice saying, 'I can't stay here! My boyfriend won't let me live in a house where there's another male!"

"If you tell him that Dan is a 17-year-old student I'm sure he won't mind".

Seeming not to hear that, still panicking, she asked, "Do you know of another house where I can live?"

Telling her that I knew of no one with no male in the house who would be able to accommodate her, she realised that she had no option but to stay......for the moment anyway.

I guessed there would be frantic phone calls to her boyfriend who was studying accountancy in London and would presumably advise her as to what she should do.

By now I was intrigued to meet the boyfriend who could trigger these fears in Karen, and it came as no surprise when he arrived on the Friday evening following Karen's arrival at my house.

He, Royce, was polite but cool, and came with an outsize sports bag, then left with Karen to go to the local supermarket. Already it was obvious that he was the dominant character, holding Karen's hand while she walked slightly behind him. There was more to come...

Having left them both to cook their meal in the kitchen I was apprehensive as they carried a meat tin filled with sizzling chicken legs, maybe 9 or 10, and proceeded to make their way across the dining room to the staircase leading up to the first floor, and from there up to a large loft room which was to be Karen's for the coming year. At this I was concerned as I had had a cream fitted carpet laid to the bedroom ready for Karen's stay for the coming year. I hoped that this was a one-off exercise but already sensed that Royce was already marking out his and Karen's territory.

The following morning Karen came downstairs carrying the large sports bag which Royce had brought in the night before, and unzipped, letting the contents fall to the floor.... all were clothes belonging to Royce which I presumed was his weekly wash load. This was beginning to look like the shades of what was to come....

Clearly, Karen felt that it wasn't necessary to ask or inform me about this concession! I still had to keep it firmly in the forefront of my mind that I needed Karen to remain in my home for the coming school year to boost my income, therefore not wishing to risk disrupting that, I made no comment.

There was something in the manner of Royce, a Greek Cypriot, that made me feel a little nervous as I could already see that he displayed a dominant attitude to women generally, and I wondered just how far he would go with me....it wasn't long before I was to discover....

I was relieved to hear from Karen that her and Royce would be sharing alternative weekends between my house and his rented room in London. On her return she would bring his weekly washing, dry and iron it ready for his visit the next weekend. Though it felt unbusinesslike of me to accept the extra demand on my energy bills, I felt rather sorry for her and didn't feel that I could let her be subjected to what might be his angry response.

June Antoinette Necchi

The following week, going to her room to change her bed, I was horrified to see photographs of Royce in military clothing, and in aggressive stances, holding

June Antoinette Necchi

rifles, plastered across the bedroom walls. It was easy to assume that he had given Karen these photographs, none of which were of her, demonstrating his control over her.

Over the next few weeks, I saw little of them, tending to leave the kitchen to them and hoping that neither of us would impose on the other. This option was to be short lived

Returning from work early one evening I was greeted by my son, Dan, who told me that in his college lunch break he had brought a couple of friends home to hear music on the mixing deck he had built into his bedroom, the room located beneath the loft bedroom of Karen. Not knowing that Royce had arrived on the previous evening, a Thursday, Dan was playing his music when there was a loud banging on his bedroom door. (Royce was now staying Thursdays to Monday's!). On opening the door Dan was confronted by a furious Royce demanding that he switch the music off, shouting, "I am studying and don't want any noise in this house. I am studying accountancy and need peace and quiet".

Dan, with his friends, left the house, and when I arrived home told me the whole story. I realised that by keeping my 'head down' Royce had assumed that I, like Karen, was submissive. How wrong he was. Time to assert myself!

June Antoinette Necchi

That evening both Royce and Karen stayed in their bedroom, but the next morning they came downstairs, Royce leading her by the hand. I was busy at the dining table with my back to them, and when Royce, in a raised voice, demanded, 'I want to speak to you', I didn't turn around instead replied with, 'Would you mind waiting for a few minutes as I'm busy?"

This was my deliberate attempt to take control of the situation though I was feeling quite nervous at what I suspected would be a confrontation. It was.

"What was it you wanted?" I asked him.

"I don't want any noise in this house when I'm studying!"

Since he did not live in my house I decided to ignore that request but instead asked Karen, "Were you here at the time, Karen?"

And when she replied, "No". I assured her that I had always warned Dan to be noise aware when Karen was in the house. I turned to Royce saying, "I'm sorry Royce but as you don't live here I have no obligation to you"

He quickly remonstrated with, "But we are like husband and wife!"

"I'm sorry Royce, but that's the way it is in my home". I answered him.

I knew that I was sailing close to the wind and possibly jeopardising my crucial income, but not to draw a line would lead to him ruling me and my son.

June Antoinette Necchi

Wondering what tactics Royce would use next I was surprised and pleased when he came down and knocked on my sitting room door. I invited him to sit down expecting an apology. He asked instead. "I want to stay from Thursday to Monday".

I responded that I felt a Friday to Sunday arrangement would fit into my routines better. I also suggested that he pay a small charge of £3 for staying. He jumped up angrily saying "But, why? "

"It's normal that there is an extra charge for another person".

"But two can live as cheaply as one", he shouted, his temper rising.

"Royc', I said," 'Every time you switch on the shower, I pay for it. There is also more wear and tear in my house, I'm sorry if you are not happy with that charge then I suggest you leave".

At which point he shouted, "Yes, I will leave!"

I found it a great relief to have a sound reason to not allow him to return to my house again. He'd shot himself in the foot. I wondered how many times he'd done that,

I hoped to settle down now, hassle free, for the remaining few months of Karen's stay. That was until the evening that my curious son went down into the basement to investigate the ongoing whirring noise coming from there. He found that the electric meter wheel was spinning around, fast. As we were using

June Antoinette Necchi

minimal electricity downstairs, obviously there was another source, presumably Karen's bedroom.

June Antoinette Necchi

Not wanting to invade her privacy, I nevertheless had to establish what was the reason for the excessive use which continued throughout the night and next morning

I went into her room after she had left for school and was astounded, and shocked, to see that she had an electric heater switched to maximum 3 drying Royce's washing hung out around the room. Not only that but there was also on a side table a small electric hob and oven! The heat in the room was overpowering, boosted by the gas radiator which I kept switched on night and day.

I needed to speak to Karen when she came from school.

How I hated these confrontations, but this one was unavoidable if I was not to be bankrupted by my energy bill. I told her quite clearly that both of her appliances were a fire hazard in a loft bedroom and my insurance company would not cover in the event of a fire due to noncompliance with terms of the agreement. Karen argued hotly insisting that she wanted to retain the stove and the fire. With slightly tongue in cheek, I told her, 'If the house burns down you simply walk away but me and my son would be homeless'.

From the first day the omens were always there but I had tried my best to retain the essential income from Karen, and to give her the security of a home while training, knowing that Royce was subjecting her to enormous pressures, but enough was enough and I

June Antoinette Necchi

knew that it was not possible for Karen to stay any longer, or for me to cope with the strained relationship. I felt sorry for her,

June Antoinette Necchi

but she was emotionally imprisoned by Royce which infected mine and my son's life.

I did wonder what kind of life she would have in Greece when married, as Royce had already destroyed her relationship with her family in the north of England leaving her isolated and completely dependent on him.

Other peoples' lives provide a kaleidoscope of personalities and relationships which a host is continually 'entertained' by, and which play out in a home which welcomes guests.

Chapter 27
LOVE STORIES
YVETTE AND DON

Unable to do a job with regular hours, having the daytime care of my daughter's two young sons, I resorted to making my home earn its keep as I had years before. I therefore registered with the accommodation officer of a Midlands University. I was given two names of trainee teachers, Yvette and Linda. Linda was to qualify as a sports teacher, and Yvette, an English teacher.

Yvette was 34, from Portadown Ireland, and had gone into college as a mature student determined to make a bid for freedom from her family home in Ireland. She was bright with a quirky sense of humour and had a twinkling smile but appeared uncertain of herself.

When she first arrived, she was devoid of makeup and dressed in shapeless clothes in neutral colours. She wore her black hair in a bob and had lovely, fair translucent skin. Her placement was at a senior school in the town.

June Antoinette Necchi

Linda, 23, was a lovely wholesome, outgoing girl. She contrasted sharply with Yvette who was quite shy, and socially unconfident. Nevertheless, a bond was quickly formed between the two girls despite their contrasting characters, both enjoying sharing their day's classrooms' experiences over dinner each evening.

By the October half term Yvette was giving us daily news about her lunchtime conversations with a teacher called Don, who taught maths at the school. Both had free periods each Friday and spent the time chatting together in the staff room.

As the days went by more information on Don trickled out. He was unmarried. He lived alone. He had his own home. And he lived ten miles away close to an area of designated natural beauty.

It became clear from our daily questioning that Don, like Yvette, was a passive and retiring individual, but it also became clear that Yvette couldn't get him out of her mind. Don began to dominate all her conversations with us, though not about the man back in Ireland with whom she had had a long-term relationship.

The man, a sports journalist, lived and worked in Belfast, was very much a man's man finding it sufficiently nurturing for a relationship to collect Yvette from her Portadown train as it pulled into Belfast station each Friday evening, and return her 24 hours later to catch the train back home …..and in time for him to join his buddies at a local pub. After 12 years it was unlikely that this relationship would go further but Yvette still lived in hope.

June Antoinette Necchi

Don's obvious enjoyment of Yvette's company daily must therefore have been quite flattering, and as an admitted born romantic, Yvette's dreams of a flowering romance, albeit with no proof of Don's interest in her, seemed to hold the relationship in suspense just as it had with her Belfast lover.

This simply wasn't good enough for Linda and me, although when I answered the weekend calls from her Belfast man I found his accent and his voice quite beguiling and wondered why it had not been possible for Yvette to fan the flame of passion in him.

She came home one day, excitedly telling us that a date had been arranged for a school staff end of year Christmas dinner, and she hoped that this would give them both the opportunity to sit near each other and spend their first sociable evening together.

At last, we had a chance to dress her up for the occasion, to be noticed. Her dowdy ageing clothes were out of the questions so we, Linda and I, made a hasty trip to my mother's house nearby to bring back a variety of size 16 tasteful outfits. Yvette was a little taken aback by this small show of glamour, but we refused to take no for an answer. Persuading her to wear a little makeup, and dare I say, small earrings, required the combined forces of me and Linda, but we won the day and Yvette left for the Christmas meal looking like the bees' knees.

We couldn't wait for her to come home, but her face told us everything as she came through the door. She

June Antoinette Necchi

looked so dejected. Apparently the seating arrangement in the big restaurant had left them sitting at opposite ends of the room and their backs to each other. This had been her last opportunity to take their casual friendship a little further as she was due to begin a new placement in the new year at another school a few miles away. The meal marked the end of term, and with it her broken dreams.

Fate is a wonderful thing, isn't it? Always with her head in the clouds, Yvette had forgotten to return a book to the school library until a card came through my door reminding her. It was then that Linda and I started plotting, plotting to find one more chance for these shy, would-be lovers, to meet.

We insisted that when Yvette returned the book to the school library that she takes a Christmas card and put it in Don's pigeonhole hoping that he would be tidying up his end of term affairs there. We even worded it for her!

HAPPY CHRISTMAS DON.

I HAVE ENJOYED MY STAFF ROOM FRIDAY AFTERNOON CHATS WITH YOU AND WILL MISS THEM. IF YOU FEEL LIKE MEETING HERE IS MY PHONE NUMBER. YVETTE.

For Yvette this was an outrageously daring thing to suggest but we now held her in sway. "What is there to lose?", we asked her.

And soon the last Friday afternoon she returned the library book and duly placed the Christmas card in

June Antoinette Necchi

Don's pigeonhole. That evening, I was not at home, and the following morning I picked up from my landline a number I didn't recognise. It proved to be a code for the town where Don lived. Yvette had gone shopping and neither of us were in for most of the day.

That evening a call came for her. It was Don! He asked to pick her up the next day from a spot out of view of my house and take her to his home where he would take her for a walk and then have tea. Wow!

Yvette came home with stars in her eyes and visited him the following weekend, failing to return that night.

I took the ritual Sunday phone call from Yvette's Belfast man friend the next day. He phoned her once a week, always on a Sunday, and always at the same time..

As Yvette was with Don when I had the call I was unable to answer his question, "Where is she?" So, telling a white lie I replied, "I have just returned home so can't help you".

This pattern of phone calls repeated themselves for the next three weeks by which time I suggested that Yvette deal with her man friend as my excuses were beginning to sound hollow.

With Don at her side, she rang her Belfast man friend telling him that she would not be returning for the Easter break.

Finally, there was a three-way conversation between him, Don, and Yvette reiterating over a two-hour call that this new relationship meant an end to the Belfast affair. Yvette, now at the age of thirty-four, had taken control of her life and of her relationships.

A few weeks later she moved into Don's house, gave up her teaching career, and made plans to get married and move to Ireland. I spent a very happy evening at Don's house with them both and was moved by their obvious devotion to each other and his delight at her quirky sense of humour.

A year later I was invited to their wedding in Portadown and stayed at the home of her brother and his family. It was a beautiful wedding of two people obviously very much in love. It took place during the week of the Orangemen march through Portadown, although the presence of armoured tanks outside the church did little to dampen the happiness of both families!

A charming chalet type hotel in the exquisite countryside was the venue for the reception where a piece of creative prose written by a friend of mine was read out rather like a fairy story about the circumstances in which they met, the obstacles along the way, and the happy ending.

Linda, the sports teacher who had become a firm friend of Yvette, achieved a distinction in her subject and married another sports teacher. Yvette never did teach but achieved her heart's dream. She was a born romantic after all.

June Antoinette Necchi

YANTO AND PHYLLIS

"June", my mother asked one day, "Would you help me to find my nieces in Wales, Marilyn and Gwyneth, Yanto's daughters?".

My letter to a Welsh valley newspaper, much to my surprise, brought a response in days. A relative of the girls responded with a telephone number, the number of Yanto's ex-wife Phyllis.

I lost no time in calling her though I wondered what her response would be.

I needn't have worried. Phyllis was delighted, though she gave me the sad news that her first daughter had passed away a few months earlier.

Gwyneth, her's and Yanto's youngest daughter, booked a coach within days to visit my mother.

As they arrived Yanto was waiting for them. Gwyneth stepped from the taxi, stretched out her arms, hugged her father, saying "Hello Dad". Those of us there were in tears..

In the house Yanto hugged Phyllis, whose luxuriant dark hair was now snow white, saying, "Where's that beautiful black hair gone, then Phyll?"

Their connection was immediate, these two sixty odd years old, reclaiming their past in minutes.

A happy reunion followed which I wove into a happy ever after story.

June Antoinette Necchi

A WELSH LOVE STORY

The morning sun is veiled by a lingering mist as I follow the path up to the cemetery in the Welsh valley.

My heart quickens welcoming the tricks my mind will play, writing its own story as it always does when I visit his grave. It is a ritual, and I know what to expect now, a rush of happiness at what might have been for him, the sailor.

But first the ritual insists that I go back in time and remember how it was all those years ago

It was 1941 Giggling and chattering with anticipation the girls from the Welsh valley made their way to the local village hall for the weekly dance which was the highlight of their week. They had left school at 14 and worked in factories, shops or 'in Service' as housekeepers or Nannies. The war which had begun 2 years earlier had sparked a spirit of camaraderie which was now firmly established, and 'wartime 'had become a way of life.

Saturday night at the village hall dance was their time to catch up with friends.... and meet boys.

The local boys who were not working in the coal mines, or on the land, had been called up into the Forces and brought with them when they returned on leave, a newly acquired worldliness, and a touch of glamour in their uniforms, which the girls found irresistible.

June Antoinette Necchi

The girls moved up the hill to the dance hall with a sense of urgency, their legs bronzed with a sand and water mix, pencilled seams, lipsticked Cupid's bows and hair caught up at the sides into a fashionable 'sweep' style.

In the village hall it was easy to pick out the servicemen from the lads who had to stay behind, and as the band struck up the opening bars of the quickstep, a curly haired sailor stepped out onto the worn wooden dance floor and made his way to the other side.

The girl who had caught his eye was olive skinned with luxuriant dark hair falling over her shoulders. Her smile as he approached her was warm.. She appeared to be surprised that the handsome young sailor had chosen her for his first partner but as they took the floor they quickly grew at ease with each other's steps. They danced and laughed together throughout the evening and afterwards the sailor walked her home and arranged to meet again the next day.

And so the sailor and the girl became sweethearts. A year later they had managed to keep their love alive by exchanging regular letters while he sailed around the world on active service with a promotion to Petty Officer aboard his ship. His rare spells of leave were spent together and were cherished by both.

At home, on leave one night, he opened the door to her mother who said, "She's having your baby...you've got to marry her". The sailor loved her, and so they married, and a daughter was born.

June Antoinette Necchi

He went back to his ship, and his wife went to work in an ammunition's factory miles from home, while her mother cared for the baby. Two years later a second child, a daughter was born, and the end of the war was in sight.

1945 at the war's end the sailor was offered a home, a prefabricated one built for returning troops.

Then the grandmother dropped the bombshell, "I've mothered these two little ones during the war and I'm not letting them go. You go and live with your sailor but you're not taking these". The young mother, her loyalties torn, felt obliged to stay with her mother and her children. She told the sailor, "Be patient, we'll be together one day".

Gradually the sailor lost hope of ever being reunited with his wife and little ones and went to live with his only surviving relative, his sister who lived miles away in England.

He became a factory worker, saved up and bought a small cottage where he spent his leisure time tending his garden. He financially supported his children but was never able to see them and seemed to have accepted that loss, until......

A letter written by me, his English niece, to a newspaper in the Welsh valleys asking for information about his daughters' whereabouts, brought a response from a distant relative.

June Antoinette Necchi

Within 24 hours a phone call had located his wife. After emotional exchanges in which she revealed that their eldest daughter had died just a few months earlier, she vowed to waste no time in making a trip to meet up with the sailor.

Things moved quickly. A coach company in her village, Pontlottyn, organised visits to the Motor Show in Birmingham and the sailor's daughter and his wife booked seats. A family member was to meet them in Birmingham and bring them the last 25 miles.

And a week later they went to visit him and his daughter, putting her arms around him, said, "Hello Dad". Though she had no recollection of him their bonding was immediate and their appearance a mirror image of each other.

Then the sailor clasped his wife remembering her words all those years ago "Be patient, we'll be together one day".

Only a few weeks later he returned to his homeland and the years slipped away on the Saturday evening as they danced on the same old wooden floor in the village hall where they had first met. Shortly afterwards he joined her in her home, and with his daughter living nearby their lives and their hearts were healed.

After 7 years of shared times the sailor passed away quite suddenly and was buried side by side with the daughter he had scarcely known.

June Antoinette Necchi

The morning mist rises as I stand before the memorial stones and scatter rose petal over the graves of the sailor and his daughter, reunited at last while the wind whispers, "be patient, we'll be together one day"

Yanto, Phyllis, me & mother

June Antoinette Necchi

Chapter 28

MY CHILDREN

RUSSELL, DONNA, MATTHEW, DAN

As the mother of four, I have countless special memories of each of them, of course.

The birth of my first child, Russell, born one month prematurely, a week after my 21st birthday was a life changing event.

I fell in love instantly with my tiny dark-haired, olive-skinned son. I hadn't realised that his birth would enable me to embark on the life I'd always longed for, one of stability, and one where I was no longer at risk from separation. We would take this journey together.

Weighing under 4 pounds Russell began life in an oxygen tent. Two days later I was able to take him in my arms. I still remember being filled with wonder at this scrap of life that had been part of me for 8 months, and of the enormous responsibility in my arms.

My once dark-haired baby, a few months later, was now golden haired, contrasting with his sun kissed skin and brown eyes. As the time passed, what was to be his gentle nature was becoming evident. He enjoyed playing alone so when I was once again pregnant I wondered would he welcome a sibling.

The expected date for my baby's birth was the 4th of July but it came and went with no sign of her arrival. A few days later the 8th I was staying with my parents, a practical decision to not be alone when I went into labour.

That day proved to be the hottest day of the year, so with doors open wide, me languishing indoors, and Russell playing in the garden, my father, a non-drinker, remembered he had once been given a bottle of cider. He thought it might be refreshing and handed each of us a glass.

At one point Russell came in and unnoticed, drank a little from my glass. Shortly afterwards a neighbour, panicking, called out that 'Russell is rolling over in the garden, and sweating badly".

The scene that followed was one of panic. In my father's car a few minutes later, Russell's face drained of colour as he lay on my lap. Rushing into the doctor's surgery, bypassing other patients, the doctor told me to calm down. I told him about the cider. He examined Russell and said, "He's blind drunk. Lay him down in a darkened room. Don't worry. He'll be okay but may wake with a hangover!"

June Antoinette Necchi

Both children were easy going and problem free giving me no warning that my next child, a son, Matthew, would break the mould.

A blue-eyed baby with a head of luxuriant dark hair, born when Donna was 7, he was the textbook 'bonny baby'. Not keen on sleep he nevertheless was a joy of a baby, inquisitive, and entertaining. Walking early opened opportunities for him to explore, open doors and try to escape. Always a freedom lover, he was the child who I'd find trying to climb out of windows and escaping from the garden. Yes, this third charming little child kept me on my toes.

At 5 he must have given some thought to the religious lesson in his Catholic school. One day when the children were told that they must love God first before anyone. He snuggled up to me that evening and whispered, "Mummy, I love you best of all but don't tell God". His first attempts to think independently. ...

After 3 children I felt blasé about having a fourth, after all I reasoned there can't be anything more to learn about child raising. I was wrong.

Dan was born 8 years after Matthew and within days of his birth he was known in the hospital nursery as 'the one that's always crying'. Of course, as his mother I made excuses.

His birth had been a very quick one, born within half an hour of me being in labour, "He must be

June Antoinette Necchi

traumatised coming into the world so quickly", I told the nurses.

June Antoinette Necchi

Once home, I told myself, he will be able to settle into calming routines.

From the beginning he was averse to sleep so much so that in desperation I went to see my doctor, "This is my fourth child, and you think I would have all the answers to child rearing but I'm back to the beginning with my last baby. He rarely sleeps before midnight and is awake at 5. He cries and the only way to soothe him is to have him in my bed".

"No. Don't do that. You are making a rod for your own back. Leave him in his cot. Go and sleep in there when he cries. He will learn".

Curled up in a sleeping bag on the floor at the side of my baby's cot in the tiny unheated bedroom, I was convinced that this would be the beginning of a new episode in our lives. I was cold, uncomfortable, but happy.

Unfortunately, despite my rocking his cot through the night he never gave up crying. Persevere I told myself. I will not give in.

Four nights later it had become a battle of wills. He persisted in crying through most of the night while I remained steadfast in my determination. On that last night, about 3 in the morning, the next-door neighbour knocked on the bedroom wall, calling out, "Will you stop that baby crying. We've got work in the morning".

June Antoinette Necchi

Dan had won and became my sleeping companion once more. And what's more this fourth child broke all the rules and walked unaided for 7 months and two weeks!

It was about this time that I sought refuge each morning at the local coffee shop leaving Dan strapped in his pram outside. This action baby decided one day to make a run for it. A passer-by called out, "There's a baby running down the pavement!".

And, yes, he was…. but taking the pram with him. This little Houdini had managed to undo one side of his reins but was still attached to his pram. No problem just took his pram with him.

He was too young to reason with so the next morning after his bath I fixed his reins under the layer of his clothes but over his vest. I was feeling quite confident at this move, satisfied that I had won this battle.

Enjoying my coffee later that morning knowing that my little son was safe outside I was taken aback to be called outside to witness Dan, again, trotting along with his pram in tow. How on earth did he do that?

Catching up with him I could only admire his determination… he'd removed his jacket, his jumpsuit and shoes and was running barefooted, his nappy hanging down and his reins over his vest.

He'd won again. Now he became my coffee buddy.

June Antoinette Necchi

Most will remember the plaintiff voice of their child, "Mummy, can we have a dog, please. My friend has a dog we can have. A collie. Can we have him?".

"Darling, you know I'm out at work. Collies need a lot of exercise ".

"I'll walk him. I promise, I'll walk him every day. I'll feed him as well".

And to clinch it with a little emotional blackmail, "All your other children had dogs".

Dan did seem to have a habit of winning I noticed....

June Antoinette Necchi

Russell, Donna & Mattew 1

Me and Dan 1

June Antoinette Necchi

Chapter 29

DAN

As mothers we look forward to reading our children's first attempts at writing, cherishing and keeping them safe in memory boxes, or pinning on the kitchen wall. I'm no exception.so looking forward to opening 7-year-old Dan's latest school exercise book I have to admit at being a little taken aback by his description of me as seen through his eyes.

"My Mother"

My Mother likes doing her Painting the Pope and Sadat. My Mum wrote a letter to Mrs Sadat and Mrs Sadat replied with a printed Egypt stamp on the letter. My Mum likes watching art programs and knitting programs. My Mum doesn't like cleaning up and tidying out the cupboards)".

This brought my housekeeping skills into sharp focus when my son was asked to write about his mother. I was more than surprised to see myself through my 7-year-old son's eyes.

Let's start with President Anwar Sadat. Yes, I did write condolences to his widow when Sadat was mercilessly assassinated as he stood to attention at a flyover in his honour. This was a man I had much admired as a man of peace. The morning newspapers showed photographs of Anwar Sadat, his smile wide as he looked skywards to the aircraft flying over in his honour. Within seconds he was gunned down. It was shocking and tragic. That day I couldn't get the horror out of my mind and found some consolation that weekend by painting a small picture of Sadat. And days later, a letter to his wife expressing my condolences of her husband who had been such a force for peace.

And, yes, obviously her reply came back with an Egyptian stamp on the envelope. No surprise there, but Dan, at 7 years old, was clearly impressed.

Now to the paintings of the Pope. Dan often came from school to see me painting yet another Pope John Paul picture.... seven in all. No wonder he remembers. His observation skills helped me one day as he arrived from school to find me struggling with a likeness. "Dan, something's not right with the Pope's face. Can you see?".

This little sharp-eyed lad told me, pointing to one of the eyes, "Mum, that eye is in the wrong place".

(He was right!).

He may have thought I was doing this for the fun of it not knowing that these commissions were keeping a roof over our heads. And watching painting programs?

June Antoinette Necchi

Very likely, but knitting programs? A bit of artistic licence on my young son's part, an art he was too perfect in later years.

Finally, the damning comment about my aversion to cupboard cleaning. Of course, it's true but had I ever told him of this? No!

Top marks for observation though, Dan!

I should have known that one day he would have to keep a roof over his own head by making full use of his imaginative and observational skills. Today, a successful designer, Dan, cut his teeth on scrutinising his mother's activities.

THE WINDSOR AFFAIR.

From the stairs of the Royal Lodge in Windsor to its new home in my son's bedroom more than 100 miles away. Surely not! Was this a dream? But there was nothing dreamlike about its installation. My knees were red raw from kneeling over the 24-inch strips sealing them to create a total floor covering.

The carpet was a quality I have never seen before, thick close pile, pile tightly woven into its backing, and a rich red colour. Yes, it had been a labour of love, but not one that I was likely to repeat, though it did feel like an achievement.

You may ask how I came to be the beneficiary of such a piece of history? Well, it was an offer from a good friend who worked for the Crown properties across

June Antoinette Necchi

London. His job was to clear out any properties that were either due for renovation, or for change of use, which meant simply removing all items, furniture, carpets, curtains etc that were no longer going to be in use. His main task was to preserve the character of the place retaining all the original features, fireplaces etc but to dispose of the rest of the contents, usually in skips.

He and his wife knew that I was looking for carpet for my son's room and suggested that I might like to have a look at some stair carpet that was due to go to a waste disposal unit.

On our visit to Windsor Lodge, I was amazed at the condition of the carpet which lined the stairs of the Lodge. There was no trace of wear, though clearly it had been laid years before. I could just imagine it in my son's bedroom and thanked my friend so much for thinking about me. Not only was it to be a gift but he was going to load and bring it to my home.

Was my son impressed with the regal carpet under his feet? I don't think so but then he raised no objections.

It was only 3 or 4 years later when driving home after a teaching session that I was to witness the demise of the carpet….

DAN'S BEDROOM

The wind and sleet swept treacherously along the open road winding its way through a landscape of pine trees and heathland. The night was moonless and bleak. The evening had been enjoyable but draining with students eager to complete their paintings and eager to have my reassurance of their continued improvement of painting skills. This followed a day of teaching under twenty one's in a local prison which had left me exhausted. A warm home and a cup of tea was all I asked for now.

I was not prepared therefore for the reception awaiting me as I arrived home. My son of seventeen having finished school with a wellspring of ideas, and all of God's hours to think about them, had come up with what he considered the most exciting yet.... Minimalism!

He began by asking my permission for what a fait accompli was already. The gruelling day had left me in a kind of stupor, but my son's persistent nature demanded that I 'have a look before I settled down to relax for what was left of the evening,

Well used to his particular brand of determination and enthusiasm, I didn't resist, while being vaguely aware that there seemed something different about the dining room as we made our way through to the stairs, following Dan to the top where he opened his door, with panache, as though introducing a theatre production.

For a moment I thought the bailiffs had been in. The room appeared to have doubled in size such was the effect of the removal of the Windsor Royal Lodge red carpet revealing the expanse of floorboards beneath. Louvred pine wardrobe doors had vanished from one side of the room instantly increasing, visually, the size of the bedroom. It was as though human life had never

June Antoinette Necchi

existed there before. The bed had gone, as had the chest of drawers. But there in the corner next to the window was a clue as to what had been different in the dining room.... a small 2-seater sofa had been secreted up the stairs in my absence, covered with bright drapes and cushions stuffed into tee shirts whose fronts expressed a wide range of musical tastes.

How long had I left my house to teach earlier? Three hours?

The transformation was admirable. "But where are the louvred doors now," I asked. "They're in the cellar, Mum. Hope that's ok".

"Your chest of drawers?". "Oh,, I popped that in your bedroom. Hope you don't mind".

OK, I could accept Dan's protestations that his cupboard was now in my room as were his clothes (keeping only the most interesting ones to hang on his rails in eye-catching fashion, or folded and stacked as though on display in some Milan designer's setting) but where was he to sleep?

Triumphantly, he pointed to the space beneath the loft bedroom staircase built into his room. There, in what seemed an incredibly small area was a 2ft x 6 ft mattress, head- end neatly inserted into what had been until a few hours ago the end section of his wall-to-wall wardrobes.

It was an inspired idea! Ever eager to encourage my offspring's creative talents. How could I complain?

June Antoinette Necchi

And the Windsor Royal Lodge beautiful carpet? Dan had laid it to rest in the cellar of our house. "Mum, if you really want it I will put it back....

BRATTO

An invitation from Dan to locate my grandfather, his great grandfather Agostino's birthplace in Tuscany came out of the blue. How could I refuse?. Though I could just about manage enough Italian to get around, Dan, because he'd had an Italian girlfriend who he met when she was studying English here, had determinedly taught himself enough to sustain their relationship. I was surprised at his natural fluency, so I felt confident to embark on an independent trip.

It wasn't a straightforward start to the trip as he was to spend a week with Alessandra at her home near Rome. Young people, Dan was twenty-two, are not wary of complicated travel plans which have the potential to fall apart, so decided to tack our trip onto his stay with Alessandra near Rome, and after a week to take a train to Pisa where with any luck we would meet up.

Pisa airport is minutes by train to Pisa, a central area, and it was outside the station we would meet. Not sure if Dan doesn't trust me let loose in Italy but he gave me a warning, "Mum, remember traffic drives on the other side of the road in Italy, so catch a taxi to meet me in the hotel.. DON'T cross the road!"

I crossed the road and walked to meet him....

June Antoinette Necchi

In the hotel room we watched devastating storms on television, and as it was early November I thought we were taking unnecessary risks. I feebly suggested, "Maybe, Dan, we shouldn't venture into the mountains tomorrow". I should have known better..

"We've come to find Agostino's birthplace and can't turn back now".

The next morning, arriving in Pontremoli by train, we booked into a local hotel. There are two rivers that flow down to the medieval Pontremoli, the Magda and the Verde which flow together at the lower end of the town. That morning, they were raging torrents but Dan, undeterred, booked a taxi to take us seven or eight miles into Bratto which was located more than a thousand metres up in the mountains.

It had been 3 weeks since Dan had called saying, "Mum, how about you come backpacking with me to look for your grandfather's village in Tuscany?"

I had agreed immediately with this son who shares my sense of family history

He proved to be a delightful companion. Whether we were sharing meals, his headphones, or simply engrossed in conversation about Italy, its language, it's culture or art.

Dan had competently organised the travel, refusing to acknowledge that the isolated mountain village of Bratto would present problems.

June Antoinette Necchi

Leaving the autostrada the taxi began to climb the narrow winding track leading to Bratto.

"I'll phone you later", Dan called to the taxi driver who waved as he left

"Wow, Mum, can you believe this?" asked Dan as we stood at the base of the village which rose up in front of us.

"I think we have been transported to another life", I answered.

Clusters of ancient stone houses, some tumbling down, cobbled alleyways and all sitting amidst the hills and glorious landscape of Tuscany.

We stopped and listened. Only the sounds of birdsong and the rustle of trees and grasses, but no human voice, broke the silence.

"Do you think it's inhabited, Mum?"

"We'll soon see, Dan, let's go and find out".

Climbing the overgrown track, we saw the first clue to human existence.....a cemetery whose gravestones with smiling photos of the dead, and adorned with vases of fresh flowers, gave a lie to our assumption that Bratto was a ghost village.

The gates to the cemetery were locked. But who held the key?

June Antoinette Necchi

Picking our way over the cobbles we came to a piazza, its flagstones cracked and sprouting weeds. A small roughhewn church stood nearby.

"Look, Mum, a plaque with our family name on it!".

The plaque attached to the church wall commemorated Israeli Necchi who died in action in 1944. This was a sobering moment for us as we stood silent.

Our thoughts then were distracted by women's voices echoing down the hills. Two women, arms laden with baskets, called out to us. We climbed the hill and introduced ourselves, "Necchi famiglia da Ingleterra", managing enough Italian to let them know we were the Necchi family from England.

"Ah, Siamo Necchi anche," she declared. "I am Maddalena".

She then continued speaking in broken English with a strong north London accent!

(As with my grandfather who left Italy for work in London, other family members had made the journey for work while retaining their homes in Bratto).

Dan asked did she know where the cemetery keys were.

"I have them from the priest, I will take you there to see the family tomb".

"But, first, let me show you your grandfather's family home."

June Antoinette Necchi

It was a touching moment, imagining my grandfather, Agostino the youngest of six children being raised there, and the hard life they would have had when his mother died when he was only 6 years old. He'd often told me of rising early with his brothers to tend the sheep on the hills. Now I could picture it all.

Making our way down to the cemetery, Maddalena stopped and pointed up at one of the houses, "A cousin of your father lives there, Italia Lusardi".

Wandering between the gravestones we had a sense of our roots beginning there in that isolated village with many of the residents bearing our name through the ages and fascinating to see their images on the stones.

In the family tomb, its marble plaques lining the walls, Maddalena pointed to a large white marble alter at the end inscribed with the names DOMENICO MATTEO NECCHI GHIRI. She announced with a sweeping gesture to include ourselves, "Domenico is the great man we all come from!"

Pointing to me, she said, "He is your great great grandfather".

We were silent realising that this tomb had brought us to the end of our journey. What we didn't know was that a meal was being prepared for us, a meal we would always remember as part of our discovery of Bratto and of family members.

At Italia's invitation we stepped carefully between the pots on the steps to reach her kitchen at the top. The simple old table was laid with cutlery, glasses of water and slabs of crusty bread. On the stove a big black frying pan was filled with small vegetables while Italia cracked eggs on the side of a basin. Holding the cracked eggs aloft she separated the shells and let the golden globes drop into the basin below, then with rapid movements whipped them to a froth before pouring them over the vegetables in the pan. She turned the gas up then deftly flipped the frittata over before bringing it sizzling in olive oil to the table.

It was the exhilaration, and the culmination of the whole authentic experience of our journey to find our past, and the meal, frittata, sent for centuries with agricultural workers to sustain them while they worked long hours on the land, and served to me and my son in that simple home, that remains forever in my memory.

As we sat in the Italian kitchen in this ages old house with few modern appliances, it's walls decorated with an assortment of family photographs, including that of her granddaughter in England, the well-known Linda Lusardi, it seemed to me that our past had been brought to life by this visit to the century's old hamlet in the Tuscan mountains.

DAN DECISION MAKING

"Mum, I've finally decided what I want to do...... Well, there are two things. I want to study music, or art in Uni".

"Wait a minute, Dan. Music? You don't play an Instrument or read music".

"Don't worry, Mum, you know I can really learn if I want to, and I was a DJ for a couple of years when I was a teenager, so it really shows I like music".

Now of course this was true, and he had saved to buy the equipment, and built a unit for it in his bedroom.

Impatient to leave school at 16, Dan had explored a plethora of money-making opportunities, one, whose prospect he found exciting, was working on a stand in the Birmingham Exhibition Centre. This did impinge on my life a little as he needed my car to get to the exhibition.

"Dan, can you put petrol in, son?"

"But, Mum, I don't get paid till the end of the month". The 'end of the month' never did materialise…

I could see that Dan happily moved from one work experience to another though his enthusiasm soon waned with those involving repetition.

Ands the list grew.

Waiting on in an Italian restaurant. Speeding around the midlands collecting parts for a local garage. Garden tidying for local houses.

It was a relief to me when he decided to be a DJ. I looked forward to a bit of financial help from Dan as

June Antoinette Necchi

after all I was raising two sons alone, and not only that it would be a positive lesson in independence for him, but as he told me when I suggested he make a contribution, "Mum, I know they pay me £50 but you know I have to keep on top of the game, and buy records every week".

"I never thought of that, Dan. Can't let your audience down, I suppose".

It was only when his older brother had left home to work in the south of England that Dan realised he felt hemmed in living in our small town and followed his brother.

Predictably, he did a few jobs but had his sights set on working with a reputable corporate bank, J.P. Morgan. With no vacancies he took the bull by the horns and through an agency was taken on for one month as a temporary clerk.

Spotting a post going in the Foreign Department, Dan applied and clinched the job with his ability to speak Italian learned when he was wooing an Italian girl.

As a mother I breathed a big sigh of relief. My son was twenty-two and excited to have landed the job he had coveted for a year.

Doesn't every mother just want her chicks to be happy? I certainly was and could relax now...... or so I thought. That was until he called me some months later.

June Antoinette Necchi

"Mum, when you visit at the weekend can we spend a day in the countryside? There's something I want to talk to you about"

June Antoinette Necchi

I couldn't imagine what the 'something' was, maybe a girl problem, or simply a day out talking about 'life', conversations Dan had always enjoyed.

Our day out began with, "Mum, I've finally decided what I want to do............".

"Look Dan, suppose you went to college, studied music, then what would you do with it?"

It's not sufficient in this world to like something. If it's a career you're after you need tons of luck as well as a love of music. Why not keep it as a hobby?

Now to the question of an art degree. Have you forgotten that you weren't in school the day they did the art GSCE? Your C.V is sadly lacking that".

"No prob, Mum. You know that pastel portrait on my wall you did. I'll take that to the interview".

"But Dan...".

Don't worry about it Mum. Leave it to me"

No mother likes to see her chick's dreams crumble, but I could hear the determination in Dan's voice and remembered the poster I'd put on his bedroom wall when he was just 3 years old. It showed a possum hanging upside down from a branch with the words, *I LIKE TO DO THINGS MY WAY*

Yes, Dan had from a toddler, loved drawing and I had no doubt that he could easily replicate my sketch, but....

June Antoinette Necchi

He turned up for his interview, my poster rolled up under his arm, (oh, dear, what if they're not impressed with my picture and he fails to gain a place)?

The anticipated questions came, but there was one he hadn't anticipated, "Can I have a look at your portfolio?".

I'm proud of my quick-thinking son. Quick as a shot, he answered, "It's back in Birmingham where I was brought up". (Strangely, he was not asked to track it down).

Whatever exchanges he and the interviewer had must have revealed his sensitivity to all things creative because he was offered a place at the end of the interview. Dan had been confident that he would pull it off...and he did.

This son still has the ability to surprise me.

Only at the end of the interview did Dan reveal to the interviewer that he would have to miss the first two weeks of the degree course as he had planned to visit his girlfriend in Italy. He was told, "take a sketchbook and bring it back for me to see".

Two weeks later when I asked to see his sketchbook with drawings of the classical Roman buildings, and the views across the multitude of roof tops, it dawned on me that Dan WAS a natural artist. The complicated perspectives were drawn accurately and beautifully, putting to rest my anxieties about Dan's ability to cope with the next 3 years in Art University.

June Antoinette Necchi

At the end of that time, he was awarded a First with Honours in Illustration Design and went on to study for a Postgraduate teaching degree and was offered and accepted a teaching post in the University!

A year later, Dan, stifled by the politics in college, resigned. He custom built two camper vans hence his interest in designing decals for campers alongside his graphic design business.

He'd come a long way from our conversation,

"Mum, I've finally decided what I want to do…"

Dan

June Antoinette Necchi

WHO IS JOYCE?

I would like to introduce my friend Joyce who is the subject of my next book

Wild black hair, piercing but playful dark eyes, a smile that reveals a cheeky gap in her front teeth that would melt the hardest heart. A colourful, magnanimous character, impetuous, charming, fearless, outrageous, and not least of all with a generosity of spirit.

She had been my friend for many years when we were young mothers together. I never expected that due to an accident one day I would become her Carer.

Joyce, a wonderful character with a heart of gold whose antics were often off the scale, and yes, I was frequently her 'partner in crime'.

Fortunately-these did not come to an end, when following a road accident, she was left with a serious form of bipolar. accentuating her Maverick character.

It was then that I became her Carer and was introduced to the complexities of this disorder.

r

June Antoinette Necchi

Joyce 1

I hope you enjoyed reading my book. Thank you so much for following me and my book journey.

I've enjoyed sharing with you my memoirs, my wartime experiences, and my attempts at painting pictures with words.

It would seem appropriate to include here my personal journey of many years,….. that of Multiple Sclerosis, and a theory I have of an environmental cause for this disease.

June Antoinette Necchi

CONTACT

Facebook

https://www.facebook.com/profile.php?id=100064937591389

YouTube

https://youtu.be/aRU3e9drllk?si=vIOMc9uOclpnoYam

Email:

junenecchiauthor@gmail.com

Printed in Great Britain
by Amazon